THE
BATTLE
OF
BRITAIN

50 YEARS ON

Patrick Stephens Limited, part of Thorsons, a division of the Collins Publishing Group, has published authoritative, quality books for enthusiasts for more than twenty years. During that time the company has established a reputation as one of the world's leading publishers of books on aviation, maritime, military, model-making, motor cycling, motoring, motor racing, railway and railway modelling subjects. Readers or authors with suggestions for books they would like to see published are invited to write to: The Editorial Director, Patrick Stephens Limited, Thorsons Publishing Group, Wellingborough, Northants, NN8 2RQ.

THE
BATTLE
OF
BRITAIN

50 YEARS ON

MICHAEL J.F. BOWYER

PSL

Patrick Stephens Limited

Front endpaper: *One of No. 19 Squadron's Spitfires at Fowlmere, in October, re-arming and refuelling.* (IWM)

Rear endpaper: *With three kill claims on its fin, a Bf 110 of ZG 26 is pushed under protective netting at its French base.* (Bundesarchiv)

First published in 1990

British Library Cataloguing in Publication Data
Bowyer, Michael J. F. (Michael John Frederick) *1928-*
    The battle of Britain : 50 years on.
    1. World War 2. Battle of Britain
    I. Title
    940.54'21

ISBN 1-85260-039-X

Patrick Stephens Limited is part of the Thorsons Publishing Group, Wellingborough, Northamptonshire NN8 2RQ, England.

Printed by Bath Press, Bath, Avon.
Typesetting by MJL Limited, Hitchin, Hertfordshire.

10 9 8 7 6 5 4 3 2 1

CONTENTS

ACKNOWLEDGEMENTS AND SUGGESTIONS FOR FURTHER READING

A 1941 official publication price 6d and prepared by two official historians and entitled *The Battle of Britain* was the first such account of the Battle. It was soon followed by an account on the wireless. After considering the contents of these accounts I referred to my diary entries made during those momentous days. Since 1940 those have been much augmented through contact with many who took part in the fight and others who observed and experienced the action.

The next milestone in the published historical record of the Battle came in 1953 with the publication of Volume 1: *The Fight at Odds*, the first of a trilogy entitled *The Royal Air Force 1939-1945* (HMSO). A paperback edition appeared in 1975. The author, Denis Richards, then Principal of Morley College, had worked with the one-time Librarian of the House of Commons, the late Hilary St George Saunders, on that first official publication. Skilfully and concisely, volume 1 of the series describes the Battle of Britain.

The next major work detailing the Battle of Britain was Basil Collier's *The Defence of the United Kingdom* (HMSO) published in 1957. This volume within the full-length official military history of the war and prepared under the overall direction of Professor J.R.M. Butler has provided a sound basis for subsequent books about the Battle. The unpublished edition contained copious references to official documents then classified and upon which the work was based. Published versions omitted these details, but examples of the fully detailed editions within the series are now available for research at the Public Record Office, Kew.

Shortly after the war Sir Winston Churchill had directed that a very detailed search be made of captured enemy documents so that an accurate listing of German losses during the Battle could be produced. Using the German Quartermaster General's record of losses and serviceability returns, and marrying these to other official documents, a team produced, after extensive study, the official record of losses during the Battle. The conclusions featured in the official histories.

Many official documents raised in 1940 and used in the preparation of these studies may now be consulted in the Public Record Office at Kew. There they have been grouped within Classes, the most pertinent being the Squadron Operations Record Books (Forms 540 and 541) gathered within Class AIR 27, and are available for microfilm viewing. Operational Records of HQ Fighter Command have been placed within AIR 24, and files on varied aspects of fighter activity may be found in AIR 16. Combat reports are held within AIR 50 and statistical and intelligence surveys in AIR 22 and AIR 40.

Bombing attacks upon the UK are extensively recorded in an assortment of material held in the Ministry of Home Security records, in Classes HO 198 to HO 202. These are far from complete and deal mainly with major incidents. Their extent reflects a wide assortment of reporting skills and styles within the 12 autonomous Civil Defence Regions. Further records of raid incidents are usually to be found in County Record Offices and vary greatly in accuracy, content and style.

Records of individual aircraft are now held on microfilm at the RAF Museum, the original Form 78s remaining in the hands of the Air Historical Branch, Ministry of Defence.

In 1961 *The Narrow Margin* (Hutchinson) by Derek Wood and Derek Dempster appeared, the first and still one of the most extensive and authoritative volumes devoted to the Battle and drawing upon the officially held material as well as other sources. Air Chief Marshal the Lord Dowding GCB, GCVO, CMG, contributed the Foreword, the book receiving widespread acclaim and the award of the Robertson Trophy, the RAF Public Relations accolade. In 1968 it formed the basis for the film *The Battle of Britain*, and appeared in March 1969 in paperback form.

Probably the best known of more recent books is Frank Mason's 1969 *Battle over Britain* (McWhirter Twins), the first published volume to carry detailed information taken from the Luftwaffe loss records. Not until ten years later did the next major work come. *The Battle of Britain — Then and Now* (After the Battle) edited by Winston G. Ramsey. This places emphasis upon the aircrew in the fight, their fates and those of their aircraft. It particularly draws upon the findings of teams of enthusiasts who have worked at crash sites to increase information. More recently After the Battle has produced a three-volume series *The Blitz — Then and Now*

along rather similar lines, in which the Battle of Britain is covered in the first volume dealing with the period up to 6 September and continuing in the second.

More specialized, but nevertheless an excellent and most enjoyable volume to consult is *Most Secret War* (Hamish Hamilton) by Professor R.V. Jones in which he describes in detail the intelligence work that he and others conducted in respect of the German use of radio beams for navigation purposes. This is also available as a paperback.

All of these works and indeed others inevitably influence any further writing about the Battle, although it is from the official material that I have mainly worked, setting its content alongside my own gatherings in 1940 and since. Crown Copyright is acknowledged for some of the basic items.

It is to a friend, Laurence Haylock, that my most sincere thanks are awarded for the fine artwork which illustrates this book. To the Imperial War Museum I express my thanks for assistance with photographs and permission to reproduce them. The Bundesarchiv in Koblenz has also most helpfully supplied photographs of German forces. Some rare illustrations have also been supplied by Michael Payne, collector of 'Me 109' photographs and ever on the look-out for more! Thus, thanks are due to a large number of people who, over very many years, have provided help, influence, companionship, and have in the process made the past five decades so full of fascination.

IN PASSING

Mention the Battle of Britain and most of us have a notion of what it was all about, whether we experienced it, distantly viewed its development, or regard it as ancient history. Precisely defining the event remains difficult, for it possessed neither clear cut opening nor sharply defined conclusion. Yet all who lived through Britain's most momentous summer were only too aware of history itself being worked out against a glorious backdrop.

So many of the Battle's parameters remain questionable. Certainly the assault upon Fighter Command, the memorable day raids and attacks both on ports and shipping preluded one aim — the reduction of Britain and if necessary by invasion. Nothing like that has happened, barely been contemplated, for little less than a thousand years. The Battle of Britain can probably be said to have begun when the bombing of Britain was stepped up in late May 1940, and may be considered to have ended when the Germans officially postponed the invasion after failing to gain mastery of both our skies and the English Channel. Although several significant daylight raids followed, as the hours of darkness increased, so the summer Battle of Britain slipped into becoming the autumn Night Blitz. During October 1940, commonly called 'Messerschmitt Month' at the time because of the amount of fighter and fighter-bomber activity, dreams — and fears — of easy German victory had vanished; the war was seen as likely to continue for some time to come. The Luftwaffe had failed in its attempt to subjugate Fighter Command, let alone destroy Bomber Command. But Britain's island status rendered it an ideal candidate for starvation, the prevention of which throughout the Battle was the prime task of all-but-forgotten RAF Coastal Command, and the Royal Navy.

Bearing those aspects in mind I have concentrated in this book upon the period from June 1940 to early October, directing attention particularly towards the play rather than the actors, many of whom have excellently recorded their personal recollections of the fight. Much has already been made of the claims and losses of aircraft. In reality the situation was far more complex than is so often portrayed, because many aircraft, even slightly damaged, were out of front line service for many months. Indeed, some were out of action far longer than others relatively far more seriously damaged. That profoundly affected the entire fight.

Before reviewing the grand acts I have attempted to set the scene by recalling life as many of those going about their daily lives would have known it. How grim those hard times seem when compared with the widespread affluence of the 1980s. Yet, if you experienced the world of half a century ago, then you will surely treasure innumerable memories: in particular of the kindness of so many people so rich in character and fascination; of the genuine concern for others not falsely related to a wish for power; the determination to succeed in a harsh world in brutal times; the sensible regard towards danger and risk taking, and the superb team spirit — all of which characterized that world, making it such a memorable experience to have known life in times which were so highly character building. Yes, character building, that's what it was, and the tragedy is that in peacetime we are quite unable to introduce the best virtues into our lives and produce such splendid folk.

Michael J.F. Bowyer
Cambridge

CHAPTER 1

BATTLEGROUND

Half a century ago? That cannot surely be — for the scenes, the exhilaration, the sounds and sorrows of the most stupendous of all summers remain as vivid as if it were yesterday. Tin hats, buckets, gas masks, shelters, first aid posts, 'ARP', static water tanks, blackout and trillions of sandbags — are they really 50 years away? Is it that long since swarms of sirens competed in the warbling stakes, the walls shook, the shelter shuddered, the guns exuded the most terrifying cacophonies? Can it be so long since the know-all's proud cry, 'It's one of ours' was understandably followed by that demand, 'Where's the RAF?', to which the communiqués seemed invariably to supply the answer either with the news that aircraft had attacked the marshalling yards at Hamm or with that familiar phrase 'mines were laid in enemy waters', and the information that 'two of our aircraft are missing'. Any who experienced those times can recall a world utterly divorced from the present, mightily more homely and considerate, despite the tyranny of King Coal belching sulphurous smoke and ruling the household and the factory (and the farm, too, for I recall once seeing some 30 traction engines smoking away quite close to one another at harvest time!); a world in which a vast, steaming, smoky railway network dominated friendly-named shires; in which the horse and cart competed with the lorry, even the steam lorry, and of course those nice little 'mechanical horses'. Iron, tin plate, fine paper, strawboard, rubber, leather, 'lino', wood — these were the foundations of Britain before plastics and chemically based products began to impinge on our lives. Flanelette, cotton, worsted, coarse wool and thick close weave vests — what security they seemed to offer, not to mention scarves, hand-knitted pullovers, grey woollen gloves and blue gabardine raincoats. How cold even the October shelter nights would have been without them — and how frigid had 'nylon' usurped their places sooner.

Precious, poky, home was mostly rented and often within a long-outdated Victorian terrace from whose assortment of chimneys smoke seemed ever to curl, from an open fire in winter and a cooking range in summer. Gas stoves were nevertheless quite common, whereas their electric cousins — so slow to warm — seemed for the more prosperous and fashionable and were to be found in an ever increasing number of smart, new, 1930s three bedroom plus bathroom suburban 'semis'. Life was certainly improving, markedly and for an increasing number, although many had still to 'make do' on less than 40 shillings a week — £2, currently inflated to around £60. Surprisingly a high proportion seemed amazingly contented with their lot, even if a 'doff' of the cap was expected by 'master'. A hall was still a luxury, a black china gas fire (remember those fragile clay-combed and curved burners?) quite 'posh', and the dangerous tall black Valor paraffin stove a smelly norm. For homes without electric light there was still the cotton gas mantle, forever crumbling in a sudden breeze and so demanding of cherishment. Curtains of net, cretton, chenille or even velvet, suspended from huge rings, slid along thick wooden poles now smartly collectable. They were ever ready to ensure non-exposure, and drawn back when their owners watched, through the sash-corded windows, the 'Sunday best' paraders. In summer a chair on the 'front tiles' provided an even better viewing platform — and in 1940 a good position from which to observe and discuss the progress of the conflict. As for those 'front tiles', they received a weekly scrub, sometimes daily attention, like the stone step by the seemingly ever open door. Not suitable for the '90s for sure, like the common habit of leaving a door key on a string accessible through the ornate metal letterbox.

When the Luftwaffe tore privacy from our homes it revealed a world now almost vanished. Countless aspidistras and ferns appeared (unless they had failed to flourish due to foul medicine being tipped upon them by a crafty child). No rubber trees swayed then — except in distant parts of the Empire. Brasses in profusion and a big clock on a wooden mantelpiece often clothed in a fringe were overlooked by a large mirror. Almost every room had its tiled fireplace, black grate and whitewashed ceilings. No emulsion paint, and only the chic used distempers.

When sickness demanded a visit from a doctor — price about 4 shillings — and recovery in the antique bed amid semi-Victorian trimmings, then the upstairs fire would blaze, an event loved by children but lit only in real need, and limited by the need to convey the coal, wood and paper to the small grate. In the 'back room' one used to sit, read, knit, play cards on the cloth cloaking the huge wooden table, legacy of times when many families were large. Letters would be written with the aid of a dip-in pen, diving into Stephen's or Swan blue-black ink. The more affluent would be guiding a Conway Stewart fountain pen or propelling pencil. What an amazing treasure a 'Biro' would have been! Children might have a paint box, stencil using thick oil paper, have coloured pencil crayons whose points seemed never sharp and constantly to snap. They could build dream cas-tles with wooden unpainted bricks and if very lucky produce a Meccano masterpiece. Wax crayons, although available, were messy. It was still the world of Dinky Toys, of Hornby, Frog, Triang, but these great names were changing into 'making things for the war effort'.

In the scullery the copper would boil clothes each Monday, traditionally washday; then from its hiding place would emerge the mangle, after which the half sodden clothes, wooden pegged, would take to the breeze. A cooking range might well help to heat 'the back room', or the scullery with its familiar brown and tan shallow earthenware sink, and often doubling up as a kitchen — minuscule compared with today's lavish creations.

Coal delivery often meant that many a 1940 coalman had to carry the load through the 'front room' of the house, the best room — all the 20 hundredweight bags. House value rose not with space for a garage but the presence of a back passage leading to the coal shed.

Glass bottles were everywhere — in the kitchen, in rarely built-in cupboards and particularly in the pantry. While tinned food played an increasingly important part, bottled fruit was plentiful. Into the Kilner jar went Dad's plums from the garden, to be boiled and hopefully sealed, to prevent them from 'working'. Refrigerators remaining rare, a thick stone 'slab' in the pantry and a gauze over the meat served to cool it and keep it safe from 'blow flies'. Milk would be boiled in warm weather and kept in cold water containers. Even so, hot weather would often curdle it, but in 1940 many discovered that milk could, with patience and dedication, be intentionally converted into tasteless butter or muslin cheese. Jam jars lurked everywhere, pressed into service as cheap vases and used by children for tadpole containment and for painting water. The jam, often home made, was staple diet for many and dripping was still spread onto bread Dickensian style. Many a pantry held an ever lingering aroma of home made pickles, milk and meat, and there was a marked absence of what many rated 'unwanted' foreign food. Rice, semolina, tapioca knew their place — in milk. Thick, tough, blue 'sugar bags' — if discarded — were replaced by tins or glass jars which also served hosts of purposes. As for spare earthenware pots, they quite likely would contain eggs preserved in the strange 'Isinglass', or water-glass — queer stuff, like transparent treacle. Of course, one had first to bring the eggs from the shop — merely in a paper bag — and then clean the shells. There seemed little more use for a medicine bottle than its primary one — but, in those careful days, one kept things 'just in case'. It was a keep, 'make do and mend', not throwaway society. The china stopper of a 1940 Corona bottle was held in place by a powerful metal catch — don't break it and you could get money back, as with many other bottles.

About half the nation's houses had one great advantage — they included a bathroom. In those without, people still bathed in time-honoured fashion, some in deep copper or zinc oval or elongated tubs, while others with gay abandon displayed themselves in giant, shallow metal 'dishes', which meant that a towel close to hand was essential in those very modest times. There was 'sex', I think, but it was rarely mentioned, which left much to be discovered! In winter, when a bath by the fire was common, there were many occasions when . . . No bubbles to provide cover, although bath salts or plain soda enlivened the effect of Lux toilet soap. When the Luftwaffe came over, someone must have been disturbed by an uninvited Hans or Johann dropping in!

Alternatively one might be more remotely entertained, on the wireless, by Lord Haw-Haw, the traitor whom many regarded more as a comedian than Nazi propagandist. When he informed the residents of Cambridge that the hands of the Catholic church needed adjusting, we were, for once, impressed by his knowledge.

We were a fit nation then, thanks to the 'Radio Doctor' and those strange 'PT' voices who each morning suggested stretching up and down to music in the 'Up in the morning, early' programme. Who says aerobics are new?

Even the smallest town garden was fully cultivated, each dwelling seeming to have both a very small lawn surrounded by flowers and a supply of vegetables. Wastage of space on patios and conifers was unknown, and many supplemented their needs with fare from the allotment.

Woolworth's was, in 1940, still trading as the 'nothing over 6d' store although prices by then had been inflated to over 1/-. Halfords was still selling bicycles, soon to be hard to buy. Liptons, International Stores, Maypole were competing with Sainsbury's for your rationing registration. Boots and 'M&S' (nothing over 5/-) traded in quite limited fashion, the former as a glorified chemists shop, the latter as the source of 'Rex' records which the better off played on the radiogram. If such shops as those had one linking feature it was high combustibility, luckily not linked to acrid oil-based smoke common in fires of the 1980s.

Such were the familiar things above which the Heinkels and Messerschmitts roamed during the Battle of Britain. Quaint they may seem to those who knew them not, making anything as wonderful as the Hurricane and Spitfire ('they can do over 300!') incredible machines. As for the rumoured secret 'beams'! . . .

. . . Herr von Ribbentrop . . . you must not underrate England. She is a curious country and few foreigners can understand her mind. Do not judge by the attitude of the present administration. Once a great cause is presented to the people all kinds of unexpected actions might be taken by this very government, and by the British nation. Do not underrate England. She is very clever. If you plunge us all into another great war she will bring the whole world against you, like last time.

Winston Churchill,
Post-war recorded recollections

CHAPTER 2

TROUBLE BREWING

'The day war broke out' — to quote Rob Wilton, delightfully funny man of those days — everybody expected instant bombing by the Luftwaffe. It seemed to have been promised as much by our government as 'theirs'! Instead, the population had to make do with false alarms, within a few minutes of the declaration of war and again the following night. In reality, the German air force was too busy with 'the Polish Question' to concern itself with the British one.

 The Prime Minister's broadcast informed us that we were already at war and he had just ceased speaking when a strange, prolonged wailing noise, afterwards to become familiar, broke from the air. My wife came into the room braced by the crisis and commented favourably upon the German promptitude and precision, and that the quarter of an hour's notice which we had been led to expect we should receive was now running out. We made our way to the shelter assigned to us, armed with a bottle of brandy and other appropriate medicinal comforts.

Winston Churchill,
Post-war recorded recollections

While the Luftwaffe rarely ventured over mainland Britain before mid-1940, it began in October 1939 a vicious onslaught upon ship-ping off the east coast. When a U-boat sank the battleship *Royal Oak* it was clear that the Royal Navy did not have control of the North Sea, and that launched the spectre of German troops landing on the east coast to prevent which the Army hastily commenced preparations. The possibility of invasion of Britain grew stronger, and when France fell in June 1940 it became highly likely, even probable. The Battle of Britain was the aerial bombardment intended to pave the way for just such an event. By October 1940 it was evolving into becoming part of the Battle of the Atlantic. To counter the air attacks, the country was exceedingly fortunate in being able to have, thanks to the wisdom of its leader, a Fighter Command still intact after the fall of France. Best of all, those gallant 'Few' were led by a brilliant commander, Air Chief Marshal Sir High Dowding.

Aloof, austere, quiet, not one to suffer fools gladly — unquestionably one of the most highly skilled military commanders — his were qualities that did not assure him universal popularity among unequals. General Pile, commander of the anti-aircraft forces in 1940, who came to know him well, was of the opinion that Dowding 'knew more than anybody else about all aspects of aerial warfare', that it is 'hard to exaggerate his influence'. that he 'always wanted more — faster'. His contribution to victory cannot be overstated.

During the period in which Dowding was Commander-in-Chief, Fighter Command, only the very best was good enough for his people. The reduction of his fighter force by the six

Hurricane squadrons sent to France at the out-break of war, with another six listed 'mobile' and available to join them, caused Dowding to fear that even more Hurricane squadrons might, in an emergency, be sucked from Fighter Command. His desire for 52 squadrons in Fighter Command remained. Minus those in France he was down to 33.

The early-morning BBC news on 10 May 1940 had come as a bolt from the blue. Although details were sparse, we were told that the Germans were bombing 'Holland' and Belgium, and attacking France. Watchers on the roof of the British Embassy in The Hague reported seeing German bombers in action. On the 8 o'clock news we heard of paratroops descending upon the Netherlands and large numbers of troop-carrying aircraft landing on

Right *Air Chief Marshal Sir Hugh Dowding, Air-Officer-Commanding, Fighter Command, main architect of the British victory.* (IWM)

Below *The Hurricane bore the brunt of the RAF's contribution to the fight. L2124 shown in 501 Squadron colours served with 7 OTU from June to August 1940, then with 5 OTU.* (G.R.S. McKay)

Presently a message arrived summoning me to the Palace at 6 o'clock. I was taken immediately to the King. His Majesty received me most graciously and bade me sit down. He looked at me searchingly and particularly for some moments, and then said, "I suppose you don't know why I have sent for you." Adopting his mood I replied, "Sir, I simply couldn't imagine why." He laughed and said, "I want to ask you to form a government." I said I would certainly do so. At last I had the authority to give direction over the whole scene. I felt as if I were walking with destiny, and that all my past life had been but a preparation for this hour and for this trial... I was sure I should not fail. Therefore, although impatient for the morning, I slept soundly and had no need for cheering dreams. Facts are better than dreams.

Winston Churchill,
Post-war recorded recollections

Above *Spitfires in traditional battle formation, altered through combat experience.*

Below *To defeat dive and low level attack on cities, Low Zone Kite Balloons were flown in barrages. These around Buckingham Palace are close hauled.* (IWM)

beaches and open spaces. German tanks were smashing their way forward over frontiers and Luxembourg was being overrun.

Within hours the British Government acted adroitly — it formed a committee. A Home Defence Executive was established to discover what must be done to prepare the British people for the possibility of an invasion by sea and air. What course that would take was uncertain, but fear of paratroop attacks on key points and within a few days led to these being guarded by troops from AA sites. A veritable army of searchlight troops acquired a vital anti-invasion role along with their 4,000 LMGs and 32,800 rifles. When Dowding and Air Marshal Sir Charles Portal, AOC-in-C Bomber Command, expressed concern that small tanks could be landed by airborne forces, it prompted them to propose an anti-tank-gun-equipped flying defence force for which a bizarre candidate was an ancient Virginia bomber armed with a hand-traversed 37mm cannon!

For ARP purposes — Air Raid Precautions, or Civil Defence as the ARP organisation later became known — the United Kingdom had been divided into twelve theoretically autonomous regions. Response to invasion would draw upon that structure, which was urgently overhauled. Rumour and false witness were reckoned to constitute a very great threat in a time of stress — more so, in fact, than the discovery of actual 'fifth columnists', enemy agents or troops landed as saboteurs.

Suitable areas for an invasion were limited not only by terrain but also by the range and duration of German fighters and the much-used Stukas whose operating radius was assessed as 100 miles. Main invasion attempts were therefore restricted to the coast between Sussex and the Wash involving only a short sea crossing. An assault from Norway, while still quite possible, would be secondary. A spearhead of paratroops, it was argued, could be landed to capture airfields to where troops would be flown in. Their task would then be to destroy coastal defences in chosen beach landing territory where troops and vehicles could land from

modified shallow draught barges common on European inland waters.

To prevent far more serious landings coastal minefields were to be extended, and the Navy was to provide over 600 guns to increase coast defences. Road blocks were hurriedly erected and a host of pillboxes — many in most unsuitable positions and remaining to this day — were quickly built as strong points. Signposts, place names at railway stations, names on vehicles and shops — all had to be removed to cause maximum confusion among invaders. Church bells would now only be rung to signal an invasion had begun.

11 May, the day after the Germans launched their Blitzkrieg, the formation of local defence forces was discussed at the War Office. The outcome was a decision that any man aged between 16 and 65 'capable of free movement' should be eligible to join the unpaid Local Defence Volunteers. (Unpaid, note; British governments never easily part with their people's money for good, sensible causes!)

Eager to involve the public and attempting to scotch any alarmist situation, the politicians for once rose to the occasion and at tea time on 14 May the Secretary of State for War, Anthony Eden, made his famous call for 'every able bodied man' to enrol in the Local Defence Volunteers at his local police station.

In less than a week a staggering quarter of a million men had registered for the LDV, one third of a million by the end of May, by which time recruiting had been boosted by the saga of Dunkirk and air raids.

As soon as the fighting in France had started, Dowding's fears were realized by calls for more AA guns and fighters to operate across the Channel. The first firm response came on 13 May, when 32 Hurricanes were ordered to be dispatched to Field Force France. Next day the French asked the British Government to quickly dispatch ten fighter squadrons to France. The Government stalled, Dowding reminding his superiors that keeping four fighter squadrons in France had, since September 1939, cost in support the equivalent of a dozen Hurricane

You ask, what is our policy. I will say: It is to wage war, by sea, land and air, with all our might and all the strength that God can give us: to wage war against a monstrous tyranny, never surpassed in the dark, lamentable catalogue of human crime. That is our policy.

You ask, what is our aim. I can answer in one word: Victory — victory at all costs, victory in spite of all terror, victory, however long and hard the road may be; for without victory there is no survival.

Winston Churchill, 13 May 1940

squadrons. However many Hurricanes were sent to France, he argued, it could not ensure the success of a counter-attack. Privately he is reported as saying, 'it's like pouring water into the sands of the desert . . . we've slender hope of getting anyone back.' Publicly he had already stated that, 'The continued existence of the nation, and all its services, depends upon the Royal Navy and Fighter Command'.

At a War Cabinet meeting on 15 May Dowding presented his case to his superiors and to Churchill against sending more fighters to France, stressing that it could result in a disastrous loss of many Hurricanes. The Allied Supreme War Council had on 23 April outlined the circumstances in which the RAF's heavy bomber force would attack targets in Germany, and it was argued that such a situation had now arisen. Dowding stated that he would rather face the Luftwaffe's expected vicious response to such operations than lose more of his squadrons to France. The War Cabinet then sanctioned the use that night of Bomber Command to bomb Ruhr targets.

Dowding's success in argument was short-lived against incessant French pleas for help. The War Cabinet, aware of the serious plight

of the French army, decided to release eight half-squadrons of Hurricanes, drastically reducing the strength of Fighter Command.

In a Hurricane-escorted 24 Squadron Flamingo, R2764, Churchill flew to Paris later on 15 May. All he heard deeply saddened him. 'We just cannot desert our ally,' he said, and late that night asked the Cabinet to agree to sending another six complete Hurricane squadrons to France. But it was impracticable, for there were only six complete squadrons remaining in Fighter Command, and no suitably sited French airfields capable of accommodating them.

Before the day was out, the War Cabinet decided that six Hurricane squadrons would instead move to advanced bases in Kent. Early each day three squadrons would fly to France and operate from there, the other three squadrons relieving them from midday.

Depletion of Dowding's home force against his advice was deeply disturbing to him. Dramatically, he told the Cabinet of a full squadron of Hurricanes lost in France in a mere 96 hours, that Fighter Command had only half the number of squadrons it needed. In a letter he stated: 'I believe that, if an adequate fighter force is to be kept in this country, if the fleet remains in being, and if Home Forces are suitably organized to resist invasion, we should be able to carry on the war single-handed for some time, if not indefinitely. But if the Home Defence Force is drained away in desperate attempts to remedy the situation in France, defeat in France will involve the final, complete and irremediable defeat of this country.'

Much moved by these sentiments, and all he had heard, Churchill on 19 May decided that whatever the need in France no more fighter squadrons must leave the country, a decision with which the War Cabinet concurred next day.

On 26 May the decision was made to bring home the BEF. The magnitude of such a task was daunting, for it meant attempting to evacuate a quarter of a million men, under fire and exposed to air attack, and ferrying them to

I speak to you for the first time as Prime Minister at a solemn hour in the life of our country, of our Empire, of our Allies, and, above all, of the cause of freedom... Today is Trinity Sunday. Centuries ago words were written to be a call and a spur to the faithful servants of truth and justice. 'Arm yourselves, and be ye men of valour, and be in readiness for the conflict; for it is better for us to perish in battle than to look upon the outrage of our nation and our altars. As the Will of God is in Heaven, even so let it be.'

Winston Churchill, 19 May 1940

England across the Channel.

Late on 26 May Operation Dynamo, the withdrawal of the BEF, swung into play. As soon as it was daylight the Luftwaffe started attacking the assembling land and sea forces.

Dowding was faced with an enormous task in which failure would mean the loss of an entire Army and rapid defeat. The fighter force gathered in the 11 Group area was too small to allow continuous operations in strength, but denuding other parts of the country would be foolish. Therefore Dowding ordered Park to mount two-squadron patrols, relying upon an 18-squadron force, and leaving only brief intervals between patrols.

The Operations Room at HQ Fighter Command. (IWM)

On 29 May Park operated four-squadron forces at peak times of embarkation. By the evening of 2 June the last British troops were withdrawn and by 4 June around 225,000 British and 112,000 French troops were safely conveyed to England, an astonishingly successful achievement.

The whole nation viewed the retrieval of a third of a million men from under the nose of the mighty German war machine as little short of a miracle. True, many returning soldiers were in a tragic state. Morale was low but not completely shattered.

Much of the south coast was still not even protected by barbed wire, one senior officer

We shall go on to the end, we shall fight in France, we shall fight on the seas and oceans, we shall fight with growing confidence and growing strength in the air, we shall defend our island, whatever the cost may be, we shall fight on the beaches, we shall fight on the landing grounds, we shall fight in the fields and in the streets, we shall fight in the hills; we shall never surrender.

Winston Churchill, 4 June 1940

*Not a scene from 'Dad's Army'
but a splendid array of 'Ironsides'.
Quickly built four-man 'armoured
cars' carrying a forward-firing
bren-gun. (IWM)*

I had succeeded generally in keeping the Spitfire squadrons out of the Continental fighting. The reason for this was that the supply situation was so bad that they could not have maintained their existence in face of the Aircraft Casualty Rate experienced in France.

When the Dunkerque evacuation was complete I had only 3 Day-Fighting Squadrons which had not been engaged in Continental fighting, and 12 squadrons were in the line for the second time after having been withdrawn to rest and re-form.

I was responsible for the Air Defence of Great Britain, and I saw my resources slipping away like sand in an hour glass.
*Air Chief Marshal Sir Hugh Dowding,
Commander-in-Chief Fighter Command*

being heard to say, 'There are so many beaches that the enemy could land on it is hardly worth doing anyway. Let's do one and hope they choose that.'

In the Army there was a lamentable lack of understanding of the need for fast, ferocious reaction to disorganize paratroops. Only in Northern Command were troops being encouraged to become a highly mobile force. Elsewhere too many commanders were preparing for 'static', cordon warfare among road blocks and trenches, while across the Channel Hitler was stirring his cauldron and casting evil spells.

CHAPTER 3
BOMBS HAVE FALLEN

All bombing raids were on Scottish or northern targets until the night of 10 May when twenty 50-kg HEs were unloaded over the Bridge Blean rural district of Kent, which was bombed again three nights later. Then a bomb landed at Swanage on 14 May, eight at Eastleigh, Hants, on the 21st and two the next night on Romney Marsh. East Anglia received its first on 22 May, close to Butley church near what is now RAF Bentwaters. Another 16 HEs fell in the Felixstowe area.

None of those events constituted much of a bombing campaign. That appears to have been launched on 24/25 May when Heinkel He 111s of KG 27 set out from western Germany to bomb a variety of targets in east and north-east England. Included were five bombs on Catterick's landing ground and 16 in the Holderness district. Another two fell on industrial Middlesbrough and 18 just outside RAF West Raynham, Norfolk. One exploded near Harleston, and two at Willow Farm, Langley, Loddon, killing a cow. Animals were to suffer as much as people.

Luftwaffe occupation of captured airfields brought a new, immense problem for Fighter Command, increased the danger to shipping and added immeasurably to the invasion threat. The Luftwaffe was only an hour's flying time from London, the world's largest, most tempting target. It could easily outflank British defences by attacking from the west and in particular devastate vital ports on Merseyside, at Bristol and in south Wales. Increased Fighter Command strength was therefore essential.

Small-scale night bombing had continued. On 2 June at Strumpshaw, for instance, a Norfolk civilian became the first East Anglian to be seriously injured. That night also brought a He 111 raid on Mildenhall, all 23 HEs missing the bomber station. With the BEF now gone from Dunkirk, enemy air effort on 5 June was switched to supporting a strong thrust towards Paris before, in the late evening and in ideal conditions, there came the largest attack yet upon Britain with enemy aircraft operating between the Orkneys and the Isle of Wight. By dawn some 30 bombers had produced 134 overland raid tracks, with ports and airfields the main objectives. Bombs fell widely — two near Wick, another near Horsham St Faith, six at Driffield and a large shower of incendiaries near Duxford. Fire bombs also fell around Gainsborough and Tilbury; ten HEs fell at Peterborough and another 14 at Louth. Flares released over Stoke Holy Cross near Norwich may have been the first such eerie objects to drift over Britain. As the total load dropped was less than expected from so many bombers, it was concluded that they must have mainly been engaged in training.

It was thought at first that the raiders established their positions by taking bearings on M/F (Medium Frequency) radio beacons, but the physicist Professor R.V. Jones, seconded to Air Ministry, suspected something more. A He 111 of KG 26 brought down on 3 April 1940 contained among its papers a reference to 'Radio Beacon *Knickebein* from 0600 hours on 315°'. Professor Jones suspected that German bom-

Typical French airfield scene early in the campaign. Bf 109Es of 9/JG 2 Richthofen and support vehicles have been roughly camouflaged using foliage. (Michael Payne)

bers were flying along a radio beam and dropping their loads soon after reaching the intersection point of a second beam. If that was so, the Luftwaffe could attack with some accuracy during darkness and bad weather, assuming its beams were correctly aligned. On 6/7 June the Germans operated on a wider scale, over 170 tracks being plotted between Yorkshire and the south coast. Aerodromes — existing or planned — had clearly been targetted, bombs falling near Beverley, Pocklington, Marham, Pulham, Upwood, Feltwell and Mildenhall. Most munitions dropped were of the 50-kg type but a clutch of 250-kg bombs was recorded at Bedfield, Suffolk.

On 7/8 June the Heinkels came again after RAF bomber bases, including Honington, and also sought major railway installations, Peterborough among them. Thereafter activity over Britain declined, the lull lasting until the French request for an armistice on 17 June. By then Professor Jones had deduced that the blind-landing receiver was the means by which German bombers flew along a beam to their targets, and an Anson aircraft was fitted out to

try to pick up one of the beams on any of the frequencies to which the receiver was normally tuned. Meanwhile, on the night of 18/19 June the biggest night operation yet against Britain was launched and the first bombs fell in Greater London, at Addington.

Forty He 111s of KG 27 and 31 of KG 4 had set out, 139 flights being traced. Some penetrated deep into Britain whereas previously mostly shallow penetrations had been made. Attacks were repeated on East Anglian Wellington squadron bases — Marham, Honington, Mildenhall, Stradishall — and Lincolnshire's Hampden stations. Other German crews aimed at railway installations, and at Cambridge two bombs undershot onto a terrace of Victorian houses, killing nine and injuring ten civilians in the worst incident so far. At Thameshaven KG 4 tried to destroy oil tanks, and by dawn bombing had occurred in at least 18 areas as far apart as Settle, Strood, Bridlington and Chatham. Of 210 HE bombs known to have fallen, 22 did not explode. Spilsby area's large share was 44, 11 of the UX type.

About 80 He 111s operated on 21/22 June, beginning their work at Parkeston Quay. Another 26 incidents followed in East Anglia, including the first bombing of Ipswich, where 10 HEs were laid across the town. What made that attack so memorable for the townsfolk were

'organ pipe' whistling devices attached to bomb tails. The night brought other novelties, the first 'oil bombs' at Melton Ross, near Brigg in Lincolnshire and at Rede, Suffolk. Within a 250-kg HE bomb shell was a mixture of explosive, incendiary and tarry liquid.

By day *Zenit* weather reporting sorties were flown off the East Anglian coast as far as Scotland. A flurry of such activity on 24 June preceded operations over the South and Midlands by about 60 He 111s. Bristol received its first raid, a clothing factory at Knowle being demolished and 23 houses hit, a school was fired and a soap factory damaged in the Old Market Street area. Five were killed by the 108 incendiaries and 20 HEs delivered. Other raiders penetrated to Liverpool. In London there were five deaths due to shock when air raid warnings were sounded.

So far the largely ineffective raids had struck at widespread targets. A more concentrated three-phase operation by about 70 bombers started just before midnight on 25 June.

Enemy activity brought anti-aircraft guns

Above *From France, the Germans took over the Channel Islands, where they requisitioned local transport as necessary. This Messerschmitt Bf 109E of JG 53 at Guernsey Airport being refuelled from petrol drums aboard Austin truck '5377' belongs to JG 53. (Bundesarchiv)*

Left *Many elderly 3-inch naval (emplaced) guns served as anti-aircraft guns. An example photographed at Portland 26 July 1940. (IWM)*

into action at Bristol, Portsmouth and Southampton which, between them, loosed off 141 rounds. The heavy AA guns were either elderly 3-inch, hefty 4.5-inch or more usually the 1934 Barrow-designed Vickers 3.7-inch whose firing trials had been held at Weybourne in August 1936. It fired a 43.1-inch-long shell which, boosted by 2 lb 5 oz of TNT, weighed 46 lb 4 oz when complete. Prominent sights on clear dark nights were the 90-cm 12½-million candle power searchlights, 96 in a regiment and each light theoretically 6,000 yards apart, allowing a cone of three beams to hold an aircraft and pass it to the next trio.

By the end of June the Heinkels had played their unforgettable 'compahhing' engine overture to much of Britain. They had operated on average at about 10,000 feet — too low for their safety. Confirmation of that were 22 night combats, success in location by searchlights, and the 11 German bombers shot down in June's raids. That score might have been higher had more attention been paid to airborne interception (AI) radar in fighters and gun-laying radar for the AA forces. Instead, wisely as it turned out, most effort had been put into developing early warning radar. Thirteen RAF airfields, 16 industrial plants and 14 port areas had so far been attacked, but little lasting damage done.

Already, many had heard the crash of bombs, seen the bright white glare of incendiaries, and some would hold loved ones no more. These early raids had provided valuable experience for the defences, and the Civil Defence organization's sirens had very widely been sounded. Realizing it would make sense to sound the alarm when raiders were very likely to be in a specific area, rather that to warn much of the country, siren sounding abated. The Germans, in exchange for night flying experience over Britain, had actually paid a higher price than they realized. On its second flight the Anson fitted with beam-searching equipment allocated to Wyton's Wireless Investigation Development Unit, and flown by Flight Lieutenant H.E. Bufton with Corporal Mackie, discovered two of the suspected radio navigation narrow beams.

One was found near Spalding and the other nearer to the Humber. Professor Jones emphasized the serious implications — accurate night attacks *were* possible, on almost any part of Britain, in particular industrial centres and vital ports, many of which were in the poorly defended western half of the country.

'Shall we sound the Siren?'

The British Isles were divided into about 130 'Warning Districts', their layout based upon the existing public telephone system. Raids were plotted on a map at HQ Fighter Command showing these districts, and when a raid was within 20 minutes of one the Air Raid Warning officer would telephone a message to the Trunk Exchanges in London, Liverpool or Glasgow. From there it would be passed to the relevant Districts who would notify Police, Fire, Hospitals, etc. This was known as the 'Yellow' warning.

If the District was still under threat 5 minutes later, a 'Red Warning' would be sent and the sirens sounded. 'Green' was the codeword for 'All Clear'. At night, when exposed lights were essential in places such as docks, railyards, etc., another warning, 'Purple', was used. It meant that all such lights should be doused and was often in force after 'All Clear' was sounded.

By midsummer 1940 a German invasion was no longer a mere possibility, more a certainty. The nation had also become aware that the Royal Navy was *not* as invincible as popularly thought — that starvation by blockade was increasingly possible. Although Britain possessed ten battleships and three battle cruisers, only three had been built since the 1914-18 war, and only five were at any one time in home waters. Ranged against our Navy was a modern, quite powerful, but smaller, combined Axis surface fleet, while under the sea roamed the chief adversary, the submarine.

The War Cabinet's assessment was that effective air defence must be the No. 1 priority. However, after reviewing the events so far, it concluded that an aerial knockout blow was probably not possible, that west coast ports could probably be kept open — just — and that with RAF intervention an invasion would prove difficult and costly. All was seen to hinge upon successful air defence of the whole country.

One invasion tactic it was thought the Germans might contemplate was seizure at night by some 5,000 paratroops of seven vital fighter airfields in the south-east for landings to be made upon them at dawn by transport and even bomber aircraft. Meanwhile some 20,000 troops would make a beach assault. Reinforcements under air cover would arrive during daylight hours.

To counter that threat eight Army divisions were ordered to man coastal defences in depth. By mid-June 1940 786 field guns were in place, either by likely coastal landing places, or inland to guard against any airborne forces landed to take coastal defence forces from the rear. The Army had not been trained, as yet, to cope with

...the Battle of France is over. I expect that the Battle of Britain is about to begin. Upon this battle depends the survival of Christian civilisation. Upon it depends our own British life, and the long continuity of our institutions and our Empire. The whole fury and might of the enemy must very soon be turned upon us. Hitler knows that he will have to break us in this island or lose the war. If we can stand up to him, all Europe may be free and the life of the world may move forward into broad, sunlit uplands. But if we fail, then the whole world — including the United States, including all that we have known and cared for — will sink into the abyss of a new dark age made more sinister, and perhaps more protracted, by the lights of perverted science. Let us therefore brace ourselves to our duties, and so bear ourselves that, if the British Empire and its Commonwealth last for a thousand years, men will still say 'This was their finest hour.'

Winston Churchill, 18 June 1940

Tanks, rare in 1940, of the 5th Royal Tank Regiment, 3rd Armoured Brigade, 1st Armoured Division passing through Thursley, Sussex. (IWM)

Bren-gun Carriers followed by bicycling soldiers, photographed at Haven Street, on the Isle of Wight. In the carriers, men of the 6th Black Watch, 12th Brigade, 4th Division, V Corps. (IWM)

fast-changing situations. Across East Anglia five defence lines, including a giant ditch — the Eastern Tank Trap — were established ahead of a main GHQ line. Another three in the south-east were for the defence of London. These defences in depth were also intended to prevent any breakdown in law and order. Behind them, from mid-June, were three mobile infantry divisions, centrally held. Churchill wanted 10,000 men to be available within six hours to reinforce any point where the enemy had landed, and groups of 20,000 ready to react as a mobile force, though, as Ironside pointed out, his troops were not trained for such activities. Tanks of the 1st Armoured Division would rush forward where needed, but it seems unlikely that they would have had the necessary mobility and firepower to be of much value. The 2nd Armoured Division with over 150 tanks was held in central western East Anglia to react towards the coast as necessary.

'I'll fight on the sands, in my trench, then my pillbox. Like the man said, I'll never surrender!' Great Yarmouth, 1 August 1940. (IWM)

By late June over 150,000 troops and civilians were preparing defences too often badly placed or wrongly orientated. East and south coast beaches were mined during June and July 1940. Simple wire net booms were floated offshore and mines attached to scaffolding, to discourage landing craft. A floating minefield sealed off the Wash, and many manned road-blocks were built on routes leading from the shore. Pleasure piers had their centre sections demolished to prevent their use as jetties. Within a host of

concrete pillboxes stores of hand grenades and so called 'sticky bombs' were established for use by the LDV, whose task was to make life extremely unpleasant for the intruders. Had the enemy penetrated far he would have faced Army reserves manning anti-tank defences and operating 167 anti-tank guns along the GHQ Line passing between natural high points from Middlesbrough to London.

With insufficient weapons though, both the Army and the LDV would have had a hard fight. All told the Army had operationally available 52 18-pdr guns, 87 25-pdr guns, 72 4.5-pdr guns and 167 anti-tank guns, and placed at its disposal were seven RAF squadrons, two of Blenheims and five flying Lysanders.

Few living at the time failed to enjoy hot gossip, none of it more spine-chilling than that concerning plans to pour petrol on the sea, set fire to it and cremate the invaders! The trials that were undertaken showed that releasing petrol onto the sea and then igniting it was not as easy as the idea sounds because of the action of the tide and the motion of the waves. Eventually, petrol was used in land-based and relatively common defence works. Perforated pipes joined to disguised petrol tanks were laid alongside roads leading from beaches. After turning on the flow an LDV member was expected to hurl a lighted torch onto the petrol, more of which would flood anti-tank ditches or flow from barrels onto the beaches themselves. Such gruesome activity was master-minded from June 1940 by the Petroleum Warfare Department.

Many critical areas remained undefended. When the military bastion, Dover, came within range of German gunners at Framzelles in the Pas de Calais it was the latter who largely controlled the Dover Straits. Dover's destroyers were forced to Portsmouth and Chatham, and British convoys had whenever possible to pass through the Straits in darkness. Few British guns had sufficient range to bombard enemy positions, such activity in any case was reckoned likely to bring unwanted retaliation. German guns and gunners had to be discouraged by the RAF — no easy task.

Harshly battered during the fight for France, the RAF, although it had lost around 1,000 aircraft, had survived more adequately equipped than the Army. Its losses were mainly of obsolete Fairey Battle bombers, and Hurricane fighters which could be replaced from reserves and ever-increasing production. German failure to destroy our aircraft production sources early in the war was a fundamental blunder.

Where did the first bombs fall?

Estimate of total weights of bombs dropped:

5/6 June	158 tonnes
18/19 June	100 tonnes
19/20 June	80 tonnes

Number of bombs dropped in June 1940:
1,388 high explosive of various sizes, mainly 50 kg 14 oil bombs, equal to 859 metric tonnes. Incendiaries — not known

Legend: ibs = 1-kg incendiary bombs
RD = Rural District
UD = Urban District (towns/cities unless otherwise stated)
Bracketted numbers = unexploded bombs additional to others

10 May

Bridge Blean, Kent	20, ibs

14 May

Swanage	1

21 May

Eastleigh (Hants)	8

22 May

Butley (Suffolk)	1
Felixstowe, in sea	5

24/25 May

Middlesbrough	2

25 May

Billericay	1
Holderness RD	16
Horsham St Faith RD	1
Loddon RD	4
Walsingham	9

2 June
Blofield and Fegg RD — 1
4 June
Mildenhall RD — 23
5/6 June
Bridlington RD — 16
Driffield RD — 6
Gainsborough — 15
Louth RD — 14
Peterborough RD — 10
Scunthorpe
6 June
East Kesteven RD — 6 (2)
Newton Cambs — ibs
Pocklington — 10
Thurruck UD — ibs
Welton — 6
Worlingworth — (4)
7 June
Depwade RD — (3)
Swaffham — 5
Peterborough — 7
8 June
Oakham RD — 8
South Kesteven RD — 15
9 June
Newmarket RD — 41
10 June
Canvey Island — 1 (1)
Hartismere RD — 5
13 June
Portland — 22 (23)
16 June
Isle of Wight — 2
18/19 June
Arundel
Benfleet — 1
Boston RD — 6
Bridlington RD — 6
Bury St Edmunds — 4
Cambridge — 2
Chesterton RD Cambs — ibs
Deben RD — 4
Docking RD — 6
Downham RD — 6
Dunmow RD — 4
Freebridge & Lynn RD — 7 (7)
Horncastle RD — 1
Huntingdon RD — 4
March — 7
North Kesteven RD — 26 (2)

North Witchford RD — 9
Rochford RD — 2 (1)
Saffron Walden RD — 2
Sevenge — 25
Southend — 4 (1)
Spalding RD — 3
Spilsby RD — 33 (12)
St Neots — 1 (1)
Strood RD — 3
Witham — 4
19 June
Settle — 10(3)
19/20 June
Billingham (Durham) UD — 22
Caistor RD — 1, ibs
Derwent RD — 11
Glandford Brig — 4 (2) ibs
Grimsby RD — 8
Hull — 1, ibs
Norton RD — 1
Southampton — 10
West Hartlepool — 12
20 June
Cardiff — 6
Cowbridge — ibs
20/21 June
South Shields — 5
21/22 June
Cleethorpes — 8
Erping RD — 12
Grimsby — 3
Romney Marsh — 2
Swale RD — ibs
Tynemouth — 2
22 June
Cosford RD — (1)
Forehoe and Henstead RD — 2
Harwich — 9
Ipswich — 10
Lothingland RD — 3
Smallborough UD — 25 (1)
Thedwastre RD — 16
Woodbridge — 6
Wymondham — 13
24 June
Chichester RD — 30
Launditch RD — 1
24/25 June
Bristol — 20, ibs
Lutterworth RD — 14 (1)
Melton Belvoir RD — 3

Rugby — 39
25 June
Battle RD — 1
Colne Valley UD — 7
Derby — 4
Dover RD — 4
Halstead RD — 2
Shardlow RD — 9
Wayland UD — 4
25/26 June
Aldridge UD — 5
Bridgewater RD — 4 (1)
Edinburgh — 5, ibs
Fleet — 3
Hinckley — 4 (1)
Midlothian, landward — 29, ibs
Newcastle-under-Lyme — 12
Spalding UD — 1
West Bromwich — 2
26 June
Chelmsford RD — 2
Cowes — 2 (5)
East Lothian, landward — ibs
Fife, landward — 1
Newport (Mon) — 9
Perth, landward — 13, ibs
Salisbury RD — 4
26/27 June
Aberdeen — 4
Amesbury RD — 4
Hawarden — 6
Stone — 12
Winchester — 5
Winchester RD — 3 (6)
27 June
Swansea — (6)
27/28 June
Brierley Hill UD — 6
East Elloe RD — 8
Meriden RD — 2
Newmarket — ibs
Selkirk, landward — 4
28 June
Angus, landward — 6
Blackwell — 12
Chepstow RD — 2
Hepton — 10 (3)
Roxborough — ibs
Wainford RD — 3 (5)
28/29 June
Poole — 2

29 June

Aberdeen RD, in sea	1
Cardiff RD	6 (1)
Neath	2
Port Talbot	10

Torpoint	2
Wells next Sea	(1)

29/30 June

West Kesteven RD	4

30 June

Chichester RD	24
Hove	2
Penarth	14 (2)

CHAPTER 4
AROUND OUR SHORES

While Britain concentrated upon building its defences the Luftwaffe trained and prepared for the invasion being planned by the High Command; but first it needed to extinguish the RAF. Although Hitler hoped the British would be sensible enough to surrender, on 2 July he enquired how long the Luftwaffe would take to obtain total air superiority. 'Four days', replied the High Command, to remove fighter protection from southern Britain.

Taking a very different view, the British Chiefs of Staff forecast a severe German economic crisis in 1941, and advised the Government to bear that in mind and continue the fight. Hitler, on 16 July, decided that Britain must be invaded and, satisfied with the plans drawn up, issued an operations directive. To the end of the first week of August the Luftwaffe

would probe British defences and attack Channel shipping. Six weeks before the invasion the Luftwaffe would launch a major offensive. It must prevent attacks on his invasion forces, smash enemy coastal defences, break initial resistance and destroy the Army reserves behind main British defences.

The Germans accepted that their foe would put up a tough fight — not only British soldiers but probably most British men, women and even children. True, very true, for many households with long memories of 'the last war' were

The Germans, far from home, had to first prepare forward bases in France, initially used for night raids by He 111s, one of which is being hidden under camouflage netting. (Bundesarchiv)

almost gleefully storing private arsenals, including garden tools, beer bottle petrol bombs, sugar rations to pour into German petrol tanks, man traps, and contemplating nasty uses for boiling water.

In addition to those four days needed to subjugate British fighter defence south of a line from London to Gloucester, the Germans reckoned it would take another three weeks to destroy the remainder of the RAF in Britain.

Both Luftflotten 2 and 3 were ordered to carry out the massacre. No. 2 based in northern Germany, the Netherlands, Belgium and north-east France was commanded by Field-Marshal Kesselring, commander of Luftflotte 1 during the Polish campaign. Luftflotte 3 in North and North West France was led by Field Marshal Hugo Sperrle, the 1936-37 leader of the Kondor Legion in Spain. These were, without doubt, the Luftwaffe's finest commanders. Luftflotte 2 would operate east of the line approximately Le Havre-Solent-Oxford-Birmingham-Manchester, Luftflotte 3 to its west. Convergent raids by both Luftflotten would split the defending effort, particularly at

Looking every inch the tough Man of the 'Master Race', Hugo Sperrle commanded Luftflotte 3. (IWM)

night. Luftflotte 5, based in Denmark and Norway and commanded by General Stumpff, would operate against northern England and Scotland, and mount diversion raids and widespread shipping attacks, thus forcing the British to summon defenders from the south. Between them they held about 3,500 aircraft. All straightforward, almost simple.

FOOD FACTS No. 1

Register now for cooking fats. On Monday July 22 cooking fats will be rationed... Butter and Margarine total weekly ration 6 oz — butter or all margarine or some of each. Tea is now rationed — 2 oz a week. You may buy from any shop you like, no registration is necessary

Newspapers, 15 July

The National Milk Scheme provides 1 pint of milk at a reduced price for an expectant or nursing mother and every child under five not attending school. All... get milk at 2d a pint. Mothers and children are entitled to free milk if the combined income of parents is less than 40/- a week, or if one parent's income is less than 27/6d...

Newspapers, 15 July

In the third week of July 1940 the German Air Force was ordered to 'full readiness' and the final, detailed operations orders were worked out.

Unit returns for 20 July from the three Luftflotten set alongside similar returns for the RAF on 22 July, as in the table opposite, make for interesting comparison. About 66 per cent of

	LUFTFLOTTEN 2 and 3			TOTAL RAF	
	Strength	Serviceable		Establishment	Serviceable
Long-range bombers	1,131	769	Long-range bombers	320	256
Dive-bombers	316	248	Light/Medium bombers	272	257
Single-engined fighters	809	656	Single-engined fighters	900	606
Twin-engined fighters	246	168	Twin-engined fighters	160	101
Long-range reconnaissance	67	48	Coastal/long-range/ strike recon- naissance	291	156
Short-range reconnaissance for army/invasion support	90	?	Lysanders (Nos. 22 and 61 Groups)	174	143
	LUFTFLOTTE 5				
Long-Range bombers	129	95			
Single-engined	84	?			
Long-range reconnaissance	48	33			
Grand totals	2,920	2,076		2,053	1,519

the German bombers were expected to be serviceable, 80 per cent of the fighters; so Luftflotten 2 and 3 could field about 800 long-range bombers, 250 dive-bombers and 820 fighters. German intelligence sources reckoned the Metropolitan RAF to have 50 operational fighter squadrons — some 900 front line aircraft excluding the Blenheim fighters — of which about 675 would at one time be serviceable.

Fighter Command strength was underestimated by the Germans. In early July it comprised 48 operational squadrons (two with Defiants and four more forming or re-equipping) — 58 if those training, etc, were included. The six Blenheim 1s in day-fighter squadrons and those equipping the Fighter Interception Unit at Tangmere usually operated at night. British anti-aircraft defences were poorly regarded by the Germans, and balloons — flown too low — very vulnerable to attack and rough conditions. Searchlight defences experienced during June were rated effective.

Balloon barrages formed an important part of British defences. Pre-war planning called for 1,450 Low Zone balloons, but only 624 were operationally deployed at the outbreak of war. Losses due to bad weather were higher than expected, nevertheless by May 1940 there were sufficient balloons to meet pre-war plans. Some saving was achieved by close hauling balloons until required. Mobile barrages for ship protection were introduced, and barges permitting waterborne barrages including the important examples at Harwich and in the Thames Estuary. That led to a shortfall of 600 balloons.

Protection of west coast ports and adjacent areas raised difficult problems in an area short of aerodromes and AA guns. Defence therefore relied largely upon balloons. Dowding proposed four new barrages in the west, increasing the size of some existing, and siting groups of ten waterborne balloons in 14 more estuaries to interfere with mining. That raised the overall total from 2,027 to 2,375 balloons. The Air Staff, believing that insufficient to protect western areas, decided by the end of July the need to be for 2,600. Balloon squadrons num-

Most 3.7-inch anti-aircraft guns were of the cheaper, fixed type. (IWM)

bered 52 by July 1940 (listed establishment 1,865, actual strength around 1,450 balloons). Monthly production — just over 200 in September 1939 — reached around 1,200 by September 1940.

The G.O.C.-in-C Anti-Aircraft Command, General Sir Frederick Pile, in mid-June 1940 had a force of 1,204 heavy and 581 light guns against an established need of 2,232 and 1,860 respectively. By late July he possessed only half the heavies and one-third the light guns he had needed even before France had fallen, when gun losses were high. Although there were seven gun divisions, each of 15 regiments, manning levels were inadequate because the Army had syphoned off the fittest troops. Gun defences were much in demand for VPs (vital points) such as aircraft factories, airfields, west coast ports, naval bases and industrial areas. Rolls-Royce Derby had 22 guns protecting it, British Aeroplane works at Filton only eight and Fighter Command HQ Stanmore only four. Shortfall of Bofors was reduced by placing almost 4,000 Lewis guns in AA Command, but the RAF believed that it would need about 850 hits from one of those to ensure a kill.

The most serious flaw in the German assessment of British capability was a failure to realize the increasing effectiveness of Britain's warning radar system. By early 1940 the coastal

'This, men is a searchlight. It moves on caterpillar tracks. The trooper on the left controls azimuth setting, the man on the right its elevation. Now, what is it Engineer?' 'A searchlight, SIR'. (IWM)

radar chain extended from the Firth of Forth to the Solent; it also protected Scapa Flow and the Bristol area but left most of western Britain uncovered. Remedial action in the spring of 1940 meant that by mid-July six CHL (Chain Home Low) and 3 CH (Chain Home) radar stations existed in south-west England and south Wales. To correlate defences in this region, a new Fighter Group, No. 10, opened on 1 June 1940 and took over four squadrons and three Sector stations from 12 Group: Pembrey, Filton (temporarily used until Colerne became available) and St Eval, where squadrons lodged on this Coastal Command station. Middle Wallop joined the Group in August 1940.

Observer Corps cover extended over the south-west and south Wales. Most of Wales, the west Midlands and north-west to the Scottish border remained under 12 Group control. Another Group was certainly needed to co-ordinate fighter and AA activity over Wales and northwards west of the Pennines. Poor land communications existed there, airfields were few, radar non existent. Although this new Group — No. 9 — opened on 9 August 1940, and a Filter Room at Preston on 13 August, it played little part in the Battle. No. 14 Group, which controlled the air defence of Scotland, began reforming on 20 July 1940. No. 13 Group, which opened on 24 July 1939 controlled air defence

Above *A typical Chain Home (CH) radar station of the type originally called an Air Ministry Experimental Station. Its 350-foot towers transmitted the signal (from an aerial array slung between them), the 250-foot type received the return.* (IWM)

Right *Spartan interior of a CH radar station, WAAF 'sparks' busy.* (IWM)

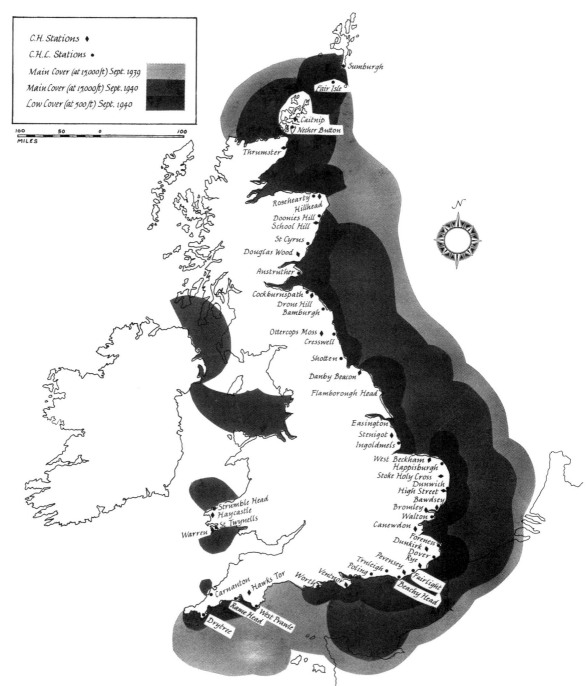

C.H. Stations ◆
C.H.L. Stations ●
Main Cover (at 15,000 ft) Sept. 1939
Main Cover (at 15,000 ft) Sept. 1940
Low Cover (at 500 ft) Sept. 1940

100   50   0   100
MILES

Sumburgh
Fair Isle
Caitnip
Nether Button
Thrumster
Rosehearty
Hillhead
Doonies Hill
School Hill
St Cyrus
Douglas Wood
Anstruther
Cockburnspath
Drone Hill
Bamburgh
Ottercops Moss
Cresswell
Sholten
Danby Beacon
Flamborough Head
Easington
Stenigot
Ingoldmels
West Beckham
Happisburgh
Stoke Holy Cross
Dunwich
High Street
Bawdsey
Bromley
Walton
Canewdon
Foreness
Dunkirk
Dover
Pevensey
Rye
Truleigh
Poling
Fairlight
Beachy Head
Strumble Head
Haycastle
St Twynells
Warren
Carnanton
Hawks Tor
West Prawle
Worth
Ventnor
Rame Head
Drytree

RADAR CHAIN, JULY 1940 and RADAR COVER, SEPTEMBER 1939 AND SEPTEMBER 1940

from the north-east to Wick.

The Observer Corps played a particularly valuable part. Its keen, skilled watchers and plotters could elaborate upon radar information, precisely identify the nature of threats by discovering aircraft types employed and often give immediate raid warning relating to lone, very dangerous attackers heading for vulnerable points.

The Germans did not realize that the Brit-

Above *Skilled Observer Corps personnel using binoculars and a type of sextant able to swing through 360 degrees. They could identify aircraft types — which radar could not — and provided vital information on height and course of friendly as well as enemy aircraft.* (IWM)

Below *Observer Corps posts, usually in clusters of three or four with up to 50 in a Group, fed information to their Group Centre, where it was displayed on a plotting table. A wall notice reminds the personnel that 'Walls Have Ears'.* (IWM)

ish had acquired their Enigma code deciphering equipment. It gave access to operational policy, planning and targeting, although just what could be derived from the assorted and often incomplete information which took time to evaluate remains speculative. What it appears not to have provided were final details of tactical arrangements to be employed by raiders, the prerogative of unit commanders. Those involved with Enigma at the time seem of the opinion that it often provided incomplete information rather too late to help much in repelling the raiders.

Other sources of vital intelligence material included the 'Y' Service (the listening service) which, from the start of the war monitored German radio chatter 24 hours a day, recorded it and sifted it. By employing radio direction finding, hearing snippets of give-away radio talk and listening to radio homing, valuable information was acquired to set alongside other intelligence. Flights by high-flying photo reconnaissance Spitfires of the PRU resulted in excellent photographs of enemy coastal areas, particularly of invasion assemblies. Add to these reports from agents and embassies abroad and the British can be seen to have been well supplied with material with which to conduct their defence.

Unravelling by Professor R.V. Jones of German 'beam riding' and radio target marking had by July 1940 led to the formation, under Wing Commander E.B. Addison, a signals expert, of No. 80 Wing whose task was to enact countermeasures to *Knickebein*. Controlled in utmost secrecy by Air Ministry and a few officers at Fighter Command, it reviewed radio jamming, production of false beams, redirecting of M/F transmissions to confuse crews and the relevance of other intelligence data.

All was of little use without men and weapons. Although planned Fighter Command pilot strength was 1,450, the number on 9 July 1940 — the 'official' starting date of the Battle — totalled 1,253. Each squadron nominally held 12 aircraft, making the number available at one time to be about 600. Had more pilots

been available that could easily have been 700. As for the pilots themselves, an increasing proportion lacked all-round experience. A high percentage already lost had been experienced and long trained, and replacing them was impossible. Many more pilots should have been trained pre-war, thus providing a pool — politically impossible in peacetime when every step towards re-armament had met with strong opposition. Had there been greatly increased pilot training facilities the number of young men physically and mentally ideally suited to becoming fighter pilots might still have proved insufficient. Attempts were made, by re-orientating the Auxiliary Air Force into a reserve fighter force, to build a reservoir of trained pilots, but recruiting and operating the

'Where's Hitler?' Bow tie, cigar, pin striped suit and splendid hat — typical of 'Winnie'. (IWM)

squadrons had to take place near large population centres where, again, the number of suitable young men was limited. It was, indeed a difficult problem, solved only after the establishment of a sufficiently large training organization.

Instead of forming more squadrons, the Establishment of many short-range day fighter squadrons (30 of Hurricanes and 6 of Spitfires) was raised by 4 aircraft to 16 each, the additional aircraft being flown in emergencies by pilots rested or nominally on leave. Further swelling of squadron ranks came when 68 Fleet Air Arm pilots were seconded to Fighter Command although ten had soon to be released for naval service in the Mediterranean theatre. From June to October an average of 60 naval pilots flew in fighter squadrons and others with Coastal Command.

By 10 July every coastal county of England and Wales had received unwelcome objects. General disruption brought by raid warnings caused official concern, but failure to alert the public could prove disastrous. At Aberdeen on 12 July, without public warning, a raid resulted in 50 casualties.

Two distinct new threats had evolved, (i) cloud cover, daytime, precision attacks hard to detect by radar and mounted by a single or small group of bombers penetrating inland to a key point, and (ii) fighter protected/supported relatively small raids, of which six occurred between 1 and 9 July. Within that period seven attacks were delivered upon Channel convoys, particular attention being paid to shipping as well as port facilities at Dover, Weymouth, Portland, Plymouth and Falmouth.

Protecting shipping was uneconomical and difficult because an attack could equally be by single aircraft cloaked by fog or rain, or a large escorted formation. Intent upon conserving its forces, Dowding ordered Park to daily move squadrons forward, from Hornchurch Sector to Manston, from Biggin Hill and Kenley to Hawkinge and from Middle Wallop to Warmwell, thus placing them close enough to provide rapid protection of Channel convoys by small

forces. Those needs were somewhat reduced when ocean-going convoys ceased to pass through the English Channel. East Coast and Channel coastal trade convoys comprising as many as 30 ships — particularly small colliers — remained tempting targets.

Popular belief that the Battle of Britain was fought over south-east England is too simplistic. Indeed, early on 1 July a He 59 air-sea rescue floatplane, D-ASAM of Seenotflugkommand probably supporting KG 26, was shot down eight miles off Sunderland by Spitfires of 72 Squadron. Morning activity over the Dover Straits was followed by Ju 87s attacking convoy 'Jumbo' off Plymouth. Hurricanes of No. 145 Squadron (P3521, P2770 and N2496) shot into the Channel a 2/KG 77 Do

Squadron Leader J.R.A. Peel, highly successful leader of 145 Squadron. (IWM)

17 which had prowled between Poole, Liverpool and Odiham. A spectacular afternoon fire was lit at the Heddon, Hull, depot of Anglo-American Oil by a lone, Stavanger-based KG 26 He 111 which narrowly escaped the wrath of 616 Squadron. Late afternoon south Wales was also attacked. About 15 He 111s of KG 55 operated there after dark, half the night force and operating from Villacoublay, while others came from Jever and Aalborg. At distant Wick, bombing by a Ju 88 of KG 30 killed 14 people. Clearly, the raids were nationwide. The tempo of the action heightened after the German High Command's order of 2 July to increase bombing Britain. At lunchtime that day KG 26 called on Saltburn's Skinningrove iron works, reducing production, also on shipyards at Jarrow and Newcastle.

Hurricanes of 32 Squadron took a major part in the fighting, among them P3522 seen here. Used by 32 Squadron 20 May 1940, damaged in action 23 August and passed to 213 Squadron on 19 September 1940. (IWM)

Lords of the Air

The British Empire proudly stands
As in the days of old,
Our fathers fought o'er land and sea,
Their history is told
In our new battlefield the sky,
Prepare to do or dare,
Let this be our new battlecry
'Britannia rules the air.'

England our island home,
Land of the free,
England unconquered yet,
O'er land and sea,
Lord of the heav'ns above,
Answer our prayer,
God keep Britannia's sons,
Lords of the Air

Michael North and Davy Burnaby

Cloud and rain shielded lone bombers which at midday on 3 July began bombing assorted targets within the area North Foreland-Ford-Midhurst-Crystal Palace. Among them was White Waltham aerodrome, where six bombs damaged seven Tigers and an Anson. Late afternoon brought a score of similar incidents mainly at coastal towns and docks. Raid M22, a He 111, sowed a line of 15 bombs across Ipswich. None exploded, but at Lowestoft a sharp onslaught by a KG 77 Do 17 set ablaze the town's main CWS store, from where sailors rescued delivery vans while firemen bravely brought out people sheltering in the basement.

Not all the raiders escaped. A cheeky Do 17Z of II/KG 77 which bombed Manston was caught by No. 56 Squadron Hurricanes (P3387, P3587, P3547) and set alight to ten minutes later off Burnham-on-Crouch. Another, which aimed six bombs at Kenley, was destroyed by a trio of 32 Squadron Hurricanes (N2463, N2670, N2671). During the day three Ju 88s of 8/KG 30 were shot down off Scotland by 603 Squadron. Such raids highlighted the difficulties in warning coastal residents of imminent attack and led to klaxon 'crash warnings'. They also emphasized the desirability of having civilians move inland, and showed the difficulty of rapidly gathering — usually from their work places — voluntary Civil Defence workers for the fire, rescue and first aid services.

On 4 July the first Stuka and fighter escorted raids were launched when at 08:30 Bf 110s shepherded 33 Ju 87s of III/StG 51 eager to demonstrate to the British six minutes of classic dive bombing. Grouped, line astern, they screamed down from 15,000 feet out of the sun aiming at Portland harbour whose defenders replied with 155 3-inch shells and 4,753 machine-gun rounds. The tug *Silverdial* was sunk before the Stukas singled out HMS *Foylebank*, a 5,582 grt anti-aircraft ship, slamming at least nine bombs into her. Aboard, and displaying enormous courage, was Acting Leading Seaman Jack Foreman Hantle who, despite horrific wounds to his left leg, continued firing a 20mm pom-pom gun even after receiving fur-

Above *Reconnaissance photograph of Portland Harbour.* (IWM)

Below *Acting Leading Seaman Jack Hantle, awarded the Victoria Cross for his valiant manning of the guns aboard HMS* Foylebank. (IWM)

ther wounds. He died by his gun, and was posthumously awarded the Victoria Cross on 3 September 1940.

Portland was subsequently attacked many times, its second raid coming mid-morning on 4 July when two bombers killed ten people in the dockyard. Twenty miles away, others of KG 77 and II/Lehr 1 attacked the last deep sea convoy to sail through the Channel, OA178. They damaged nine large merchantmen (including *Argos Hill* of 7,178 grt, *City of Melbourne* of 6,630 grt, *William Wilberforce* of 5,004 grt and *East Wales* of 4,358 grt), escaping before 213 Squadron Hurricanes could catch them.

Meanwhile nine small ships off Dover had received attention from two Staffeln of Do 17s protected by about 30 Bf 109s. Eight 79 Squadron Hurricanes scrambled from Hawkinge to intercept lost one of their number. At about the same time He 111s skilfully using cloud cover attacked a variety of targets. Bristol's Filton works received four HEs before a hectic chase by three 92 Squadron Spitfires ended in the bomber's destruction at Ref. U2454/Weston-super-Mare. Driffield was also bombed, barrack blocks and the NAAFI being damaged by six HEs. Further bombs fell near Maidstone, Yeovilton, Ramsgate and Plymouth's Storr Point.

Early in the evening Hurricanes of 32 Squadron[1] engaged Raid 20, three Staffeln of Bf 109s which shot down two Hurricanes without loss. Before darkness fell three Spitfires of 64 Squadron (including P9450 and R6700) snooping high over the Pas de Calais encountered Bf 109s of JG 51 which shot down Pilot Officer Milne (P9507). Over 50 bombers drawn from KG 27, KG 51 and KG 54 operated particularly over Kent and Eastern England after dark.

Poor weather resulted in little activity on 5 July. Although cloud and rain on 6 July continued to restrict activity they provided cover for raiders including a He 111 which after circling Thorney Island headed in undetected near Littlehampton. It flew to Aldershot where at 16.15 hrs it unleashed nine HEs which fell on Gullemonte Barracks, two cottages, Wellington

The Ministry Says...

What do I do when I hear guns and air raid warnings? I keep a cool head, I gather my family and gas masks, I go quietly to my shelter or refuge room. I do NOT try to have a look, I do not run about alarming people. I remember a lot of the noise is good noise, our guns firing at the enemy... Cut this out and keep it.

From the newspapers, space presented to the nation by the Brewers' Society — 4 July

Only highly trained pilots of the RAF can take up the Spitfires and Hurricanes but you, the citizens, can provide the planes, the ships, the weapons with which the Battle of Britain can be won. Buy 2½ per cent National War Bonds.

Newspaper advertisement

What do I do if a raid catches me in the street and I go into a public shelter? I say to myself "this is where I keep calm and steady. It's human to be a bit nervous, but I'm not going to show it. I don't talk loudly nor crack silly jokes because that does not help others and, much as I want to, I do not smoke because it would make the shelter stuffy." Cut this out.

From the newspapers, space presented to the nation by the Brewers' Society.

Urgent! Great events turn upon your response to this message. There are two gigantic tasks before us — to defend our island fortress and prepare the ground upon which we shall finally win victory. Every shilling you now spend on your own pleasure now means part of the nation's resource is lost, wasted. Every shilling you put into National Savings directly helps to defend our country and bring about the defeat of the enemy. There is no time to lose...

Newspaper advertisement

LIGHT ANTI-AIRCRAFT GUNS AS DEPLOYED 7 JULY 1940

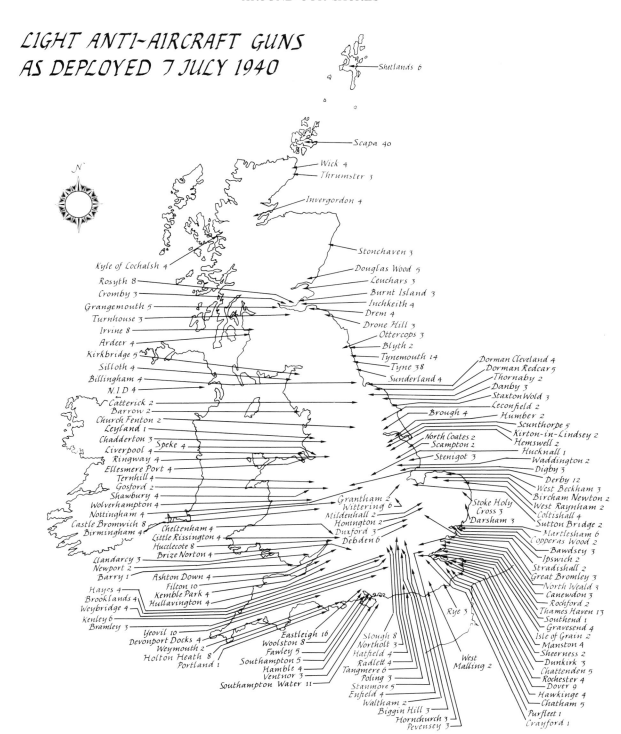

Shetlands 6

Scapa 40

Wick 4
Thrumster 3

Invergordon 4

Stonehaven 3

Douglas Wood 5
Kyle of Lochalsh 4
Leuchars 3
Rosyth 8
Burnt Island 3
Cromby 3
Inchkeith 4
Grangemouth 5
Drem 4
Turnhouse 3
Drone Hill 3
Irvine 8
Ottercops 3
Ardeer 4
Blyth 2
Kirkbridge 5
Tynemouth 14
Silloth 4
Tyne 38
Billingham 4
Sunderland 4
N.I.D 4

Dorman Cleveland 4
Dorman Redcar 5
Thornaby 2
Danby 3
Staxton Wold 3
Leconfield 2
Brough 4
Humber 2

Catterick 2
Scunthorpe 5
Barrow 2
Kirton-in-Lindsey 2
Church Fenton 2
North Coates 2
Hemswell 2
Leyland 1
Scampton 2
Hucknall 1
Chadderton 3
Speke 4
Stenigot 3
Waddington 2
Liverpool 4
Digby 3
Ringway 4
Derby 12
Ellesmere Port 4
West Beckham 3
Ternhill 4
Bircham Newton 2
Gosford 2
West Raynham 2
Shawbury 4
Grantham 2
Coltishall 4
Wolverhampton 4
Wittering 6
Stoke Holy
Sutton Bridge 2
Nottingham 4
Mildenhall 2
Cross 3
Martlesham 6
Castle Bromwich 8
Honnington 2
Darsham 3
Copperas Wood 2
Birmingham 4
Cheltenham 4
Duxford 3
Bawdsey 3
Little Rissington 4
Debden 6
Ipswich 2
Hucclecote 8
Stradishall 2
Llandarcy 3
Brize Norton 4
Great Bromley 3
Newport 2
North Weald 3
Barry 1
Ashton Down 4
Canewdon 3
Filton 10
Rochford 3
Hayes 4
Kemble Park 4
Thames Haven 13
Brooklands 4
Hullavington 4
Rye 3
Southend 1
Weybridge 4
Gravesend 4
Kenley 6
Isle of Grain 2
Bramley 3
Yeovil 10
Eastleigh 16
Slough 8
Manston 4
Devonport Docks 4
Woolston 3
Northolt 3
West
Sheerness 2
Weymouth 2
Fawley 5
Hatfield 4
Malling 2
Dunkirk 3
Holton Heath 8
Southampton 5
Radlett 4
Chattenden 5
Portland 1
Hamble 4
Tangmere 6
Rochester 4
Ventnor 3
Poling 3
Dover 9
Southampton Water 11
Stanmore 5
Hawkinge 4
Enfield 4
Chatham 5
Waltham 2
Biggin Hill 3
Purfleet 1
Hornchurch 3
Crayford 1
Pevensey 3

100   50   0   100
MILES

43

HEAVY ANTI-AIRCRAFT GUNS
AS DEPLOYED 7 JULY 1940

Shetlands 12

Scapa 88

Wick 4

Invergordon 4

Kinloss 2

Lossiemouth 2

Kyle of Lochalsh 4

Aberdeen 4

Forth 40

Clyde 27

Ardeer 4

Acklington 2

Tyne 54

Tees 30

Thornaby 4

Linton 4

Driffield 4

Sheffield 24

N.I.D 7

Humber 38

Barrow 3

Derby 36

Leeds 20

Nottingham 16

Manchester 20

Grantham 4

Liverpool 52

Leighton Buzzard 4

Ringway 4

Marham 2

Crewe 8

Feltwell 2

Birmingham 63

Watton 2

Duxford 2

Coventry 44

Wattisham 4

Daventry 4

Martlesham 4

Brockworth 36

Ipswich 4

Newport 4

Harwich 15

Cardiff 12

North Weald 4

Rochford 2

London 92

Stanmore 4

Thames & Medway North 44

Manston 8

Thames & Medway South 70

Dover 18

Hawkinge 7

Portland 6

West Malling 2

Plymouth 18

Biggin Hill 4

Falmouth 8

Tangmere 4

Hounslow 4

Holton Heath 8

Brooklands 16

Southampton 43

Langley 28

Portsmouth 44

Bramley 8

100   50   0   100

MILES

Avenue and Knolly's Road, and killed seven and injured 24. About the same time a score of raiders were approaching Aberdeen in four groups, while more operated over the Forth Estuary. Nine more were turned away by fighter reaction. KG 55 was also operating, against Plymouth and Falmouth. After dark He 111s of Schiphol's KG 4 operated over the Durham area, five bombs falling two and a half miles from Shotton Colliery. Maynsforth Colliery was also raided, and KG 26's choice included a colliery near Dunfermline, while KG 1 operated against ports in the south-west.

Civilian casualties in the 24-hour period ending 06:00 included 62 killed. Losses were not all one-sided for three Do 17P convoy spotters were brought down early on 7 July by Hurricanes of Nos. 43[2], 145[3] and 601[4] Squadrons. Bombers of seven Geschwaderen brought about incidents at many sites, including Ipswich and Eastbourne; at the latter, nine homes were demolished and 60 badly damaged. Bf 109s made forays along the south coast, defending gunners claiming one which crashed at Ref. R7859. No. 54 Squadron's Green Section tackling a He 111 was bounced by Bf 109s which forced down Pilot Officer A.R. Campbell (P9398) and Flying Officer E.S. Coleman

(P9399) at Barton's Hall (Ref. T7865). Flying Officer D.A.P. MacMullen nursed his damaged Spitfire (P9389) into Manston and the squadron diarist recorded 'a most disastrous day'.

Over the Channel KG 1, 2 and 51 sought shipping; KG 3 and KG 53 attacked docks, one of these a damaging attack at 17:45 on Falmouth, where four bombs severely damaged the docks, stores, the Shell installation and an RAF depot. Three houses were demolished and five civilians killed. Evening saw Do 17Zs of I and II/KG 2 strike at a CE convoy, sinking one ship and damaging three. Spitfires of 65 Squadron arriving too late were bounced by Bf 109s which destroyed three. Two Bf 109s were however claimed and 64 Squadron damaged two Dorniers. Hurricanes of 79 Squadron were also engaged and Squadron Leader J.D.C. Joslin, shot down by a Bf 109, crashed at Ref. R726586. At night Gruppen 106 and 126 continued mining activities.

Attacks on shipping continued on 8 July, when eight bomber groups were operating, mainly against Portsmouth, Devonport, Hull

Off the South Downs, a Channel East (CE) convoy comes under air attack. (IWM)

No. 610 Squadron airborne possibly at an early stage of the Battle. (IWM)

and off Sunderland. Around 14:00 nine Do 17s trying to bomb a Channel convoy were driven off. An hour later a more strongly escorted force took their place and again 610 Squadron[5] was ordered to defend the ships. Supporting them was 79 Squadron, two of whose Hurricanes were soon overcome and lost near Dover. Further west, Ju 88s attacking a convoy were driven off by Spitfires of 234 Squadron. Skinningrove iron works again came under attack and naval barracks at Devonport when 70 bombers operated in darkness. Soon after dawn Norwich suffered a sharp attack. Barnard's was hit and a total of 16 people were killed and 70 injured.

Through cloud and rain German aircraft reconnoitred the Thames Estuary on 9 July gathering details of a large FN convoy assembling. Come 12:45 and a Luftwaffe strike force was radar detected, also a Bf 110 diversion by III/ZG 26 approaching the south coast. No. 43 Squadron (P3796, P3464, N2621) engaged those, damaging two, Squadron Leader C.G. Lott (P3464) delivering a head-on attack before serious splinter wounds forced him to ditch.

The main force was engaged by six 11 Group squadrons. Soon after 13:00 'A' Flight 151 Squadron left North Weald, its Station Commander Wing Commander Victor Beamish flying Hurricane P3807 being with them. Within a few minutes six Hurricanes were facing about a hundred enemy aircraft, bombers at around 12-15,000 feet protected by top cover Bf 109s up to 20,000 feet. One Hurricane section went for the bombers but '151' was fighting for its life. Midshipman O. Wightman, shot down, was rescued by a trawler. But the bomber formation had been split, and all but one group was making for home. The ships remained undamaged.

Mid-afternoon brought another 70 German aircraft. They faced just seven Spitfires[6] of 65 Squadron operating from Manston. Escorted above and flanked by Bf 110s and Bf 109s the bomber formations again parted as the Spitfires dived upon the II/JG 51 Bf 109s, Flight Sergeant N.T. Phillips destroying one. A straggling I/KG 53 He 111, possibly from the force, was shot down at sea by Hurricanes (P2588 Pilot Officer G.R. Bennette, P3673 Pilot Officer K. Manger, and Sergeant G. Griffiths) of 17 Squadron guarding FN convoy 'Ancient'.

Then came He 59s seeking missing German

Above *Heinkel He 59B-2 floatplanes — Boulogne based and carrying Red Cross insignia — were unexpectedly used to rescue Luftwaffe airmen from the sea.* (Bundesarchiv)

Below *As the Junkers Ju 87b Stukas (A5+DH of I/StG 1 shown here) entered a steep dive their engines emitted an horrendous scream. Their course was fairly easy for gunners to predict and, being fairly slow, they were also picked off during climb away.* (Bundesarchiv)

airmen. No. 54 Squadron[7] halted those proceedings by forcing down a He 59 (D-ASUO) on the Goodwin Sands. Following capture, it was towed to Deal. What might be construed as a mercy mission certainly had operational reconnaissance content. Spitfires had engaged the escorting Bf 109s, again of II/JG 51, and in the fierce combat that ensued Flight Lieutenant A.C. 'Al' Deere shot down one before, during a head-on pass by another, its propeller brushed the canopy of his Spitfire. Deere, his engine stopped, force-landed near Manston and his Spitfire caught fire. Pilot Officer J.W. Garton was shot down and killed near Manston and Pilot Officer A. Evershed died in the sea.

Rounding off the daylight raids, 27 escorted Ju 87s of I/StG 77 again tried to wreck Portland. Green Section, 609 Squadron[8], des-

troyed a Stuka and lost Pilot Officer Drummond-Hay in R6637. The day's fighting cost the RAF seven fighters destroyed and three pilots killed. After dark about 50 hostiles sought East Anglia's bomber bases.

By deploying a handful of fighters Dowding had surprisingly thwarted large enemy forces, but for how long could that continue? The Germans clearly thought 'not long', reckoning that southern England would become unprotected in a matter of days. To clear the Channel zone, II and VIII Fliegerkorps were chosen under, respectively, Generals Lorzer and Richthofen, with HQs in the Pas de Calais and Le Havre.

Maintenance of German aircraft in France was carried out using makeshift equipment on primitive airfields. (Michael Payne)

Throughout the campaign Major Adolf Galland, here taxiing his Bf 109, proved himself an excellent leader. His telling Göring that what the Luftwaffe needed were Spitfires must have required enormous courage too. (Bundesarchiv)

Lorzer, with the tougher task at the Dover end, chose Johannes Fink as Channel Battle Leader, whose Battle Group comprised Kampfgeschwader 2 — about 75 Do 17Zs, 60 Ju 87s in two Stuka Gruppen and some 200 Messerschmitt 109s equipping JG 26 commanded by Major Adolf Galland and JG 53 led by Major Werner Molders. The other Fliegerkorps would operate between Portsmouth and Portland.

CHAPTER 5

'IT'S THE BATTLE OF BRITAIN' — OFFICIAL!

...The Battle may be said to have started when the Germans had disposed of the French resistance.

...I have, somewhat arbitrarily, chosen the events of the 10th July as the opening of the Battle. Although many attacks had previously been made on convoys, and even on land objectives such as Portland, the 10th July saw the employment by the Germans of the first really big formation (70 aircraft) intended primarily to bring our Fighter Defence to battle on a large scale.

Air Chief Marshal Sir Hugh Dowding,
Commander-in-Chief Fighter Command

Around 10:00 on 10 July a Do 17P of 4(F)/121 protected by Bf 109s of JG 51 began viewing shipping movements off Kent. Four Spitfires of 74 Squadron (two damaged in combat) engaged them, damaging the spy and a Bf 109. No. 610[9] Squadron facing more 109s lost Flight Lieutenant E.B.B. Smith in P9503.

Radar detected an enemy build-up beyond Calais at around 13:00 so Hurricanes[10] of 32 Squadron were ordered to protect a CW convoy off Folkestone. Soon facing 27 Do 17s of I/KG 2 and 40 Messerschmitts of I/JG 3 and I/ZG 26 they called for assistance which materialized as 16 Hurricanes of Nos. 56 and 111 Squadrons and six Spitfires[11] of 74. A fierce

air battle involving 100 aircraft developed over Dungeness, something never hitherto seen thereabouts. Most successful was 'Treble One' Squadron whose contribution opened with a head on attack in which Flying Officer T.P.K. Higgs crashed into a Do 17Z and both fell in the sea. Flying Officer Ferris, who put a Bf 109 into the water, was immediately set upon by others and was lucky to reach home. Another Hurricane crash-landed at Hawkinge and a fourth was damaged, as were three 74 Squadron Spitfires. The Dornier force, baulked by 'Treble One', unloaded 150 bombs wide, sinking only a small Dutch sloop. As the enemy was withdrawing at 13:40 six of 64 Squadron's Spitfires[12] arrived on the scene and engaged the Bf 110s without success.

In analysing the event Fighter Command concluded that tragic losses were inevitable and faster reaction times essential. Several Sectors had been involved, their co-operation good, but more elaborate data was needed from radar warnings in order to select the most suitable reaction time and extent. Committing too many squadrons would leave large areas exposed; too few could bring total disaster.

Single aircraft had also been active throughout the day over the south-west. Nine workers were killed when two cranes were hit at Kings Dock, Swansea. Two Ju 88s, Rd 179H, dropped 12 delayed action HEs on the Royal Navy oil installation at Llanreith. One bomb resting on a tank was made safe, its fuse having in any case not been set. Another produced a leak in a 164,800-gallon container. A raider circled for

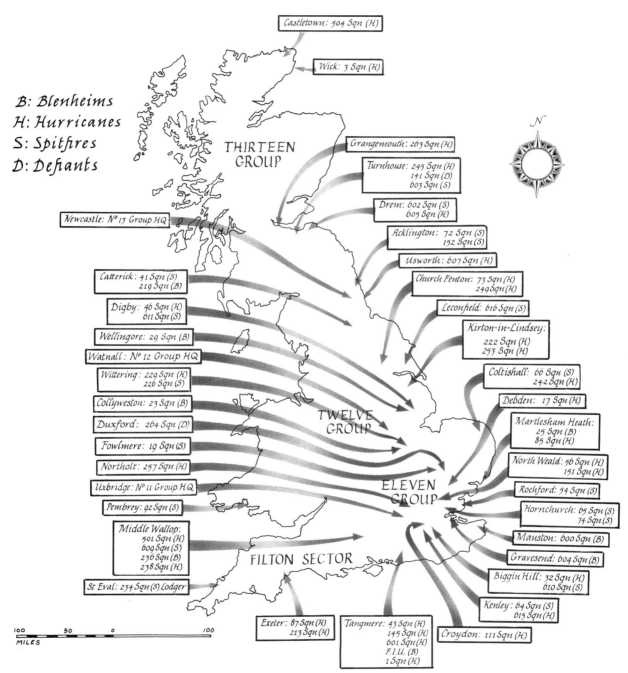

B: Blenheims
H: Hurricanes
S: Spitfires
D: Defiants

Castletown: 504 Sqn (H)

Wick: 3 Sqn (H)

THIRTEEN GROUP

Grangemouth: 263 Sqn (H)

Turnhouse: 245 Sqn (H)
141 Sqn (D)
603 Sqn (S)

Drem: 602 Sqn (S)
605 Sqn (H)

Acklington: 72 Sqn (S)
152 Sqn (S)

Usworth: 607 Sqn (H)

Church Fenton: 73 Sqn (H)
249 Sqn (H)

Leconfield: 616 Sqn (S)

Kirton-in-Lindsey:
222 Sqn (H)
253 Sqn (H)

Coltishall: 66 Sqn (S)
242 Sqn (H)

Debden: 17 Sqn (H)

Martlesham Heath:
25 Sqn (B)
85 Sqn (H)

North Weald: 56 Sqn (H)
151 Sqn (H)

Rochford: 54 Sqn (S)

Hornchurch: 65 Sqn (S)
74 Sqn (S)

Manston: 600 Sqn (B)

Gravesend: 604 Sqn (B)

Biggin Hill: 32 Sqn (H)
610 Sqn (S)

Kenley: 64 Sqn (S)
615 Sqn (H)

Croydon: 111 Sqn (H)

Newcastle: Nº 13 Group HQ

Catterick: 41 Sqn (S)
219 Sqn (B)

Digby: 46 Sqn (H)
611 Sqn (S)

Wellingore: 29 Sqn (B)

Watnall: Nº 12 Group HQ

Wittering: 229 Sqn (H)
226 Sqn (S)

Collyweston: 23 Sqn (B)

Duxford: 264 Sqn (D)

Fowlmere: 19 Sqn (S)

Northolt: 257 Sqn (H)

Uxbridge: Nº 11 Group HQ

Pembrey: 92 Sqn (S)

Middle Wallop:
501 Sqn (H)
609 Sqn (S)
236 Sqn (B)
238 Sqn (H)

St Eval: 234 Sqn (S) Lodger

TWELVE GROUP

ELEVEN GROUP

FILTON SECTOR

Exeter: 87 Sqn (H)
213 Sqn (H)

Tangmere: 43 Sqn (H)
145 Sqn (H)
601 Sqn (H)
F.I.U. (B)
1 Sqn (H)

100   50   0   100
MILES

N

FIGHTER COMMAND~OPERATIONAL LAYOUT
10 JULY 1940

ten minutes in cloud before dropping nine HEs on Carmarthen's Royal Ordnance factory, killing nine and injuring 15 workers, and escaping from AA guns in four areas. Cardiff docks were raided and at 15:10 a Ju 88 in the face of 31 rounds of 3-inch shells dropped five HEs to cause a small fire at Llandarcy, Neath's National refinery. Moments before, two Ju 88s dive bombed Falmouth, scoring hits on a crane and jetty. They also sank the 6,499-ton tanker SS *Taskulsa* and left the SS *British Chancellor* burning. Night activity resulted in 13 noteworthy incidents including bombing at Longtown, Cumbria, eight miles north of Worthing and at Newport, Essex, near Debden airfield. Most of the 170 HEs counted fell wide, yet 29 peo-

ple were killed and 94 injured in the 24 hours to dawn on 11 July. No mean alarm was caused when a mustard gas release was falsely signalled from Winchester. Although such was always possible, public opinion rated it unlikely on the basis that the enemy would suffer heavy retaliation. The Government, to the end of the war, viewed it far more likely.

The Luftwaffe made an early start on 11 July. Squadron Leader Peter Townsend, flying Hurricane P2716: VY-F of 85 Squadron and dealing with a Do 17 off Harwich, was shot down by its return fire and soon rescued by a naval launch. Squadron Leader Douglas Bader, flying Hurricane P3048 of 242 Squadron, shot down a Dornier off Cromer, another of which

'Scramble!' Pilots of 85 Squadron race to their Hurricanes. (IWM)

No. 85 Squadron's Hurricanes in traditional threes early in the fight. Markings were far from standardized, these Hurricanes having various sized underwing roundels in varying positions on under surfaces of various blue shades. (IWM)

was damaged off Yarmouth by 66 Squadron.

A convoy in Lyme Bay attracted a dozen Ju 87s and 20 Bf 109s of Luftflotte 3 which, on arrival, found Spitfires of 609 Squadron[13] and three Hurricanes of 501 Squadron[14] awaiting them. Half the Spitfires tried for the Ju 87s, but before reaching them German fighters picked off two (L1069 and L1095) both pilots, Flight Lieutenant Barren and Pilot Officer Mitchell, being killed. Hurricane N2486 was also shot down and Sergeant F.J.P. Dixon drowned. The Stuka bombs fell wide.

Employing such small numbers of fighters against large enemy forces was causing resentment on the squadrons. No. 609's diarist recorded that the 'utter futility of sending small numbers of fighters to cope with intense enemy action is bitterly resented. The fact they have so often been sent off in a Section or Flight only to find themselves outnumbered is discouraging because the British fighter then finds himself unable to do his job... our contacts with the enemy have taken place when the numerical odds were too unreasonable.'

Cloud and poor visibility in the north cloaked a raider which at 08:03 bombed an army camp at Melbourne, south of Derby, killing seven soldiers and wounding nine. Less effective were four bombs placed on Skipsea bombing range, but mid-morning HEs which exploded at Bridlington's town hall and railway station killed six and caused an ammunition truck to explode.

By late morning the weather in the south improved sufficiently for reconnaissance aircraft to operate. Six 601 Squadron Hurricanes[15] set forth to tackle one over Lyme Bay only to be confronted by 15 Stukas and over 30 Bf 110s of III/ZG 76. Help was summoned as '601' swept down on the intruders out of the sun. Two Ju 87s were in the sea before their escort reacted, and only one merchantman was hit. Four Bf 110s were destroyed, two by 601 Squadron and one each by the reinforcing 87 and 238[16] Squadrons.

When in the late afternoon a dozen KG 55 He 111s escorted by Bf 110s approached from Seine Bay just six Hurricanes of 601 Squadron[17] met them. Sergeant Woolley was soon shot down by AA fire and baled out wounded, leaving his Hurricane, P3681, to crash at Cranmore, Isle of Wight. Although they shot down one and caused two Heinkels to collide, 601 Squadron was unable to prevent them dropping a score of bombs on Portsmouth at 18:00, thereby carrying out the first daylight bombing raid in strength on a British city. Reinforcements from Tangmere Sector arrived too late to prevent hits on a floating dock, timber yard, and a hotel. Airspeed's Hilsea factory and a gas holder, which detonated, then burnt itself out in 40 minutes. Casualties amounted to 17 killed, 50 injured.

The prevention of target bombing was of course the essential purpose of the fighter effort, not just the destruction of enemy aircraft. Whereas radar stations in Kent could warn of a raid up to 20 minutes away, radar cover elsewhere was often less effective. From warning to receipt for plotting was taking four minutes, in which time a raid could almost cross the Straits of Dover. Fighters needed around 15 minutes to reach battle height, which gave controllers precious little time to react and a need for excellent judgement to produce correct instructions and identify feints. Already it was clear that the Messerschmitt 109 was a most formidable fighter, whereas the Bf 110 had shown itself no match for a Hurricane. British fighters needed constant-speed propellers and fire-protected fuel tanks, but incorporating such modifications meant withdrawing aircraft from front line. While the Luftwaffe possessed a well thought out air/sea rescue service, the British relied upon small naval boats to save the precious lives of their pilots and indeed those of the foe.

Although enemy crews were briefed to bomb military and economic targets their bombing easily strayed, as on the night of 11/12 July when Rochester and Chatham, both with many 'legitimate' targets, were attacked, killing 36 and injuring many. Ten bombs fell on marshland on the Isle of Grain from a bomber estimated to be at 24,000 feet. Another bomb exploded half a mile from the ground, search-lights illuminating a grotesque, giant smoke ring.

MEDIA — 1940 style

12 July . . . 'Göring's Century with RAF Aid' — 102 planes lost on raids since June 18. Göring has now reached his century but neither he nor his captain, Hitler, will be happy about it.

Cloud and rain reduced German operations on 12 July, bringing only one major engagement, off the East Anglian coast where a large FN convoy, 'Booty', attracted Raid 31 — Do 17s of II/KG 2 and He 111s of II/KG 53. Hurricane pilots of 'A' Flight, 17 Squadron, Martlesham, set out to patrol the convoy when the raid was on its way, while Blue Section 85 Squadron, 'A' Flight 19 Squadron[18] and 11 Hurricanes of 151 Squadron[19] tackled the bombers en route. Then it was No. 17 Squadron's turn, which did well in shooting down two Heinkels before its Hurricanes turned their attention to the leading Dornier which, flown by Hauptmann Machetzki, Staffelkapitan, was also forced into the sea. The tight Dornier formation concentrated its fire upon the Hurricanes, shooting down Flying Officer J.H.L. Allan (NZ) (P3275). Another Hurricane, P2557, flown by Sergeant L. Jowitt of 85 Squadron, came down off Felixstowe. The cloudy day allowed the Luftwaffe to operate widely. Bombs at Hamble fell on a boat yard and shelter, while at Aberdeen at 12:55 ten bombs hit Hall, Russell & Co. ship repair yard, six houses and a public house. No warning had been sounded and 26 men were killed and 79 people injured, 32 of them seriously. A He 111 of KG 26, possibly responsible, was shot down by 603 Squadron near Aberdeen. Scotland also suffered after dark when two tenements in Greenock were damaged.

Memories of the summer of 1940 are usually of hot days and blue skies but there were many days when rain and cloud prevailed. Although

13 July was mainly overcast it did not prevent Ju 87s of II/StG 1, protected by Bf 109s of JG 51, operating against shipping in the Portland area. Patrolling 56 Squadron[20] claimed seven Stukas although none can be confirmed from Luftwaffe records. Two Hurricanes were, however, lost in the action. Later Nos. 54[21] and 64[22] Squadrons fought Bf 109s over Dover, 54 Squadron's Pilot Officer Colin Gray in R6893 scoring the first of his 14 kills. Forced to land damaged Spitfire P9795 at Hawkinge, Sergeant A.E. Binham attributed his predicament to zealous AA gunners.

Cloudy conditions persisted on 14 July, Ju 87s of LG 1 escorted by JG 3 carrying out the now usual afternoon Channel raid near Portland. Sixteen Hurricanes of 151[23] and 615[24] Squadrons and a dozen 610 Squadron Spitfires[25] engaged them and shot down one Stuka, but Pilot Officer M.R. Mudie's Hurricane of 615 Squadron was shot down. Taking part in the engagement with 151 Squadron were Wing Commander V. Beamish in P3871 and the first twin-cannon armed Hurricane, L1750 of 151 Squadron, flown by Flight Lieutenant R.L. Smith, whose fire brought down a Bf 109 on the French coast. This was the day when orders were issued to shoot down air-sea rescue He 59s, of which about 30 were available.

Poor weather over the next four days must have irritated the Luftwaffe, eager to decimate the RAF. Overnight bombing on 14/15 July occurred south of a line Newport-Ipswich, three passes resulting in the railway to Avonmouth being cut. While thick cloud on the 15th prevented KG 2 accurately bombing a convoy, LG 1 placed a dozen bombs on Westland's Yeovil factory but lost a Ju 88 to 92 Squadron near Cardiff. Barry, Mount Batten and Brixham were also being raided. No. 603 Squadron struck lucky, putting another KG 26 He 111 into the sea off Peterhead. Very little action took place on the 16th, but Flying Officer W.H. Moorhouse, son of Second Lieutenant W.B. Moorhouse, VC, and serving with 601 Squadron, shot down a Ju 88 of II/KG 54 off the Isle of Wight.

KG 26, active over Scotland on the 17th, sent six Heinkels to wreck Ayrshire's Ardeer explosives factory, where they destroyed the detonator house. One attacker ended its days off Fraserburgh. No. 92 Squadron drew blood yet again, near Bristol where a Ju 88 of 1/KG 51 was caught. Some 11 HEs had been laid across the Newton Ashford marshalling yards.

The Ministry Says...

Join Britain's silent column. Sensible people who know when not to talk. Here's something you can do, and keep on doing. It's not spectacular. You will wear no uniform, you'll not spend nights on lonely duty. Your only weapon will be your conscience, your ears and your tongue. You will be doing a duty as wide as the making of munitions. Keep it to yourself — and make others do the same.

Newspaper, 16 June

Early on 18 July three small bombs cratered Gooseley Lane off the Barking-East Ham bypass, another falling close to East Ham gasworks. Possible evidence of enemy frustration was seen around 09:00 on the 18th when 610 Squadron patrolling off Dover was furiously bounced by nine Bf 109s which shot down Spitfire R6765-T flown by Pilot Officer Litchfield, Green Leader. Small-scale operations over southern England resulted in KG 27's commander being shot down by 145 Squadron. Near Aberdeen a He 111's gunner brought down a 603 Squadron Spitfire. KG 26 was very active at this period and on 18 July three of its He 111s attacked Montrose aerodrome, where fighter pilots were trained on Miles Master 1s. Another scored a hit on the Long Shed at Leith docks.

July 19's brighter weather brought a memorable day's fighting. Initial success came to 145 Squadron[26] around 07:00 when a Do 17P of 4(F)/121 after reconnoitring Surrey, was

brought down off Brighton. At 10:40 KG 26 attacked Glasgow's Rolls-Royce engine factory, the Cardonnell Royal Ordnance factory, Govan and the Scotstown area.

Park had already ordered squadrons to forward bases, among them the Defiant-armed and inexperienced 141 Squadron which left West Malling for its advanced base at Hawkinge. In perfect, cloudless conditions — visibility 13 miles — Raids H47 and H49 were detected at 12:15, 30 Do 17s and Ju 87s in three or four groups at 12,000 feet approaching from the south-west to dive-bomb a destroyer at a two-convoy intersection in the Straits. Dover's AA guns fired at 12:23, as a dozen Defiants were ordered off. To protect the harbour AA gunners fired a 164-shell barrage, battery D1 claiming a direct hit on a Dornier. Only nine serviceable Defiants[28] took off to patrol led by Squadron Leader W. Richardson. South of Folkestone they were suddenly bounced by about a dozen Bf 109s of II/JG 2, the 'Richthofen Geschwader', which dived upon them before zooming up to rake their belly blind spots. Desperately banking to allow their turret gunners to take aim, the Defiants were overtaken by more 109s delivering head on attacks. Within moments four Defiants — from which only Pilot Officer J. Gard'ner survived — were shot out of the sky. Then Flight Lieutenant I. Donald's L7009 crashed in Dover. Only the arrival of 'Treble One' Hurricanes saved the four remaining Defiants. Flight Lieutenant M. Loudon's gunner baled out, to become the only one surviving that way, before his aircraft (L7001) crashed in Hawkinge's circuit. Pilot Officer MacDougall's mauled Defiant L7014 was immediately declared a write off. Of his gunner who had baled out nothing more was ever seen. Dowding never wanted turret fighters which, in this instance, were not being fielded in a situation for which they were designed — i.e. for attacking unescorted bomber formations.

To fill the sudden gap, No. 32 Squadron[29], which hastened to the scene, attempted to drive Ju 87s away from Dover. It was the usual story, with protecting '109s' sweeping in to pick off

Above *The ill-fated Boulton Paul Defiant turret fighter, which had been intended to destroy bombers with attacks from below. German fighters easily disposed of it.* (IWM)

Below *Photographs, including this of Dover, were taken pre-war from German civilian aircraft.* (IWM)

yet another Hurricane. No. 43 Squadron[30] in Tangmere Sector also tangled with German fighters, losing Flight Lieutenant J. Simpson, 'A' Flight Commander, in P3410, and Sergeant J. Bush, flying P3351, who died in the sea off Shoreham. Before darkness fell Ju 87s tried again to damage Portland.

Five Fighter Command pilots died on 19 July, five were wounded and eleven aircraft lost. In nearly every engagement the squadrons had been overwhelmed. Strengthening each response could be costly, even foolhardy; but what were the alternatives? Hitler yelled 'surrender', but with British morale extremely high that was popularly greeted with derision. Nevertheless he could be reasonably pleased with his Luftwaffe's achievements, and certain of victory he upgraded Hermann Göring to Reichsmarschall.

The handful of aviation enthusiasts of those days craved one sighting — a Junkers four-engined bomber. Despite official records deeming that almost an impossibility, and the knowledgeable words of some born decades beyond those times, there remain old hands who still swear to seeing a fighter-escorted Ju 89 or Ju 90 (and not a Stirling) south of Croydon one bright 1940 day. Liverpudlians were certainly assaulted by several Focke-Wulf Condors, but

Do 17Z F1+KL and others of KG 76 shortly after taking off and heading for England. It is easy to see why 'flying pencil' was bestowed on the ricketty-sounding Dornier. (Bundesarchiv)

The Ministry Says...

What do I do if I come across German or Italian broadcasts when tuning my wireless? I say to myself now this blighter wants me to listen to him. Am I going to do what he wants? I remember German lies over the air are like German troops dropping on Britain. I remember no one can trust a word the Haw Haws say, so I make them waste their time. I switch them off or tune them out...
22 July Newspaper — space donated by, yes, the good old Brewers!

Remember — Careless Talk Costs Lives. Keep the enemy in the dark...

22 July, Newspaper

the most satisfied of such customers must have been those living between Hartlepool and Sunderland on the night of 19/20 July when searchlights picked up a Fw 200 of I/KG 40 promptly forced into the sea by AA shells. Mining too close to the shore, it was one of a pair that perished at this time, the other sinking off Northern Ireland. Two prisoners taken ashore in Northumberland confirmed their somewhat exotic means of transport.

Come the morn of 20 July and another two He 59s, combining humanitarianism with observation of Convoy CW7 which sailed from Southend at 07:00, were disposed of by Hurricanes. Four fighter squadrons then guarded the convoy and not until 18:00 did protected Ju 87s of II/StG 1 attempt to cause trouble. No. 32 Squadron[31] by diving through the top cover sent a pair of Stukas into the water and damaged two more. No. 615 Squadron[32] was also at hand, Flight Lieutenant L.M. Gaunce (P2966), Pilot Officer Hugo (P2963) and Fly-

ing Officer Eyre bagging a I/JG 27 Bf 109 without loss. Here was proof that, given a good start, Hurricanes could dispose of nimble Messerschmitts. Also witnessing the convoy raid was No. 610 Squadron[33] which fought the 109s near Folkestone. As for the convoy, the SS *Pulborough* was sunk, and the damaged SS *Westown* took shelter in Dover. Destroyer HMS *Brazen* was damaged and sank under tow. The final tally showed a Hurricane and a 610 Squadron Spitfire missing, the latter flown by Pilot Officer G. Keithley who crashed at Lydden, near Canterbury. By dusk six British fighters had been shot down. The enemy had lost 13, including four Bf 109s. Encouraging, very encouraging.

At dawn and dusk every day Lysanders scoured the coastline looking for invaders. LX:T N1294 belongs to 225 Squadron, Tilshead. (IWM)

Using the 'Lyssies'

Under Fighter Command control was No. 22 (Army Co-operation) Group whose squadrons were each equipped with Lysanders. Purpose built to support the Army, their main purpose was reconnaissance. Able to land in confined spaces, they had proven large for the role and vulnerable, but by the summer of 1940 they were given two special tasks.

The entire coastline between Land's End and Duncansby Head was divided into 'beat' areas allocated to Lysander squadrons which, at twilight and dawn, starting on 1 July, operated pairs of aircraft for patrols seeking enemy invaders.

In May 1940 they were given another task — gas spray. Fear of gas attack remained to the end of hostilities, Britain being prepared to resort to chemical warfare only in retaliation for German first use. Five Lysander squadrons (Nos. 2, 4, 26, 225 and 614) and some Blenheim bomber squadrons were trained to lay gas. Each Lysander squadron was allocated 47 × 250-lb 26-gallon Smoke Curtain Installation containers, sufficient for two sorties by each of its 12 aircraft. The containers emptied in 15 seconds of spraying. From between 250 and 500 feet a dense curtain could have smothered invaders within an area 600 yards long, 60 yards wide (600 yards wide if sprayed from about 3,000 feet). Training in gas spray operations for a pilot and one senior NCO from each squadron was undertaken at RAF Halton.

Although the Lysander's main task remained Army reconnaissance, it could carry a 500-lb bomb load (12 × 40-lb or 16 × 20-lb) on Light Series Carriers, on its spat stubs and/or beneath the fuselage, for close support. In June 1940 it was given another role, that of anti-tank. A 20 mm Hispano cannon firing 12 rounds per second was fitted to each bomb stub, tested at AFDU Northolt, and then by No. 110 Canadian Squadron, who found it cut the aircraft's already slow speed by 12 mph. Only ball ammunition was available — useless against tanks! Nevertheless, on 21 October the Air Ministry decided that 50 per cent of squadron Lysanders should carry cannon... Early in September each Lysander squadron had its IE cut appreciably from 18 to 12. A new squadron, No. 231, was formed from 416 Flight in Ulster, where the Government believed a landing was possible — with support from the then-dormant IRA.

CHAPTER 6

WEAR THEM DOWN

The last week of July and the first two of August saw the Luftwaffe waging a war of attrition prior to the launch of its main attack. Although Fighter Command responded in increased strength, Dowding held back as much of his force as possible. Anti-shipping operations figured prominently in enemy activity, considerable mining of the Mersey early on 21 July attracting an 83-round AA barrage. Although six mines were soon exploded by sweepers, Mersey ports and also Holyhead were closed for some time.

Larger fighter reaction was fielded on 21 July, relay patrols covering Convoy CW7 which eventually came under attack at 14:30 by 40 Do 17s ten miles south of the Isle of Wight. Just three Hurricanes P3782, P3781, and N2621 of 43 Squadron parted the bomber formation before III/JG 27 engaged them, each side losing one fighter. Then Blue Section No. 238 Squadron came on the scene as 15 Bf 110s surprisingly started dive-bombing the convoy crawling at 7 knots south-west of St Catherine's Point. The discovery that Messerschmitt 110s (of V/LG 1) could perform as fighter-bombers provided no mean shock to the British who named them 'Jaguars'. Flight Lieutenant Walsh (P3618) claimed one, and another badly damaged by Pilot Officer B.B. Considine (P3599) crashed at its French base. The strike disorganized the convoy, sank the SS *Terlings*, left the SS *Kollskegg* burning and caused the SS *Ninaborthen* to return to Portsmouth. No. 238 Squadron Hurricanes (P3823, P3462, P2947) forced down a reconnoitring Bf 110 at Goodwood, and at 15:15 Hurricanes P3599 and P3618 of the squadron destroyed over Blandford a rare Do 17M. Thunderstorms over southern England failed to discourage an evening bomber from dropping a salvo off Portland near the Dutch steamer *Stuyvesant*.

Among the incidents on 22 July, a cloudy day of reduced activity, was the bombing of a German PoW camp at Banff, where six inmates were killed and 18 injured. Leith docks, Torpoint, Margate, Pembroke Dock, were all bombed and at 01:35 RAF Ternhill attracted 11 Hes. In the 24 hours ending 06:00 23 July 140 HE bombs were reckoned to have fallen on Britain, and during the night Tangmere's Fighter Interception Unit scored the first kill with the aid of AI radar.

Mid-afternoon on 23 July brought two of those ever memorable lone Dornier penetrations. One was to Pulham, where bombs dropped from 700 feet exploded in the old airship shed causing an eerie moaning and sighing to engulf the giant cavern. The other, Raid UB56H, came in west of Shoreham. Skilfully using cloud cover the crew slipped into the circuit at the Vickers-Armstrong Weybridge works at 15:19 while two Wellingtons were being air tested and lots of Tiger Moths were active from nearby schools. Cunningly the Dornier crew courted the other fliers at 4,000 feet, then put the bomber's undercarriage down and lined up for a bombing run. Fighters had in vain already sought the raider and, immediately it was recognized, Bofors gunners loosed off 51 rounds AEB and the four 3.7-inch guns another five, many

Right *Bofors guns were very useful against low-level minelayers. This example was sited by the River Mersey.* (IWM)

Below *Long-range Focke-wulf Fw 200 Condors of KG 40 mined off the west and east coasts, this example reputedly being Fw 200C-1 F8+EH which crashed off Hartlepool.*

shells bursting prematurely for such was the haste of the response. An initial salvo of six bombs fell along the landing ground's edge, a second six at St George's Hill and another five at the Wandsworth Gas Co. premises in North Road, Walton. Vickers and Brooklands had a lucky escape.

Heinkel 111s resumed mining the Mersey early on 24 July, searchlight crews illuminating one which fired upon their sites at New Brighton. That, or another Heinkel, was then illuminated again and held lit for three minutes. Coastguards at Hoylake and Formby Point independently claimed that it crashed in the sea as a result of dazzle. Could it have been a Fw 200 of I/KG 40 repeatedly reported as crashed in the Irish Sea off Belfast?

The damaging potential of sneak raids was further demonstrated early on 24 July, this time by a low-flying He 111 whose HEs and incen-

diaries were hurled onto Glasgow's Hillington Industrial Estate, damaging a printing works, a sugar and oil cake factory and injuring 18 people. Soon after, Welsh-based 92 Squadron Spitfires (K9998, N3167, N3297) engaged over Porthcawl a Ju 88 of KG 51 into which 87 Squadron's Pilot Officer R.P. Beamont later poured more shots, ensuring its demise near Lynton.

Late morning brought what 54 Squadron dubbed 'The Battle of the Thames Estuary', when 18 Do 17s escorted by JG 52 attempted to bomb a convoy, forced a ship to run for shallow water and provided the squadron[34] with its 'biggest fight since Dunkirk'. So furious and confused was the fight over Margate that '54' claimed 16 '109s. Luftwaffe records suggest two, possibly three, a more likely score. Pilot Officer Allen (R6812) engaged one near Margate, then his engine stopped. When it came to life again he tried to reach Manston, but instead his aircraft spun in and crashed on an electricity substation in Omer Road, Cliftonville. Sergeant G.R. Collett (N3192) chased a Bf 109 for a considerable distance, only to run out of fuel and crash at Sizewell, Suffolk. As for the Messerschmitts, one came down in Dane Valley Road, another in Byron Avenue, Margate, where the pilot became a prize for local AFS men. Nos.

65[35] and 610 Squadrons had been vectored to Dover to engage the BF 109s when the latter were getting short of fuel and vulnerable. Unfortunately the plan misfired when a fresh formation of Bf 109s arrived to deal with just such schemes. Fighter Command lost a pilot and two aircraft in the engagement and the Germans five Bf 109s of JG 26 and JG 52.

For formation raiding 25 July proved ideal, its clear blue sky spelling trouble for the British. The first major attack came in at 10:40, Ju 87s of III/StG 1 trying again to damage Portland. No. 152 Squadron later bagged a Do 17M west of Eastfleet, as well as one of those Ju 87s west of Portland Bill.

Bf 109s and several bombers approaching Dover around noon provided a temptation British fighters could well have ignored. Instead, 65 Squadron went into action. Flight Sergeant

Spitfires of 65 Squadron. YT:N R6712 served with 65 Squadron 10 July to 25 October 1940 and with 53 OTU in May 1941. Written off in a ground collision at Heston on 11 May 1941. YT:M R6714 which joined 65 Squadron with R6712 was written off after diving into the ground near Auchtermuchty, Fife, while patrolling on 16 October 1940. The photograph was taken on 13 August. Note the censor's marks on the skyline to prevent the aerodrome from being identified. (IWM)

Franklin by manoeuvring extremely low in N3164 caused a chasing Bf 109 to plunge into the sea. No. 32 Squadron's Hurricanes[36] joined 615 Squadron[37] in another battle resulting in limited success. Pilot Officer V.G. Daw of 32 Squadron mixing with six '109s received leg wounds and was forced to land a badly damaged P3677. A few bombs fell harmlessly in Dover harbour and four more behind the cliffs at Swingate, near which sheep were cruelly machine-gunned.

Convoy CW8 comprising small ships carrying coal, cement and general cargo sailed at 07:00 from Southend. By 14:30 it was off Dover while many British fighters were rearming, at which time Ju 87s steeply dive-bombed the convoy, sinking three small ships and damaging two. Defence had rested with AA gunners, Dover Site D1 claiming a Ju 87 before frantic calls brought along Spitfires of 54 Squadron[38] then 65 Squadron upon which a hoard of Bf 109s immediately pounced. They destroyed two Spitfires, including R6707 flown by 54 Squadron's 'B' Flight commander, Flight Lieutenant

Hurricanes of 17 Squadron return from patrol, 25 July. (IWM)

B.H. Way, who was killed. Little wonder '54' called this 'Black Thursday'.

When eight Spitfires of 64 Squadron[39] arrived they faced another onslaught, this time by 30 Ju 88s of III/KG 4 accompanied by 50-plus Bf 109s. Three more 64 Squadron Spitfires (N3230, R6700, L1035) soon reinforced their companions, also 12 Hurricanes of 111 Squadron, and although they engaged the bombers they could not prevent the sinking of two more ships. Sub Lieutenant Dawson Paul, RN, flying L1035, in which he had earlier claimed a '109, was shot down. The convoy had now lost SS *Corhaven, Henry Moon, Leo, Polgrange* and *Porslade.* Five ships were damaged.

It was at 16:21 that Spitfires of 54 Squadron patrolling off Dover signalled that they had spotted E-Boats leaving Boulogne. Two destroyers, HMS *Boreas* and *Brilliant*, along with two MTBs, hastened out of Dover and soon two E-Boats were foundering off Calais. That brought a fierce response, Ju 87s which dive-bombed the destroyers further pestered by gunfire from the French coast. *Boreas* was hit, called for smoke and tugs, then more Ju 87s screamed down upon her. Both damaged destroyers slowly headed for Dover, whose No. 4 LAA gunsite claimed a Stuka. More Spitfires of 54 and 64

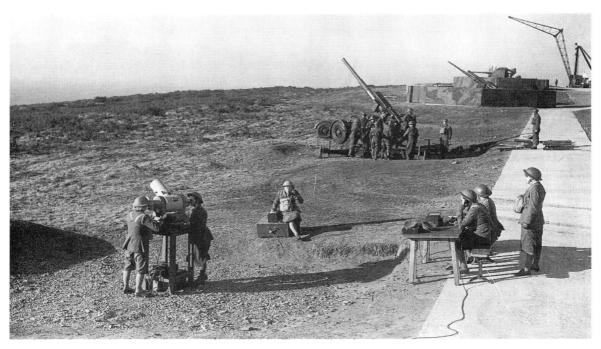

Squadrons tried to protect the warships, along with Hurricanes of 56 Squadron even though they were challenged by over 100 enemy air-craft. Just as the destroyers came under further attack 610 Squadron's Spitfires arrived to bag a couple of JG 52's Bf 109s and damage several

Above *A 3.7-inch mobile gun at Dover, 29 October 1940. Near the predictor, operators maintain a telephone link with control.* (IWM)

Left *In less than a year the strict style of RAF flying dress had changed to suit individual tastes and, one suspects, comfort! In the centre stands Squadron Leader D.O. Finlay, who flew with both 41 and 54 Squadrons.* (IWM)

Balloons for Dover

Few targets provided such understandable fascination for Messerschmitt pilots as Dover's balloons. The question of a Dover barrage was first raised on 15 May 1940 when Dover was the main port for crossings to Calais. Balloons, it was argued, would prevent dive-bombing. Eight sites were suggested, manned by 956 Squadron. The Air Ministry was strongly against the idea, arguing that it would interfere with RAF operations, and the notion lapsed.

The intensity of raids on Dover in July 1940 led to a revival of schemes for a Dover Low Zone Balloon Barrage. On high-level authorization the go-ahead was given on 30 July, suggestions being for balloons to be waterborne, possibly flown from six barges withdrawn from the Thames Yantlet Barrage.

Events moved with astonishing speed. A new squadron, No. 992, was formed in 30 Group at 23 Marine Parade, Dover, by midnight on 30 July, by which time 17 sites had been chosen. Next day Fighter Command escorted to Dover three drifters, two power barges and their balloons from Southend — the balloons withdrawn from Sheerness-based 952 Squadron. By midday 16 land sites were in use and eight waterborne balloons floated above their moorings.

The Dover balloons seriously handicapped the area's anti-aircraft gunners, who were initially ordered to fuse their shells to burst above 3,000 feet.

The successful dive-bombing of HMS *Codrington* in Dover on 27 July, which had contributed towards the Navy's decision to move its destroyers to Portsmouth or Sheerness, had worried the Navy, whose MTBs, with less fire-power than E-Boats, would not have been able to prevent landings on the south coast before destroyers arrived. The Navy, therefore, was eager to have the destroyers back in Dover and hoped that balloon cover would permit that. During the recent major raid Stukas and Bf 109s had successfully dived through the AA fire.

The first attack upon Dover's balloons developed at 14:30 on 30 July during an aerial battle over Folkestone involving nine Bf 109s at 15,000 feet. One Bf 109 then dived using light cloud cover to attack, with the balloons at 4,500 feet. First to fall in flames was one on a cliff edge site, and by keeping close to the balloons the pilot shot down a second.

To discourage such pursuits orders were then given to fly each balloon independently and just above the base of any thick cloud, at 8,000 feet if there was no cloud and just above 4,500 feet if fewer than four aircraft were attacking, because that made balloons harder to destroy. AA gunners therefore had to be careful not to score a balloon! On 5 August the entire barrage was reorganized as 961 Squadron with 24 balloons, eight of them waterborne.

more without loss. While the remnants of CW8 later ploughed into an uncertain night, Flying Officer Haynes of 600 Squadron tried in vain to deal with a rescue He 59 brightly lit off Foulness by searchlights. In the early hours of the 26th E-Boats fired on the convoy again before it was ordered to anchor in St Helen's Roads.

Tough fighting over the Straits had been supported by the usual activity around Portland. There No. 1 Squadron[40] entered the campaign, for it had temporarily replaced 43 Squadron at Tangmere. Its patrolling Hurricanes met Bf 109s of III/JG 27, destroying one which fell to Pilot Officer G.E. Goodman.

The daylight fighting had cost six Spitfires — three each from 54 and 64 Squadrons — and four pilots killed, in the most hectic day's fighting so far. So prominent among the 15 RAF fighter squadrons operating was No. 54 that it was time for the squadron to rest, and it moved to Catterick next day from where it was replaced by 41 Squadron. During July 12, 54 Squadron Spitfires had been shot down, five pilots were killed and three wounded. An astonishing 504 sorties had been flown by its handful of pilots during three weeks of bitter fighting in the course of over 800 hours operational flying. No mean achievement by some of the first of The Few.

Rain and low cloud swept in to reduce visibility and activity on 26 July although No. 238 Squadron[41] managed to fight with JG 27, Sergeant R. Little (P3702) having part of a boot shot away and two bullets in his parachute. Off Portland Flight Lieutenant S.C. Walch (P3618) destroyed a Bf 109.

German night activity, more widespread than of late, included ten HEs deposited upon the Fraserburgh Consolidated Pneumatic Tool Co. At Chigwell houses suffered, also at Staple Hill Bristol, Dagenham and on Canvey Island. Bombs intended for the ICI plant at Winnington, Cheshire, fell instead, without exploding, among houses at Northwich. Off Flatholme, Wales, a sand ship was blown up (possibly by mines) eight crewmen being lost. Night raiders were mostly dropping salvoes of from two to four bombs and multiples of 36 incendiaries.

Fine weather returned to the south on 27 July, the Germans taking advantage of it by dispatching about 30 Stukas of I/StG 77 escorted by JG 27 to deal with a convoy off Swanage. Just as three Hurricanes (P3462, P3823, P2947) of 238 Squadron arrived, the Ju 87s were peeling off into the attack and Flying Officer Davis (P3462) managed to destroy one. By the time the second wave arrived, three Hurricanes and Spitfires of 609 Squadron[42] were protecting the ships.

Thundery weather rolling over southern England calmed the contest until late afternoon, when the second of two attacks on Dover damaged the barracks and marine station and, more spectacularly, resulted in four direct hits on the destroyer HMS *Codrington* which caused its boilers to explode. That event, and the discovery that the enemy was building near Calais emplacements for heavy calibre long-range guns, forced the Admiralty to move the destroyer flotilla from Dover to the Nore. Dowd-

ing received that news with relief, considering it to diminish the harbour's importance. Air Ministry, though, stressed its continuing usefulness, in consequence of which the number of fighter squadrons in the south-east increased to 28 and Hawkinge and Manston became increasingly used as forward bases.

Codrington was not the only destroyer lost that day. HMS *Wren* was bombed and sunk off Aldeburgh by He 111s of KG 53 and another destroyer was damaged. At 18:46 Hurricanes of 615 Squadron (P2801, P3161, P3111, P3158, P2587, P3162) downed an air-sea rescue He 59 off the Foreland.

Not all patrols and scrambles resulted in combat. Throughout the day 145 Squadron had sections patrolling but only made one contact. Spitfires were in action against Bf 109s 20 miles south of the Needles and Blue Section 145 Squadron joined them. Three 109s latched onto Flight Lieutenant A.D. Boyd and P3221 and try as he did he was unable to shake them off until at sea level he reached the French coast. He was lucky then to escape and at the end of a two-hour flight had only five gallons of fuel left after landing.

Whenever a warship was lost it was bad for national morale. Sustained protection of shipping from air attack demanded repeated sorties for each pilot each day, and could easily have brought exhaustion to both them and the ground crews. Dowding, realizing the seriousness, ordered that each pilot be given eight hours rest a day, one day off per week. That assumed sufficient pilots remained on hand to fight.

A night attack on Belfast highlighted the inadequacy of night defences and the vulnerability of the west. A score of bombers had operated over Ireland and Anglesey, while others were busy over the south-east dropping 60 HEs and an oil bomb on Gillingham as well as bombs on Maidstone and near Sevenoaks.

German conclusions that British pilots must be getting exhausted might have seemed confirmed when, during fine weather on 28 July, a large morning gathering over the Channel

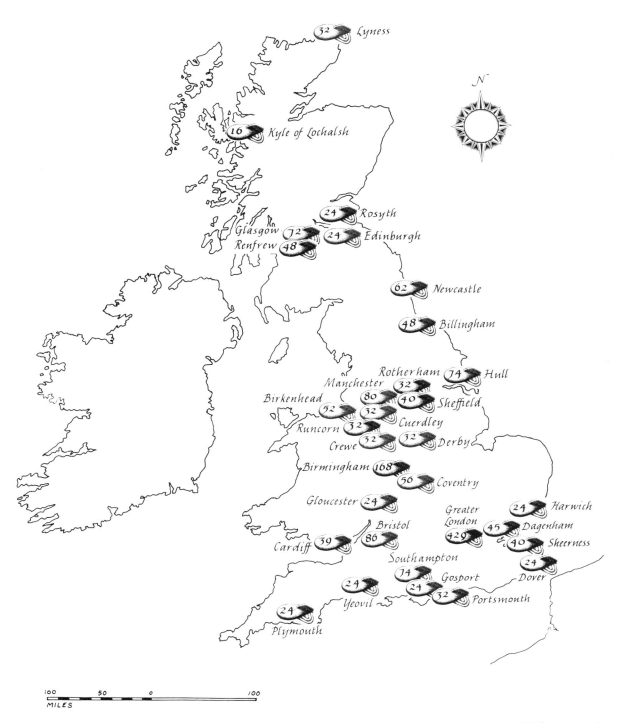

BARRAGE BALLOONS AS DEPLOYED AUGUST 1940

FOOD FACTS Nº 2

...cut out extras, cut out waste, don't eat more than you need.

TEA TIPS: You can save that extra one for the pot if you get the best out of your tea so remember: i) As soon as the water is boiling really fast you should be ready with a well warmed tea pot. The tea pot should come to the kettle, not the kettle to the pot. You should give the tea enough time to brew, and stir it just before pouring...

Don't make the mistake of using lettuce just as a salad. Lettuce cooked in a little water makes a delicious vegetable. You can enjoy the outside leaves even...

You can hear unusual tips on the wireless at 8.15 every morning.

Bake any stale bread in slices and use as toast or serve as rusks with soup or stews...

Cut a medium sized marrow in two and scoop out the seeds. Fill with stuffing made of two heaped tablespoonfuls of bread crumbs, two of minced bacon or cold meat, one of chopped suet, one small onion grated and a sprinkling of mixed herbs. Add pepper and salt... if preferred the bacon or meat may be omitted... more suet should then be included...

Spitfires[43] of 74 Squadron led by the famous South African 'Sailor' Malan, thus popularly known from his merchant navy days, waded among 36 Bf 109s of I/JG 51 over Dover, while Hawkinge's Hurricane squadrons set about the bombers. Such clear division of effort, probably overdue, meant that squadrons would whenever possible no longer split at the battle site. Maybe the enemy detected a tactical change, for the bombers readily turned about, leaving their escort battling with RAF fighters.

A sharp fight ensued, with 41[44], 74, 257[45] and 111 Squadrons combating I and II/JG 51 led by Major Werner Molders, who had to force-land his Bf 109 in France after it was badly damaged by 'Sailor' Malan. No. 74 Squadron did extremely well, Squadron Leader Malan (N3091), Pilot Officer Freeborn (R6706) and Flight Lieutenant Kelly (K9878) each destroying a Bf 109. Another three were damaged, for the loss of two Spitfires and Pilot Officer J.H.R. Young.

He 59 seaplanes arrived to snatch German survivors from the sea, only to encounter No. 111 Squadron, which destroyed one and seriously damaged another. Darkness cloaked much more sinister floatplanes, He 115s which accompanied He 111s and Ju 88s to extensively mine British waters, while bombers operating on a greater scale than of late attacked Newcastle, where a dozen HEs fell in a line parallel to and a mile from the Tyne, and Barry, Port Talbot, Colchester, Salford, Newcastle-under-Lyme, Seaford, Staplehurst, Ashford, and Edenbridge. Two bombs that failed to explode had the cheek to fall near the beautiful Cotswold Slaughters. Midlothian, Cheshire and the Otmoor bombing range also attracted the enemy.

When the morning mist cleared on Monday 29 July it revealed Britain splendidly bright and sunlit, conditions advantageous to the foe. After the feints of the previous day, controllers cautiously committed aircraft to engagements, but when radar detected a large enemy force clearly by-passing two convoys and obviously heading for Dover that certainly needed interception. Spitfires of 41 Squadron[46] scrambled from

failed to attract attention. Fighter Command, though, was conserving its strength for such as the large enemy bomber force which advanced on Dover at around 14:00, and had placed eight squadrons at forward airfields. A dozen

Manston at 07:25 to engage the enemy on his northern flank, leaving ten Hurricanes of 501 Squadron to race in from the sunward side. But as they met the Luftwaffe, they realized they were facing one of the largest raids yet, four formations of 80-plus which assembled near Cap Gris Nez and were revealing themselves as Bf 109s escorting two waves of Stukas which were soon screeching down from 12,000 to 1,000 feet to dive-bomb Dover. There they sank the previously damaged *Gronland* and started a fire aboard a submarine depot ship. No. 41 Squadron went after the Stukas but Bf 109s bore down upon the Spitfires. The squadron, forced to split, engaged both, and lost one aircraft in combat and four more in crash landings for the destruction of one Messerschmitt. Nos. 64[47] and 56[48] Squadrons had been vectored to help, the latter's Hurricanes engaging the 109s. No. 501 Squadron[49] had penetrated to the Stukas, shooting down two into the sea. Incendiaries and HEs which had fallen on the Royal Navy oil depot broke a supply pipe from which spilt fuel gushed, then blazed upon the water. Dover's AA guns merrily adding to the confusion claimed 501's Ju 87s!

WHAT'S ON AT THE PICTURES?

July — *Susannah of the Mountain* (Shirley Temple)

Hardy and Son (Mickey Rooney and Lewis Stone), *Hollywood Cavalcade* — in Technicolor (Alice Faye and Don Ameche), *The Great Victor Herbert* (Allan Jones and Mary Martin...yes, 'JR's' Mum!), *The Saint Strikes Back*, *The Gates of Alcatraz* (Walter Connolly and Oslo Stevens), *Drums Along the Mohawk* (Claudette Colbert and Henry Fonda).

At the Regal all next week: Sam Goldwyn presents *Raffles* with David Niven and Olivia de Havilland.

29 July — For six days only (no Sunday opening) — *Melody of Youth*, two prices only — 6d and 1/-.

Soon after midday attention switched to Channel convoys. Off Dungeness one was subjected to a low-level onslaught by Ju 88s of KG 76, whose lead aircraft clouted a ship's balloon cable. Another was claimed by ships' gunners. No. 610 Squadron's[50] Spitfires arrived too late to participate, the raiders having approached below radar's capability to detect them. Convoy 'Agent' off Essex then came under attack by a mixture of 36 fighter and fighter-bomber Bf 110s engaged by 151 Squadron. From 45 miles off Felixstowe a snooping Do 17 was chased as far as the Dutch coast, and three pilots of 85 Squadron shot down a He 111 approaching 'Agent'. A few minutes later another was destroyed off Lowestoft. Meanwhile, off Portland, bombers had achieved a notable success by sinking the destroyer HMS *Delight*. Among limited raids the following night were nine on north-east England. At Hull five shops and a public house were damaged. Near Bury St Edmunds, soon after midnight a Ju 88 crashed due to circumstances never established. Penetrating cloud and drizzle on 30 July, a Dornier at 06:04 released 15 HEs onto Norwich which caused considerable damage, killed 10 and injured 16 residents. Additional to other cloud cover attacks over the east, south, Scotland and the Orkneys there was a follow-up anti-shipping foray off Suffolk by Bf 110s of Erpro 210 during which one was shot down by 85 Squadron. Unusual was an early evening bombing raid on Esher's balloon sites, when an ARP post was hit. Night operations — including plentiful mining of Liverpool Bay partly by Fw 200s — were mainly directed at Wales and in particular Barry Docks. At Monmouth 13 HEs fell, Heysham, Lancashire, being another target.

Hazy conditions on 31 July generated more lone aircraft operations until Bf 109s of JG 2 began shooting down Dover's balloons. An increasing number of 74 Squadron Spitfires arriving to deal with the Messerschmitts found them to have a height advantage which they rapidly exploited to bring down the Spitfires of Sergeant Eley (P9398) and Pilot Officer Gunn (P9379) for the loss of one Bf 109 which crashed in France.

The following night many raiders operated widely south of a line Newcastle-Liverpool, while 50 aircraft mined off the east coast. A procession of bombers crossed the Beachy Head-Shoreham area to the Thames region, to release their loads at Croydon, Romford, Gravesend, also Ipswich and Martlesham.

A British analysis at the end of July suggested that 1,921 HE bombs, an unknown quantity of incendiaries, 162 oil bombs and 19 mines of uncertain types had been recorded as falling on the United Kingdom during a month which had seen activity on every day and night, and included several days of greatly enhanced enemy operations — and the Luftwaffe was only playing the overture.

Luftwaffe Losses during operations by operational units, 1-31 July 1940

Captured Luftwaffe Quartermaster General's ledgers listing losses and accidents to the end of 1943 form the basis for official statistics of losses, along with further material from unreleased documents. The listing here and later is based upon the Quartermaster General documents.

a indicates shot down, *b* crashed after action and written off, *c* seriously damaged.

July	1			2			3			4			5			6			7		
Type	a	b	c	a	b	c	a	b	c	a	b	c	a	b	c	a	b	c	a	b	c
Do 17M	—	—	—	—	—	—	—	—	—	—	—	—	—	—	—	—	—	—	—	—	—
Do 17P	—	—	—	—	—	—	—	—	—	—	—	—	—	—	—	—	1	—	2	1	1
Do 17Z	6	1	1	1	1	—	1	—	—	—	—	—	—	—	—	—	1	—	—	—	1
Do 18	—	—	—	—	—	—	—	—	—	—	—	—	—	—	—	—	—	—	—	—	—
Do 215	2	—	—	1	—	—	—	—	—	—	—	—	—	—	—	—	—	—	—	—	—
Fw 200	—	—	—	—	—	—	—	—	—	—	—	—	—	—	—	—	—	—	—	—	—
He 59	1	—	—	—	—	—	—	—	—	—	—	—	—	—	—	—	—	—	—	—	—
He 111D	—	—	—	—	—	—	—	—	—	—	—	—	—	—	—	—	—	—	—	—	—
He 111H	—	1	—	—	—	—	—	—	—	—	—	—	1	—	—	—	—	—	—	—	—
He 111P	—	—	—	—	—	—	—	—	—	1	—	—	—	—	—	—	—	—	—	—	—
He 115	—	—	—	—	—	—	—	—	—	—	—	—	—	—	—	—	—	—	—	—	—
Ju 87B	—	—	—	—	—	—	—	1	—	—	—	—	—	—	—	—	—	—	—	—	—
Ju 88A	1	—	1	—	1	—	3	—	—	—	—	1	—	1	—	—	2	—	—	—	—
Ju 88C	—	—	—	—	—	—	—	—	—	—	—	1	—	—	—	—	—	—	—	—	—
Me/Bf 109	—	—	—	—	1	—	—	—	1	—	—	—	—	1	—	—	—	—	2	1	2
Me/Bf 110	—	—	—	—	—	—	—	—	—	—	—	—	—	—	—	1	—	—	—	—	—
TOTALS	10	2	2	2	3	0	4	1	1	1	0	2	1	2	0	1	4	0	4	2	4

July	8			9			10			11			12			13			14		
Type	a	b	c	a	b	c	a	b	c	a	b	c	a	b	c	a	b	c	a	b	c
Do 17M	—	—	—	—	—	—	—	—	—	—	—	—	—	—	—	—	—	—	—	—	—
Do 17P	—	—	—	—	—	—	1	2	—	—	—	—	—	—	—	—	—	—	—	—	—
Do 17Z	—	—	—	—	—	—	3	—	1	—	—	—	2	2	—	—	—	—	—	—	—
Do 18	—	—	—	—	—	—	—	—	—	—	—	—	—	—	—	—	—	—	—	—	—
Do 215	—	—	—	—	—	2	1	—	—	—	—	—	—	—	—	—	—	—	—	—	—
Fw 200	—	—	—	—	—	—	—	—	—	—	—	—	—	—	—	—	1	—	—	—	—
He 59	—	—	—	1	—	—	—	—	—	1	—	—	—	—	—	—	—	—	—	—	—
He 111D	—	—	—	—	—	—	—	—	—	—	—	—	—	—	—	—	—	—	—	—	—
He 111H	2	—	—	1	—	—	1	—	—	4	—	2	4	—	1	—	—	—	—	—	—

July	8			9			10			11			12			13			14		
Type	a	b	c	a	b	c	a	b	c	a	b	c	a	b	c	a	b	c	a	b	c
He 111P	—	—	—	—	—	—	—	—	1	—	—	—	—	—	—	—	—	—	—	—	—
He 115	—	—	—	—	—	—	—	—	—	—	—	—	—	—	—	1	—	—	—	—	—
Ju 87B	—	1	—	1	—	—	—	—	—	2	1	—	—	—	—	—	1	1	—	—	—
Ju 88A	1	—	—	—	1	—	—	—	—	2	1	—	1	—	2	—	—	—	—	1	—
Ju 88C	—	—	—	—	—	—	—	—	—	1	—	—	—	—	—	—	—	—	—	—	—
Me/Bf 109	4	1	1	2	—	—	2	—	—	—	1	—	—	—	—	2	—	2	1	—	—
Me/Bf 110	—	—	—	—	4	—	1	1	1	—	4	—	—	—	—	—	3	—	—	—	—
TOTALS	7	2	1	9	1	3	8	1	2	15	3	5	7	1	1	6	0	6	2	1	0

July	15			16			17			18			19			20			21		
Type	a	b	c	a	b	c	a	b	c	a	b	c	a	b	c	a	b	c	a	b	c
Do 17M	—	—	—	—	—	—	—	—	—	1	—	—	—	—	—	—	1	—	1	—	—
Do 17P	—	—	—	—	—	—	—	—	—	—	—	—	1	—	—	—	1	—	1	—	—
Do 17Z	—	—	—	1	—	—	—	—	1	—	—	—	—	—	—	—	—	1	—	—	—
Do 18	1	—	—	—	—	—	—	—	—	—	—	—	—	—	—	—	—	—	1	1	—
Do 215	—	—	—	—	—	—	—	—	—	—	—	—	—	—	—	—	—	—	—	—	—
Fw 200	—	—	—	—	—	—	—	—	—	—	—	—	—	—	—	2	—	—	—	—	—
He 59	—	—	—	—	—	—	—	—	—	—	—	—	—	—	—	2	—	—	—	—	—
He 111D	—	—	—	—	—	—	—	—	—	—	—	—	—	—	—	—	—	—	—	—	—
He 111H	1	—	1	—	—	—	1	—	—	—	—	—	—	—	—	—	—	—	—	—	—
He 111P	—	—	—	—	—	—	—	—	—	—	—	—	1	—	—	—	1	—	—	—	—
He 115	—	—	—	—	—	—	—	—	1	—	—	—	—	—	—	—	—	—	—	—	—
Ju 87B	—	—	—	—	—	—	—	—	—	—	—	—	—	—	—	2	—	—	—	—	1
Ju 88A	1	1	—	1	—	—	1	1	—	2	—	1	—	—	—	1	—	—	—	1	—
Ju 88C	—	—	—	—	—	—	—	—	—	—	—	—	—	—	—	—	—	—	—	—	—
Me/Bf 109	—	—	—	—	1	—	—	—	—	—	—	—	1	—	—	5	—	—	2	—	1
Me/Bf 110	—	—	—	—	—	—	—	—	—	—	—	—	—	—	—	—	—	—	1	—	1
TOTALS	3	1	1	2	1	0	2	1	2	4	0	1	4	0	0	11	4	1	6	2	3

July	22			23			24			25			26			27			28		
Type	a	b	c	a	b	c	a	b	c	a	b	c	a	b	c	a	b	c	a	b	c
Do 17M	—	—	—	—	—	—	—	—	—	1	—	—	—	—	—	—	—	—	—	—	—
Do 17P	1	—	—	1	—	—	—	—	—	—	—	—	—	—	—	—	—	—	—	—	—
Do 17Z	—	—	—	1	—	—	—	—	—	1	—	—	1	—	—	—	—	—	—	1	—
Do 18	—	—	—	—	—	—	—	—	—	2	—	—	—	—	—	—	—	—	—	—	—
Do 215	—	—	—	—	—	—	—	—	—	—	—	—	—	—	—	—	—	—	—	—	—
Fw 200	—	—	—	—	—	—	—	—	—	—	—	—	—	—	—	—	—	—	—	—	—
He 59	—	—	—	—	—	—	—	—	—	1	—	—	—	—	—	1	—	1	—	—	—
He 111D	—	—	—	—	—	—	—	—	—	—	—	—	—	—	—	—	—	—	—	—	—
He 111H	—	—	—	—	—	—	—	—	—	—	—	—	—	—	—	—	—	—	—	—	—
He 111P	—	—	—	—	—	—	1	—	—	—	—	—	—	—	—	—	—	—	—	—	—
He 115	—	—	—	—	—	—	—	—	—	—	—	—	—	—	—	—	—	—	—	—	—
Ju 87B	—	—	—	—	—	—	—	—	—	1	—	—	—	—	—	1	—	—	—	—	—
Ju 88A	—	1	1	1	1	—	1	1	—	1	—	—	—	—	—	1	—	—	1	2	—
Ju 88C	—	—	—	—	—	—	—	—	—	—	—	—	—	—	—	—	—	—	—	—	—
Me/Bf 109	—	—	—	—	—	—	6	—	—	—	5	—	1	—	1	—	—	—	3	—	3
Me/Bf 110	—	—	—	—	—	—	—	2	1	—	—	—	—	—	—	—	—	—	—	1	—
TOTALS	1	1	1	3	2	0	8	3	1	7	9	1	2	0	1	4	0	1	4	4	3

July	29			30			31			GRAND TOTALS		
	a	b	c	a	b	c	a	b	c	a	b	c
Type												
Do 17M	—	—	—	—	—	—	—	—	—	3	1	0
Do 17P	—	—	—	—	—	—	—	—	—	9	2	2
Do 17Z	—	—	1	—	—	1	—	—	1	15	5	9
Do 18	—	—	—	—	—	—	—	—	—	2	3	0
Do 215	—	—	—	—	—	—	—	1	—	4	1	2
Fw 200	—	—	—	—	—	—	—	—	—	3	0	0
He 59	—	—	—	—	—	—	—	—	—	6	1	1
He 111D	—	—	—	—	—	—	—	—	—	1	0	0
He 111H	2	1	—	1	—	—	—	—	—	22	5	4
He 111P	1	—	—	1	2	1	—	—	—	5	3	3
He 115	—	—	—	—	—	—	—	—	—	2	—	—
Ju 87B	4	—	—	—	—	—	—	—	—	10	4	3
Ju 88A	3	1	2	—	—	—	—	1	1	26	15	6
Ju 88C	—	—	—	—	—	—	—	—	—	—	2	—
Me/Bf 109	—	—	—	—	—	1	—	1	1	29	14	15
Me/Bf 110	—	—	—	1	—	—	—	—	1	14	2	7
TOTALS	10	2	3	3	2	2	0	3	4	151	58	52

RAF bomber, coastal and fighter aircraft losses, 1-31 July 1940

General note relating to loss tabulations:

British and German losses in the accompanying tables are grouped within three basic entries — *a* shot down, *b* write off due to battle damage, *c* suffered major damage but repairable. All the entries relate to loss or damage sustained during operational flying. Tabulations such as these can only give a general picture of the results of combat flying. Some damaged aircraft were quickly returned to front line service while others even with little damage were not repaired until many weeks, even months, had passed. Others, particularly on the British side, were removed for repair by civilian contractors which led to their return to RAF squadrons and units via Aircraft Storage Units (MUs) where sometimes they tarried long and underwent modification programmes. Generally, if the fuselage of an RAF aircraft survived an accident sufficiently well for it to be repairable, the identity number (its 'serial') was retained — even if other major components needed replacing. Thus, the mainplanes of a written off aircraft could well be wedded to a repairable fuselage of another. The Luftwaffe assessed the damage of its aircraft on what seems a rather imperfect percentage basis. An aircraft with 40 per cent or more damage required considerable attention, that rated at 60 per cent and over being very badly damaged. Just how complete the German records were can only be surmised, although without recording a loss a unit would not have received its replacement. Certainly the German records became ever more detailed as the fighting developed. Indeed, earlier omissions are often included at much later dates. British individual aircraft record cards (Form 78s) were generally amended some time after the events they record, in some instances at the end of the relating calendar month. Their brief entries cover wide possibilities, as, for example, when the category of damage was amended and not always recorded on the card. Fates and dates, too, for a variety of reasons, may differ from those listed. The subject of losses is indeed a highly complex one.

WEAR THEM DOWN

Legend: *a* Failed to return from operational flight/shot down, *b* destroyed as a result of battle damage — written off, uneconomic to repair, etc., *c* seriously damaged — needing contractor's attention

July 1–7

Type	1			2			3			4			5			6			7		
	a	b	c	a	b	c	a	b	c	a	b	c	a	b	c	a	b	c	a	b	c
Blenheim F	—	1	—	—	—	—	—	—	—	—	—	—	—	1	—	—	—	—	—	—	1
Defiant	—	—	—	—	—	—	—	—	—	—	—	—	—	—	—	—	—	—	—	—	—
Hurricane	—	—	1	—	—	—	1	1	2	—	—	1	—	1	—	—	1	—	1	—	1
Spitfire	—	1	—	—	—	—	—	1	—	—	—	—	1	1	1	—	1	—	5	1	—
Blenheim B	—	—	—	1	—	—	—	—	—	1	—	—	2	—	—	1	—	—	2	—	—
Hampden	—	—	—	1	—	—	—	—	—	—	—	—	—	—	—	—	—	—	—	—	—
Wellington	—	—	—	—	—	—	—	—	—	—	—	—	1	—	—	1	—	—	—	—	—
Whitley	1	—	—	—	—	—	—	—	—	—	—	—	—	—	—	1	—	—	—	—	—
Coastal Cmd	—	—	—	2	—	—	—	—	—	2	—	—	—	—	—	2	—	—	—	—	—
TOTALS	1	2	1	4	—	—	1	2	2	3	—	1	4	3	1	5	2	—	8	1	2

July 8–14

Type	8			9			10			11			12			13			14		
	a	b	c	a	b	c	a	b	c	a	b	c	a	b	c	a	b	c	a	b	c
Blenheim F	1	—	—	—	—	—	—	—	—	—	—	—	—	—	—	—	1	—	—	—	—
Defiant	—	—	2	—	—	—	—	—	—	—	—	—	—	—	—	—	—	—	—	—	—
Hurricane	3	—	—	2	1	—	1	—	1	4	1	—	2	5	3	2	2	1	1	—	1
Spitfire	2	1	—	2	1	—	—	—	3	2	—	—	1	—	—	1	1	—	—	—	—
Blenheim B	—	—	—	—	1	—	—	—	1	—	—	—	—	—	—	—	—	—	—	—	—
Hampden	2	—	1	—	—	—	—	—	—	—	—	—	—	—	—	—	—	—	—	—	—
Wellington	—	—	—	—	—	—	—	—	—	—	—	1	—	—	—	—	—	—	1	—	—
Whitley	1	—	—	1	—	—	—	—	—	—	—	1	—	—	—	—	—	—	1	—	1
Coastal Cmd	1	—	—	1	—	—	1	—	—	1	—	—	1	—	—	1	—	—	3	—	—
TOTALS	10	1	3	6	3	—	2	—	5	9	1	—	3	6	3	3	3	3	6	—	2

July 15–21

Type	15			16			17			18			19			20			21		
	a	b	c	a	b	c	a	b	c	a	b	c	a	b	c	a	b	c	a	b	c
Blenheim F	—	—	—	—	—	—	—	—	—	2	—	—	—	—	—	1	—	—	—	—	—
Defiant	—	—	—	—	—	—	—	—	—	—	—	—	5	1	1	—	—	—	—	—	—
Hurricane	1	2	2	—	—	—	—	—	—	—	—	1	4	—	1	4	1	—	1	—	—
Spitfire	—	—	—	—	—	—	2	—	—	3	1	3	—	—	—	1	1	—	1	—	—
Blenheim B	—	—	—	—	—	—	2	—	—	1	—	—	—	—	—	1	—	—	—	—	—
Hampden	—	—	—	—	—	—	—	—	—	—	—	—	1	—	—	4	1	—	1	1	—
Wellington	—	—	—	—	—	—	—	—	—	—	—	1	1	—	—	1	1	—	2	—	1
Whitley	—	—	—	—	—	—	—	—	—	—	—	—	1	—	—	—	—	—	1	—	—
Coastal Cmd	1	—	—	—	—	—	—	—	—	4	—	—	—	—	—	—	—	—	—	—	—
TOTALS	2	2	2	—	—	—	4	—	—	11	1	6	12	1	2	12	4	—	6	1	1

July	22			23			24			25			26			27			28		
	a	b	c	a	b	c	a	b	c	a	b	c	a	b	c	a	b	c	a	b	c
Type																					
Blenheim F	—	—	1	—	—	—	—	—	—	—	—	—	—	—	—	—	1	—	—	—	—
Defiant	—	—	—	—	—	—	—	—	—	—	—	—	—	—	—	—	—	—	—	—	—
Hurricane	—	2	—	—	3	—	—	2	—	1	—	1	2	1	—	—	1	1	1	1	—
Spitfire	—	—	3	—	1	—	1	2	—	6	2	1	—	1	2	1	1	—	2	1	1
Blenheim B	—	—	—	1	—	—	1	—	—	1	—	1	—	—	2	—	—	—	—	—	1
Hampden	—	—	—	1	—	—	—	—	—	2	—	—	2	—	—	—	—	—	1	—	—
Wellington	—	—	—	—	—	—	—	—	—	2	1	—	—	—	2	—	—	—	—	—	—
Whitley	1	—	—	—	—	—	—	—	—	—	—	1	—	—	—	—	—	—	—	—	—
Coastal Cmd	—	—	—	2	—	—	—	—	—	2	—	—	2	—	—	—	—	—	—	—	—
TOTALS	1	2	4	4	4	—	2	4	—	14	3	3	7	2	6	1	2	2	4	2	2

July	29			30			31			GRAND TOTALS JULY		
	a	b	c	a	b	c	a	b	c	a	b	c
Type												
Blenheim F	—	—	—	—	1	—	—	—	—	1	3	4
Defiant	—	—	—	—	—	—	—	—	—	5	1	3
Hurricane	1	1	2	—	—	—	—	2	—	33	29	19
Spitfire	1	1	5	—	—	—	2	1	1	32	28	20
Blenheim B	1	—	—	1	—	—	2	—	—	17	1	6
Hampden	—	1	—	—	—	—	1	2	—	17	5	1
Wellington	—	—	1	—	—	—	—	—	—	10	2	5
Whitley	—	—	—	—	—	—	—	—	—	10	0	1
Coastal Cmd	—	—	—	—	—	—	3	—	—	29	0	0
TOTALS	3	3	8	1	1	—	8	5	1	154	69	59

CHAPTER 7
NOT MUCH BANK HOLIDAY FUN THIS YEAR

By August invasion was a serious possibility, and everyone knew that. If such things engendered fear, then it was rarely exposed. A strange style of August Bank Holiday — then the first Monday of the month — pertained, injected with a mixture of stay put holiday spirit and determination. Like those around us, my father and I spent the day tending his roses and checking our arsenal of petrol bombs while overhead Spitfires from Fowlmere reminded us we were 'safe'. Yes, I think like many I experienced a curious sensation of being safe and I know I believed, even in those dark days, in ultimate victory, encouraged like millions more by 'Winnie'. By now he had become the grandest of champions, and shortly before his speeches were broadcast the streets would fall quiet, empty; for a high proportion of the nation was eagerly awaiting the latest round of his grand oratory. Unforgettable those quiet, frightening summer evenings. Unforgettable his voice, castigating the 'Narzies'. . . 'If we fail' — but no, we wouldn't fail. We were all in it together. Somehow we would win through.

On 1 August it was the turn of shipping off Yorkshire to come under attack, raiders escaping into cloud before Nos. 607 and 616 Squadrons arrived on the scene. A very unusual event occurred ten miles south of Hastings when No. 145 Squadron destroyed a Henschel Hs 126 army co-operation machine of 4(H)/31; it fell to Pilot Officer E.C.J. Wakeham (P3163) aided by Sub Lieutenant I.H. Kestin (P3155), who was shot down by return fire. Later, a He 111 of I/KG 4 managed a highly effective sneak raid, temporarily closing the Norwich Boulton & Paul factory and bombing Thorpe Station goods facility and a timber yard. In the evening Ju 88s of 9/KG 4 attempting to sink ships in convoy 'Pilot' off Norfolk were discovered by a trio of 242 Squadron Hurricanes, one bomber being destroyed.

What the Papers had to say:

2 August: 'First Leaflet Raid on Britain Last Night . . . They have a streamer heading ''The Last Appeal to Reason by Adolf Hitler''. The printing is good, the paper of fair quality.' (*Does one detect some disappointment with Britain's blockade?*)

2 August: from an Air Ministry announcement and a Swedish diplomat — about two German towns bombed by the RAF: ''Hamburg is said to be in ruins. Within a gigantic circle we've inflicted irreparable damage on such places as Duisburg, Düsseldorf, Essen . . . and Wesel.'' (*Does one now detect optimism?*)

Customary night-mining followed, and some 47 HEs and incendiaries were spread over Pembroke Dock, Bristol, Southend and Montrose. Highlight of the night was, without doubt, the first arrival of a large supply of curious yellow and green leaflets freely distributed to the residents of Backwell, Clevedon, Axbridge, Brecon, Taly Uyn, Southampton, Marchwood and Epping. Carrying Hitler's 'Last Appeal to Reason', they were eagerly sought trophies greeted with a mixture of delight and derision. Sold for 6d each in Bristol they aided the national effort to 'help the Red Cross help our boys'. Others performed well in a less glamorous but most useful manner... The Government in essentially British style applauded, in an Official 'Secret' report, 'the quality of paper and print'! Wartime charity sales to which the leaflets found their way were nothing new — at one such sale, two chickens 'murdered' by a German cannon shell at Fleet End provided the Red Cross with £16. Cheerful approach to tragedy was essential, especially when 'incidents' happened such as one the night before, caused by a parachuted mine which exploded near Taunton, producing a 60-foot crater 18 feet deep. Neither Social Security Office nor social workers were on hand, or needed, in those times; you more sensibly sorted yourself out — if you survived!

Shipping again bore the brunt of interest throughout 2 August. Off Harwich, fighter bombers of Erpro 210 sank HM Trawler *Cape Finisterre* with a direct hit. Gunners aboard the SS *Highlander* in convoy off Scotland managed to bring down one of two KG 26 He 111s attacking the ship, landing themselves a most unusual catch — the Heinkel on their deck a conspicuous trophy as the vessel sailed into Leith. The following night the Luftwaffe left noisy calling cards on RAF property at Halton, Catterick, Farnborough and Rochford. An impertinent, ineffective attempt was also made to break the Forth Bridge.

Dull weather on 3 August much reduced German Channel effort. Nuisance sorties included one by a Ju 88 which flew so low by Wembury Cliff searchlight site that gunners there fired down upon it. Scotland, Tyneside, Humber, Harwich, Crewe — all had night raids, and mining continued. Cornfield fires in Essex aroused an erroneous suspicion that the Luftwaffe might use oil bombs to burn ripening grain after the manner of the RAF's use of phosphorus-impregnated strips dropped upon Germany — 'razzling' as it was called. About 5,800 HE bombs were reckoned to have so far fallen on land in all the raids on Britain.

FOOD FACTS Nº 3

Save sugar — stew apples with chopped figs. It's a new way, a nice way, and you'll need less sugar.

Use the remains of today's rice pudding to thicken tomorrow's soup...

Plums are in season. Make less use of tinned fruit which should be kept for winter.

If everyone in Great Britain wasted ½ oz of bread daily we'd be wasting 250,000 tons of wheat a year. Thirty ships would be required to carry that amount. (*I wonder how much we presently waste each day?*)

Do you throw away scraps of food rather than bother to make them up? Do you have odd snacks during the day? Do you eat just a little more than you need at mealtimes? In peacetime these indulgences don't matter.
6 August, newspaper

About 4 per cent of them as 250-kg, the others 50-kg variants.

Cloudy weather throughout 4 August brought some respite to both sides, then at night bombs fell around Mildenhall, Ely, Newark and near Debden. Monday 5 August was hot, hazy, ideal for lazing and bathing but not on a barbed and mined south coast beach in 1940 — and especially with six Spitfires of 64 Squadron[51] skirmishing overhead with JG 54's Bf 109s. Two

Spitfires were shot down and yet another '109' made it across the Channel only to crash in France. Main activity came later, when escorted Ju 88s seeking Channel shipping were engaged off Dover by 151 Squadron[52] and a Bf 109 was shot down.

August 6 turned out to be cloudy and breezy, limiting operations to Channel forays and a handful of inland sorties. Off East Anglia three 85 Squadron Hurricanes[53] led by the highly successful Sergeant Geoffrey Allard provided a watery grave for a Do 17 of III/KG 3. Improved weather on 7 August brought more anti-shipping sorties and a convoy attack off Cromer. Early on the 8th two misplaced parachute sea mines exploded near Stannington Sanatorium near Plessy Viaduct and four miles south or Morpeth, bringing down the boiler house roof and generally blasting the hospital. A supposedly magnetic mine fell late that day on Lower Marsh Farm, Fairlight, by which time Salford's residents had been smothered with free reading matter, courtesy of the Führer.

On a showery, bright 8 August the heaviest assault yet developed, including three major raids on the Channel convoy CW9 codenamed 'Peewit', comprising 29 ships plus naval escort.

Sailing from the Thames late on the 7th, the convoy hoped to avoid trouble in the Dover Straits by passing through in darkness. German shore radar detected it. E-Boats roared out and two coasters (*Holme Force* and *Fife Coast*) were sunk and others damaged. Off Portland the sister CE Channel convoy was proceeding easterly when, at 06:39, two of its balloons were shot down. The enemy had signalled awareness of both convoy positions. With bomber forces almost ready for the long-awaited big blow, German commanders must have decided to practise their skills. At 08:30 Ju 87s escorted by JG 27 and LG 1 sallied forth from the direction of Cherbourg. Now it was the turn of British radar to do some detecting, which enabled five 11 Group squadrons and one from 10 Group to tackle the attackers. Between 08:49 and 09:43 two assaults each of 100-plus raiders attacked

. . .It is difficult to fix the exact date on which the 'Battle of Britain' can be said to have begun. Operations of various kinds merged into one another almost insensibly, and there are grounds for choosing the date of 8th August, on which was made the first attack in force against land objectives in this country, as the beginning of the Battle.

. . .'The essence of their Strategy was so to weaken our Fighter Defences that their Air Arm should be able to give adequate support in an attempted invasion of the British Isles.'

. . .'Long after the policy of "crashing through" with heavy bomber formations had been abandoned owing to shattering losses incurred, the battle went on. Large fighter formations were sent over, a proportion of the fighters being adapted to carry bombs, in order that the attacks might not be ignorable. This last phase was perhaps the most difficult to deal with tactically.'

Air Chief Marshal Sir Hugh Dowding, Commander-in-Chief Fighter Command

the convoy (15 miles west of the Isle of Wight), which lost SS *Conquerdale* and SS *Empire Crusader*. Once more in the thick of battle were Squadron Leader J.R.A. Peel's Hurricanes of 145 Squadron[54]. By the end of the engagement RAF fighters could accurately claim five of the enemy, and gunners at St Catherine's Point another two.

At about 12:45 the second assault on CW8 developed, just east of the Isle of Wight, delivered this time by 60 Ju 87s of three Stuka Geschwaderen — Nos. 2, 3, and 77. After disposing of the balloon cover the Stukas dive-bombed and scattered the ships. But the contest was far from one-sided, for Hurricanes

The Bofors performed well against Ju 87s. These belonged to 9/StG 2, and T6+AT in the foreground is carrying two bombs beneath each outer mainplane. (Bundesarchiv)

drawn from Nos. 43[55], 145[56], 238[57] and 257[58] Squadrons and Spitfires of 609[59] Squadron — over 50 fighters — were on hand, 257 Squadron led by Flight Lieutenant N.M. Hall opening the firing off St Catherine's Point. Participants in so many early actions, J.R.A. Peel's 145 Squadron were again busy and dived between flanking Bf 109s to pick off a couple of Ju 87s. In all, three Stukas were shot down and four damaged, the enemy also losing a Bf 110 of V/LG 1 and three Bf 109s, three more '110s and a '109 being damaged. Cost to the RAF? Three pilots and their Hurricanes. After the engagement, No. 238 Squadron's commander, Squadron Leader H.A. Fenton, recently returned to command after being wounded, went back in P3827 to search for his two lost men. In doing so he tackled a He 59, was brought down by its return fire and was rescued by a trawler.

Late afternoon saw another Stuka swarm emerge from the Cherbourg direction to again pester the now re-organized convoy. Seven well-placed squadrons met them, Peel's Hurricanes[60] at 16,000 feet confronting many Bf 109s stepped up to 20,000 feet. This time advantageously placed up-sun, the Hurricanes swooped upon the Stukas, undetected by the enemy fighters. Flight Lieutenant R. Dutton, Flight Commander of 145 Squadron, destroyed two Stukas before limping home with engine trouble and Squadron Leader Peel (P3164)

claimed two Messerschmitt 109s. No. 43 Squadron[61], which operated three times during the day also did well, possibly shooting down II/JG 27's Gruppenkommandeur. During the actions Solent guns fired 27 rounds.

By dusk, competing contemporary analysts were crediting the RAF with 24 German bombers and 36 fighters destroyed, while the Luftwaffe was settling for 49 RAF fighters. Likely true scores are 31 German aircraft shot down, and 19 RAF fighters. An exceptionally high score of ten destroyed and one damaged seems certainly to have been achieved by 145 Squadron, its claim of 21 being unsubstantiated. Three rounds of bitter fighting had however taken from the squadron five pilots. Seven merchant ships had been sunk, six naval ships damaged, and only four ships finally made Swanage. Little wonder that those aboard were strongly questioning the point of coastal voyagers risking their lives conveying goods able to travel safely on land. By diverting enemy effort from more worthwhile targets ashore these were playing, at a price, a useful part in the battle.

By 9 August the fine weather had again vanished, clouds shielding lone operators

WHAT THE PAPERS HAD TO SAY:

8 August: 'Latest score — today's successes bring total . . . to 275 since 18 June, 349 since war was declared.'

including a *Zenit* crew flying from Schiphol to Mildenhall and London. Daily meteorological reconnaissance flights were very necessary, accurate weather information essential, for next day was scheduled the beginning of the main attack plan, *Adlerangriffe* — 'Eagle Attack'. Bombers were active, too. KG 26 visited Wearmouth, dropped 14 bombs over shipbuilding and railway facilities and injured 73 people. Saltburn's Skinningrove was attacked — yet again. Sunderland's shipyards also came under attack before 79 Squadron disposed of the offender. At both Shorts and Pobjoy's Rochester works bombs narrowly missed their targets. Dover's balloons at 16:50 flared again, to the guns of JG 51's Bf 109s, before 64 Squadron

and the local gunners drove the intruders away. That night the Luftwaffe, roaming between Wiltshire and Wallasey, called on Harwich, Yeovil, Liverpool, delivered 19 bombs to Warkworth in Northumberland, and donated biased literature to Oxford's dons. By dawn on the 10th 190 HEs had fallen in 24 hours, killing seven and injuring 100.

However mighty the Luftwaffe conceived itself to be, it could not arrange the weather to its liking. Squalls and thundery conditions on 10 August again forced postponement of *Adlertag*, 'Eagle Day', the opening of the main assault. Instead, Channel tantalization continued, and Bf 110 pilots of the élite fighter-bomber Erpro 210 attempted a surprise evening strike on Norwich. A lone, undetected Do 17 put 11 HEs close to RAF West Malling despite 501 Squadron's attempts to stop it.

Skinningrove iron works was the subject of bombardment in the First World War, and again in 1940. The works survived, until recent closure. It is always hard to visualize terrible events taking place in such a superb landscape as this. (A.M. Alderson)

Activity the following night included serious damage to Llandore GWR viaduct near Swansea where a direct hit on a shelter killed four.

Maintaining huge forces at high efficiency is always difficult, and not surprisingly 11 August saw a spate of *Zenit* flights able to report fine weather but with clouds looming. With increased operational tempo feasible, Bf 109s at 07:00 also began three hours of tempting feints off Dover, with Erpro 210's Bf 109s and '110s attacking its balloons and aiming 60 HEs at the harbour area yet producing little damage. After a Channel convoy was threatened, the Luftwaffe picked on Dover again and was greeted by a mixture of AA gunfire and fighters from Nos. 32[62], 64[63] and 74[64] Squadrons which dealt effectively with two '109s. As the fighters were battling over Dover, radar stations detected a large formation heading for the Weymouth area. The Dover Activity had been a diversion.

Fighter Command rapidly responded, ordering off 38 Hurricanes of Nos. 87[65], 145[66], 213, 238[67] and 601[68] Squadrons along with Spitfires of Nos. 152 and of 609[69] Squadrons.

Challenging them were over 150 raiders — Ju 88s of I and II/KG 54 and He 111s of KG 27 escorted by Bf 109s of III/JG 2 and Bf 110s of I and II/ZG 2. A novel feature was a smokescreen laid west from the Needles behind which the raiders approached before splitting into two formations to simultaneously approach the target from both east and west. As they ran in at 10:30 two destroyers hurriedly put to sea to engage the attackers, some of which came in very low to attack Portland's Vrne and Citadel oil tanks while a furious engagement was fought high overhead. Neither high-level nor dive-bombing could be prevented, and 70 HEs rained down onto the naval hospital, two oil tanks including a 40,000 gallon underground variant, the floating dock, a signal box and the barracks at Portland. At Weymouth 120 private houses, a brewery, public utilities and ships in the bay were bombed. In protecting the installations gunners fired 162 large rounds and over 27,000 rounds of small arms fire.

As the large force withdrew, Dover's balloons again received attention from Bf 109s maintaining the pressure. From Lille and Antwerp bombers then made shipping raids between Dover and Lowestoft until bad weather forced abandonment. An unusual strike to set fire to waterborne He 59s off France had meanwhile been carried out by two 604 Squadron Blenheims (L6728, Pilot Officer E.D. Crew, and L6774, Squadron Leader M.F. Anderson) escorted by three 152 Squadron Spitfires.

In dangerous moonlight on 11/12 August 33 HEs were distributed upon Cardiff and Bristol's residential areas of Sneyd Park, Knowle and Shirehampton. Searchlight Site 53725 held in its beam He 111H-3 1G + AC of Stab II/KG 27 which enabled a Hurricane to cause its demise near Wimborne and bring 10 Group its first night success. Merseyside, Yorkshire and Devon were also raided; the Bristol Channel and Plymouth Sound were mined. Off Pendennis Point a mine exploded on impact with the sea, and another damaged Boveisand Lodge.

Claims and losses on the 11th reveal both sides incurring similar misfortunes. Fighter Command lost 32 aircraft, the enemy 38, of which 13 were Bf 109s including six of JG 2. Another 10 were Bf 110s, two of them belonging to Erpro 210 lost during anti-shipping operations off East Anglia. In the continuing saga of losses and claims some were from the start certainties, among them a Ju 88 which arrived intact near St George's Church, Blacknore, and west of which another plunged into the sea, joining a third which smashed itself in West Bay. From a He 111 off Chesil Beach five prisoners were taken, after two burning aircraft plunged into the sea west of Wyke Regis. A He 111 crashing near Searchlight 53531 yielded another four prisoners. A Hurricane in flames came down at 54172, another force-landing at U.6715.

With the weather improving, and better conditions on the horizon, the Luftwaffe command decided that 12 August would see and hear the overture to the grand slam. Destruction of fighter airfields and radar stations was to begin, while pressure on shipping and harbours was maintained. No more mild probing, this was the real thing. Large-scale escorted raids on inland targets to wipe our the RAF. . . then — THE INVASION!

Bf 109s in strength launched the day's activity over the Channel and Kent by probing towards Dover. About 200 were involved, 11 raids recorded. Four RAF Squadrons responded, a fierce engagement developing over Dungeness between 610 Squadron Spitfires[70] and nine Bf 109s of II/JG 52. As '610' went into action another 12 Bf 109s swept down. Flight Lieutenant E.B.B. Smith (H-K9818) after receiving face and neck burns from two cannon shells in his cockpit baled out and was rescued from the sea. Flight Lieutenant Gardiner (N3124-N) was wounded and his aircraft badly damaged. Two Bf 109s were destroyed, nine claimed damaged, but along with four more Spitfires, making it an expensive quarrel.

Around 09:00 a high-flying spying Dornier surveyed our Channel coast secretly, making a final assessment of the situation prior to the most dangerous attack yet. It was delivered by Bf 110 fighter-bombers of the legendary Erpro 210. Making full use of the 2,000-foot cloud base the raiders flew unobserved along the Channel, shedding flights which released HEs and oil bombs on vital south coast radar stations. Here was something new, exceedingly disturbing.

Anti-aircraft gunners at Dover's CH Station had just been 'stood down' and were gun cleaning when Raid 59H swept in almost silently, coming in line astern and out of the sun to bomb from 600 feet. Before the Bofors guns could respond, 12 HEs fell, the nearest of the five-foot-wide yet shallow craters being 60 yards from a pylon. Three bombs lay unexploded around five demolished huts. Although the RDF equipment was undamaged, one person was killed and 25 injured. At 09:40 it was the Rye CH Station's turn and there 10 HEs fell, one a mere 20 feet from a pylon. At Poling and Pevensey it was a similar story, with electricity cables to the latter station being cut. Shortly after the Dover attack Bf 109 fighter-bombers made a follow-up strike, one of the nearby balloons being set on fire and falling near the base of an RDF mast. Adding to the variety of

Many a Bf 109E 'Emil' only just made it to France, this one by the narrowest of margins. (Bundesarchiv)

assault five 8.2-inch shells arrived near Dover gas works at 10:15 and others were hurled at Deal, Folkestone and Dover. Although not seriously damaged by bombing, the CH stations had, apart from Rye, been put out of action — but for only some six hours. Radar stations were not all that easy to destroy, their tall pylons prohibiting very low attacks. Elsewhere, though, the Luftwaffe was to be more successful.

The middle of the morning saw about 80 Ju 88s of KG 51, some 120 Bf 110s of ZG 2 and ZG 76 and 25 Bf 109s of JG 53 organize themselves into a huge formation over France then head for Brighton before turning towards the Isle of Wight. Park and Brand, realizing a major threat was developing, ordered up 48 Hurricanes and 10 Spitfires from Tangmere, Middle Wallop, Warmwell and Exeter to patrol — 58 fighters to engage over 200 of the enemy — off the Isle of Wight. Soon, the Bf 110s had formed a huge battle circle and were trying to draw off and distract the British fighters while the Ju 88s formed two attack groups. The reasons for another early-morning Do 215 W2 weather sortie across the area at 22,000 feet

soon became apparent.

Twenty minutes ahead of this main force, fighter-bombers had raced in to deal with the Portsmouth balloon barrage, bombed two balloon sites and killed eight men. They were followed by about 50 Ju 88s which, from out of the brilliant sunshine, began at 12:10 delivering at least 57 HEs from varying heights during a classic, level formation attack on Portsmouth, the first of its type upon a British city. A direct hit was scored on a 200-person shelter in St George's Square, and other bombs exploded behind White's furniture store in Penroy Street. The harbour pier was demolished, its station set ablaze. Brickwood's Brewery was hit, the pontoon dock holed, but the main dockyard escaped damage and most bombs fell on old Portsmouth. Serious fires broke out and casualties totalled 96, 17 fatal. Gosport was also bombed by Ju 88s and recorded another 39 casualties — 15 fatal. From 16 heavy gun and

A huge fire rages at Portsmouth Harbour Station, bombed on 12 August. (Courtesy: The News, Portsmouth)

eight Bofors sites a tremendous barrage of 624 and 409 rounds respectively was hurled at the raiders attacking at between 8,000 and 12,000 feet. AA gunners in the area claimed two Ju 88s and as the bombers retired 213 Squadron picked off the leading aircraft flown by the Geschwaderkommodore.

As the '88s ran in to Portsmouth Bf 109s and '110s were circling the Isle of Wight. It became apparent that they were providing top cover when a group of about 15 Ju 88s turned towards the island, broke formation and delivered steep diving attacks on the CH radar station above Ventnor. After they had dropped 72 HEs and ten delayed action bombs on the site almost every building there was demolished or put at risk. Bofors gun defence was lost, and vital aerials between the 350-foot towers brought down. Civilian buildings also suffered in Ventnor and Bonchurch. Spitfires of 152 and 609 Squadrons arrived too late to prevent the bombing.

Loss of Ventnor radar was exceedingly serious, for its task was to watch over the approaches to Portsmouth and Southampton. Yet the outcome of the raid was not entirely one sided. By sparingly employing the Hurricanes against the bombers, and making a break by top cover German fighters barely worth while for fear of British attacks from above, our fighters were able to pick off eight Ju 88s. Park, by carefully positioning 615[71] Squadron, had a dozen Hurricanes ready to prevent Bf 109s sweeping in to bring support to the bombers. No. 609 Squadron[72], concentrating upon escorting fighters, claimed seven of them.

Already the enemy was building on what he felt sure was earlier stunning success, and the action returned to Kent when, at 12:45, Bf 110s of Erpro 210, taking advantage of the damaged radar chain, hurried low across Manston aerodrome bombing and strafing the vital forward base. Within moments many more HEs began raining down from 18 Do 17s of KG 2 flying at 14,000 feet in the second carpet bombing pass of the day. Try as it could, No. 54[73] Squadron, now back in the fray, was unable to prevent the raid. Among the bursting bombs 65 Squadron

tried to get airborne, one of the few pilots succeeding being the famous Supermarine test pilot Geoffrey Quill on secondment to the squadron. Eight Hurricanes of 56 Squadron also tackled the raiders, but only as they were retiring. As for Manston, 141 of the 242 HEs dropped fell on RAF property, causing 12 casualties. They destroyed its workshops along with a 600 Squadron Blenheim, damaged two hangars, also a Proctor, Magister and Puss Moth and cratered its landing ground. Nevertheless, the station was soon operational again although No. 600 Squadron was forced to switch night operating to Hornchurch, the parent station. Ramsgate had also received 17 stray bombs.

While Manston was being attacked two groups of Ju 87s tackled convoys and managed to hit two small vessels. By this act the Germans were revealing themselves unaware that Foreness CHL radar was fully functioning, and that their approach could be observed. However, the six Spitfires of 65 Squadron sent to ward them off arrived too late to prevent the dive-bombing and instead became embroiled with escorting Bf 109s. Just as the Spitfires landed at Manston for re-arming, the second Ju 87 formation arrived over a convoy off Deal and was confronted by a dozen Hurricanes of 501 and three of 151 Squadron which prevented effective bombing — albeit at a cost of two pilots and four aircraft.

There was little time for rest, the pressure on the RAF being maintained by recourse to large-scale Channel sweeps between 14:00 and 15:00. They preluded the next major onslaught of the day during which serious damage was caused to airfields. Fortunately, Kent's radar stations were fully operational again despite the German belief that they had been wiped out. Two large forces came in to deliver heavy attacks at 17:30 upon the relatively unimportant satellite fighter station at Lympne and on Hawkinge. At the former 170 bombs were reckoned to have fallen on the airfield and 70 on its surrounding fields and the Bekesbourne-Patrixbourne area. During the second bombing run Ju 88s of II/KG 76 using the canal leading from Dymchurch as their approach line demolished two hangars, station workshops and four fighters. Casualties totalled five killed and seven seriously wounded. Despite the severity of the Lympne attack the station was operating next day. Aerodromes would be very hard to put out of action, extremely difficult to destroy.

At 17:28 Ju 88s of KG 76 arrived over Folkestone. Two minutes later they were involved in a mixed attack upon Hawkinge, which was dive-bombed and also carpet bombed from 18,000 feet. Enemy aircraft arrived from out of the sun at between 3,000 and 5,000 feet, the raid damaging some buildings and putting the landing ground out of use. Much official interest surrounded one giant crater on the aerodrome. Two level attackers were hit by anti-aircraft fire. One at 17:42 had its tail unit seriously damaged and the aircraft was claimed to have come down in the sea off Dover.

While these heavy raids were taking place fighter-bombers were once more slipping in, this time to tackle the radar station at Dunkirk, west of Canterbury. They were first spotted, about half a dozen of them, circling over the target at about 12,000 feet and in line astern. Then they dived, each releasing a bomb from about 2,500 feet. The attack much interested observers who recorded that the bombs on the Bf 109s were 'carried below the cockpit'.

Widespread night operations followed, including a sharp raid on Cardiff, whose guns had earlier engaged a high He 111 at 27,000 feet. Bekesbourne was among many other places bombed, among them Stratford-on-Avon, Birmingham, Bircham Newton, Newport, Hereford, Ipswich, Plymouth, Felixstowe, Westbury-on-Severn and Eastchurch. Free reading matter was donated to the people of Worksop.

By the end of the day the Germans were claiming 71 RAF aircraft shot down. In reality the RAF, in mounting 196 patrols and flying 798 sorties, lost 22 fighters. German casualties arising from about 1,200 sorties totalled 31 aircraft in the toughest day's fighting yet.

Patrols and sorties flown by Fighter Command 10 July-12 August 1940

Surviving statistics list slight variations in totals, probably due to the inclusion or otherwise of dusk, dawn and night patrols. The listing includes all Fighter Command interception sorties, patrols, escorts, etc.

Date in the 24-hour period ending at 06:00 on the given date	Fighter Command		
	Patrols	Sorties	
	Day	Day	Night
July			
10	200	609	32
11	151	479	47
12	207	670	30
13	143	449	24
14	163	593	19
15	154	470	—
16	128	313	7
17	70	253	13
18	166	549	34
19	175	701	34
20	191	611	44
21	120	571	25
22	208	611	26
23	182	470	25
24	?	561	?
25	191	641	?
26	144	584	28
27	141	487	35
28	220	794	29
29	185	724	35
30	205	688	?
31	130	395	21
Aug			
1	?	659	61
2	147	477	24
3	144	411	26
4	?	261	4
5	99	402	26
6	?	416	?
7	?	393	?
8	152	621	33
9	142	409	14
10	116	336	11
11	165	679	62
12	196	732	?

RAF losses during operations 1-12 August, 1940

a Failed to return/shot down, *b* written off — battle casualty, *c* seriously damaged.

August	1			2			3			4			5			6			7		
Type	a	b	c	a	b	c	a	b	c	a	b	c	a	b	c	a	b	c	a	b	c
Blenheim F	—	—	—	—	—	1	—	—	—	—	—	—	—	—	—	2	—	1	—	—	—
Defiant	—	—	—	—	—	—	—	—	—	1	1	—	—	—	—	—	—	—	—	—	—
Hurricane	1	—	2	—	—	1	—	—	—	—	—	1	—	—	—	—	2	—	—	2	1
Spitfire	—	1	—	—	2	—	—	—	—	—	1	—	—	2	—	—	2	—	—	2	—
Battle	1	—	—	—	—	—	—	—	—	—	—	—	—	—	—	—	—	—	—	—	—
Blenheim B	1	—	—	2	—	—	—	1	—	—	—	—	—	—	—	—	—	—	—	—	—
Hampden	2	—	—	—	—	—	1	1	—	1	—	—	—	—	—	1	—	—	1	1	—
Wellington	—	—	—	1	—	—	—	1	—	—	—	—	—	—	—	—	—	—	—	—	—
Whitley	—	—	—	—	—	—	—	—	—	1	—	1	—	—	—	—	1	—	—	—	—
Coastal Cmd	3	—	—	2	—	—	—	—	—	4	—	—	1	—	—	2	—	—	3	—	—
TOTALS	8	1	2	4	3	2	1	3	—	6	2	2	3	—	2	3	5	1	4	5	1

August	8			9			10			11			12			GRAND TOTALS		
Type	a	b	c	a	b	c	a	b	c	a	b	c	a	b	c	a	b	c
Blenheim F	1	—	—	—	1	—	—	—	—	—	—	—	—	—	—	1	2	3
Defiant	—	—	—	—	—	—	—	—	—	—	—	—	—	—	—	—	1	1
Hurricane	11	—	2	—	1	1	—	—	—	23	2	4	12	—	2	47	7	14
Spitfire	3	2	2	—	—	2	—	—	1	5	—	2	5	3	5	15	12	12
Blenheim B	1	—	—	—	—	—	2	—	—	1	—	—	—	—	—	7	0	0
Hampden	1	—	—	—	1	—	1	—	—	1	—	—	—	—	—	9	3	0
Wellington	—	—	—	—	—	1	—	—	—	—	1	—	—	—	—	0	4	1
Whitley	—	—	—	—	—	—	—	—	—	—	—	—	—	—	—	1	0	2
Coastal Cmd	2	—	—	1	—	—	—	—	—	3	—	—	—	—	—	21	0	0
TOTALS	19	2	4	1	3	4	3	—	1	33	3	6	17	3	7	101	29	33

Where did bombs first fall?: 1 July-12 August 1940

1 July
Barry — 20
Caerphilly — 5 (3)
Gosport — 1 (1)
Wick — 2

2/3 July
Frome RD — 5
Ledbury — 6
Newcastle-on-Tyne — 3

3 July
Bognor — 4
Catown — 3
Deal — 1
Hailsham — 4 (1)

Hambledon RD — 3 (1)
Lowestoft, in sea — 16
Newhaven — 12
Pen-y-Bont RD — 13
Seaford — 4

3/4 July
Tendring RD — 2, ibs

4 July
Pontypool — 6 (1)
Sodbury RD — 2

4/5 July
West Ashford RD — 2

5 July
Lowestoft — 14

Ramsgate — 9 (1)

5/6 July
Folkestone — 1 (2)

6 July
Plymouth — 5
Farnham — 3

6/7 July
Dover — 10

7 July
Falmouth — 4
Shoreham — 1
Ventnor — in sea 2

8/9 July
Inverness, landward — 6

Moray, landward	20
9 July	
Abercarn	14
Gower	17 (3)
Llanelly	5
Lleynrd RD	4
Norwich	
Tadcaster RD	6
10 July	
Aberdare	11
Berwick, landward	8
Brecknock RD	1
Carmarthen	10
Crickhowell RD	10
Cwmaman	1
Hadleigh	1 (1)
Looe	12 (2)
Llanelly RD	13
Pembroke	4
Pontarllawerd RD	1
11 July	
Argyllshire	5
Ely RD	9
Great Yarmouth	7
Portsmouth	20 (2)
11/12 July	
Tavistock RD	10 (1), ibs
Upton-on-Severn RD	4
12 July	
Ryde	2
12/13 July	
Banff, landward	3
Bdwast Machen UD	2
Dumbarton, landward	8
Greenock	9
Tiverton RD	1
Wadebridge	4
13 July	
Lanark, landward	1
Magor & St Mallons RD	9 (2)
Mountain Ash	3
Pontypridd	3, ibs
Renfrew	18 (1)
14/15 July	
Amesbury RD	9
Brixham	6
15 July	
Narbeth RD	4 (8)
16 July	
Fraserburgh	4
Peterhead	7

17 July	
Auchtermuchty	11 (1)
Custon RD	6
Montrose	16
18 July	
Braintree	1
18/19 July	
Chatham	2
19 July	
Edinburgh	7 (1)
Glasgow	8
Horsham RD	4
20 July	
Dumfries, landward	3
Stirling	2 mines
20/21 July	
Sunderland	1
22 July	
Banff	5 (1)
Maldon RD	6
22/23 July	
Cleethorpes	ibs
Drayton RD	11
Hocktonprice UD	? 4
Newtown and Llandeilo RD	7
23 July	
Llwchwr	? 2
Neyland	2
Worthing	3 (1)
24 July	
Renfrew	11, ibs
Samford RD	17
Waltham and Weybridge	17
26 July	
Brentwood	5
26/26 July	
Faversham	2
Sheppey	3
27/28 July	
Penllyn RD	2 (1)
Sevenoaks RD	12 (2)
Truro RD	4
Wenlock	2
West Penwith	4
28 July	
Kidwelly	3
Runcorn	2
28/29 July	
Lydd	5
Maidstone RD	1
Wellington RD	14

West Lancashire RD	8
Wrexham RD	1
29 July	
Belper	ibs
Crewe	3
Dorking RD	3
Neath	ibs
Salford	6
30 July	
Merthyr Tydfil	11
30/31 July	
Clun RD	7
Colne RD	2
Denbighshire RD	18 (2)
Devizes RD	6
Leominster RD	3
Ross and Whitchurch RD	1
Welshpool	5
31 July	
Monmouth	5
Monmouth RD	8
Morecambe and Heysham	11
1 August	
Ellesmere Port	1
Hornchurch UD	9 (1)
2 August	
Dundee	24
3 August	
Frimley	8
4 August	
Cwnbrau	4, ibs
7 August	
Exeter	5
8 August	
Truro	5 (1)
8/9 August	
Birmingham	4
9 August	
Birkenhead	6
10 August	
Abergavenny	7
Malling RD	15 (11)
Rochester	10
Wallasey	11
11 August	
York	2 (1)
11/12 August	
Wilton	6
12 August	
Broadstairs	11
Eastly RD	30 (8)

Incidents involving 8 or more high explosive bombs
1 July-12 August

1 July			**19 July**			**6 August**		
Holderness RD		12	Narbeth		10 (1)	Swansea		10
3 July			Plymouth		21	**6/7 August**		
Battle RD		26	**19/20 July**			Midlothian		12, ibs
Swale RD		14	Dumbarton, landward		9	**7 August**		
6/7 July			Lanark, landward		8	Poole		8
Aldershot		6	**20/21 July**			**8 August**		
8/9 July			Orkney		11	Midlothian		14
Billingham UD		8	**21/22 July**			Truro		12
9 July			Derby		10	**8/9 August**		
Benfleet		24	**22 July**			Meir and Tisbury RD		9
Sodbury RD		6 (8)	Banff, landward		9 (1)	**9 August**		
10 July			Pembroke		20	Rochford RD		6 (3)
Neath		4 (12)	Shardlow RD		8	Sunderland		10 (5)
10/11 July			**22/23 July**			**9/10 August**		
Bridlington		8	Swale RD		26 (2)	Bournemouth		12
Spilsby RD		9	**23 July**			Salisbury and Wilton RD		23
12 July			Cardiff RD		2 (8)	South Shields		1 mine
Aberdeen		16	Pembroke		15	**10 August**		
Aberdeenshire		23 (1)	**26/27 July**			Swansea		26 (4)
Cardiff		12	Aberdeenshire		9	**10/11 August**		
12/13 July			**27 July**			Weymouth		(14)
West Hartlepool		24	Canvey Island		17 (1)	**11/12 August**		
13/14 July			**28/29 July**			Bristol		50
East Lothian, landward		8	Aberdeenshire		24	Plymouth		2 mines
14/15 July			Berwick, landward		27	**12 August**		
Dover RD		12, ibs	Calne		11 (1)	Cardiff RD		28 (1)
15 July			Newcastle		27	Folkestone		150 (1), ibs
Cowbridge		4 (6)	**1 August**			Gosport		40 (1)
Hove		8	Pembroke		9 (1)	Havant		6, 1 OB
16 July			**2 August**			Portsmouth		18 (1), 1 OB
Orkney		18 (3)	Bridge Blean RD		200 (4), ibs	Ramsgate		17
18 July			Swansea		10 (3)	Ventnor		30 (6)
Neath		9	**3 August**			Isle of Wight RDs		24 (4)
18/19 July			Swansea		10	**12/13 August**		
Lanark, landward		8				Plymouth		12 (3)

CHAPTER 8

DEUTSCHLAND UBER ALLES

'Destroy the enemy air force as soon as possible', an impatient Adolf had decreed, suggesting 5 August as a suitable day but leaving the final choice to Göring and his staff.

To destroy Fighter Command its operational layout needed to be understood, also the early warning radar network, and the positioning of squadrons, the purpose of dispersal and forward aerodromes; most of all the skill and determination of the opposition needed to be realized. Instead, the Germans were less informed than some schoolboys. July they had wasted instead of using the time to cripple Britain's aircraft factories and aircraft storage units.

Without knocking out the radar stations, and by working to a poorly conceived battle plan, the great assault was about to be frittered away, hurled against irrelevant objects whose destruction could have little bearing on the outcome of the battle.

FOOD FACTS No 4

Never waste anything, never eat more than enough. You'll be fitter, you'll save money. Every time you cook you can help or hinder Hitler. Always scrape paper in which margarine or butter is wrapped.

Newspaper, 12 August

Group Captain 'Sailor' Malan, who earlier flew with 74 Squadron. (IWM)

13 AUGUST ~ MORNING ACTION

Even the weather provided a final pause, giving time to stop and think; for dull, cloudy conditions over southern England and northern France on 13 August forced a last-minute delay until the afternoon. So poor was the overall direction of the operation that even postponement orders failed to reach all units, and in murky weather *Adlertag* was mistakenly launched.

A Do 17P was shot down at 06:20 off Kent by Squadron Leader A.G. Malan, in K9953 and partnered by Flying Officer J.C. Mungo Park (R6084), soon after the first signs of daylight activity were detected. As early as 05:30 radar stations identified two forces, about 60 aircraft, assembling slowly over France, so 11 Group ordered two squadrons, No. 64[74] from Hornchurch and No. 111 from Croydon, to protect damaged Hawkinge and Manston, assuming the enemy would, logically, hit them again.

Hurricanes of North Weald's 56 Squadron, US:P in the foreground possibly R4093 shot down on 13 August, with US:G (R2689), T (V6628?) and E airborne. (IWM)

Hurricanes from North Weald took station over a Thames convoy, while others watched over Tangmere. As the enemy formation advanced, another of about 100 was detected off Dieppe and soon about 40 more aircraft off Cherbourg before a smaller group was found by radar near the Channel Islands.

To oppose these strong forces a section of Hurricanes from Northolt flew to the Canterbury area, others from Tangmere barring the way between Arundel and Petworth. From Middle Wallop more fighters hurried to protect Warmwell before Hurricanes of Nos. 43[75] and 601[76] Squadrons scrambled from Tangmere to guard 11 Group's western flank. Additional fighters from Kenley protected the Thames Estuary and No. 10 Group the Exeter area. About 120 dispersed fighters mainly over Kent — particularly in sections, and not squadrons — were deployed to face maybe 300 attackers.

Escort for about 80 Luftflotte 2 Dornier 17Zs of I, II and III/KG 2 had been cancelled due to dense clouds around 5,000 feet, but the bomber crews pressed on, swinging left shortly before 07:00, then splitting into groups heading for Coastal Command's aerodrome at East-church and Sheerness dockyard, curious target choices. Above thick cloud the larger formation headed for Eastchurch and, near Whitstable, engagement by 74[77] Squadron. Off the North Foreland, Hurricanes of 151 Squadron engaged the others and L1750, the first cannon-armed Hurricane, flown by Flight Lieutenant R. Smith, scored the special aircraft a certain success. 'Treble-One' went into action near Herne Bay, and the combined effort forced KG 2 to jettison its load. The other element dropped about 100 bombs on Eastchurch where hangars, airmen's quarters and the Officers' Mess were hit. Ammunition and equipment stores burned, and the Operations Block and a Spitfire of 266 Squadron on the station to support Coastal Command Battles were destroyed and several Blenheims damaged. Two Bofors guns fired 25 rounds, but 16 men were killed and 48 injured. The station was fully operational by evening. Five Do 17s were shot down.

A second morning attack was mounted by two groups of Ju 88s of KG 54 which approached in poor weather intending to bomb Farnborough and Odiham — more irrelevant choices. These were greeted by Hurricanes of 43[78], 257 and 601[79] Squadrons vectored from Canterbury and 64 Squadron's Spitfires[80]. The Ju 88s soon abandoned their operation.

Next came 30 Bf 110s of I/ZG 2 heading in from Cherbourg. By noon, and without the Ju 88s they were expecting to escort, the Mes-

In France, the harvest was being gathered, as in England, while bombers such as this He 111 A1+L? of KG 53 taxied by. (Bundesarchiv)

serschmitts found Hurricanes of 87, 213 and 238 Squadrons closing in as they approached Portland. Five Bf 110s were claimed, though Luftwaffe records show the loss of only one.

An improvement in the weather having arrived, the first mighty blow was launched. *Adlerangriff* came underway a bit late, at around 16:00, with a massive attack spread along a 40-mile front. Around 40 Ju 88s of KG 54 and I, II, III/LG 1 of Luftflotte 2 were on course for Southampton and Middle Wallop. To their west were about 30 Ju 87s of II/StG 2, with 50 more Stukas of StG 77 following closely escorted by JG 27. A formidable array indeed to be entering the 10 Group area. Forward support for them all was provided by Bf 109s of JG 53 which swept between the Isle of Wight and Lyme Bay until, low on fuel, they were chased off by 152 Squadron, which also engaged the dive-bombers.

Already 10 Group's squadrons had scrambled, supported by 43 and 257 Squadrons, but they could not prevent LG 1's Ju 88s from reaching Southampton, where at least 23 bombs fell at 16:23 on the International Cold Storage Company's premises and the dock warehouses, killing five and injuring 25 workers. Later a delayed-action bomb exploded at Empress Dock.

KG 54 heading for Portland met Nos. 152, 213, 238[81] and 601[82] Squadrons, the latter destroying three escorting Bf 110s. As the first

Stukas of II/StG 2 arrived so did No. 609 Squadron[83]. Unfortunately for the dive-bombers their escort, short of fuel, had left for home, allowing Spitfires to dive out of the sun and slaughter six of them. Other Ju 87s, seeking Warmwell and failing to locate it, released their bombs over a wide area. Another KG 54 attack, on Middle Wallop, strayed — a few bombs falling near the Wallops and others on Andover, mistaken for the target.

Afternoon saw the arrival of yet more Ju 87s and Bf 110s, this time more sensibly targetted upon Rochford aerodrome but, finding thick cloud, they abandoned the operation. No. 56 Squadron[84], operating for the day from there, intercepted its would-be attackers over Kent, forcing them to unload through cloud in the Canterbury area. Accompanying Bf 109s of JG 26 then drew off No. 65 Squadron[85], opening the way for another 40 Ju 87s of LG 1 to devastate Detling. They destroyed its hangars, operations block, severely dealt with 22 aircraft, cratered its tarmac and killed 67 including the Station Commander, Group Captain E. David. Yet within hours Detling was functioning again.

Small-scale shipping attacks continued

Spitfire R6769 PR:D of 709 Squadron damaged during the bombing of Middle Wallop on 12 August. Quickly repaired it remained with '609' until 10 September 1940. It later served with 64 Squadron and Nos. 57 and 61 OTUs and was finally written off after crashing at Hatton, Cheshire, on 3 October 1943.

throughout the day, after which He 111s of KGr 100 attempted a night precision attack on Castle Bromwich's Spitfire factory dropping 11 × 250-kg bombs and damaging offices and the tool room. Two were killed, 50 injured. Incendiaries blazed on open ground, and 20 HEs falling wide damaged a school and cottages at Wootton Wawen. Another 16 HEs fell on farmland near Wolverhampton and a dozen at Bacton, Herefordshire. Other KGr 100 crews bombed the Short & Harland Belfast works, destroying five precious Stirling bombers in an advanced state of construction. By dawn, the Luftwaffe, which in 24 hours had lost 46 aircraft (39 directly to the defenders), had flown 1,485 sorties (about two-thirds by fighters), had attacked three non-Fighter Command aerodromes and damaged Southampton, Castle Bromwich and a number of other places, as a result of which 100 casualties were recorded. Fighter Command in mounting 727 fighter sorties lost 13 aircraft and 7 pilots, and realized only too clearly that it did not possess sufficient strength to rout the attackers. But it was highly organized, disciplined, ingeniously managed and equipped with men and aircraft equal to the task.

German effort on 14 August amounted to almost 500 sorties, the proceedings being opened by a high-speed low-level attack on Manston while 'A' Flight of 56 Squadron was flying a precautionary patrol above cloud over the aerodrome and oblivious to a dozen Bf 110s of audacious Erpro Gr 210 racing in very low, bombing and strafing the station. Only four bombs hit the aerodrome, one causing the end of a hangar to be blown in onto a Puss Moth. Two more exploded in a hangar on the east side containing two 600 Squadron Blenheims. The fourth produced an impressive crater 12 feet deep and 30 feet across. Two oil bombs fell on the nearby village. Ground Defences brought down two Bf 110s which crashed on the edge of the landing ground, three out of the four crew men being killed. The fourth revealed that the formation had set forth from Denain, refuelled at St Omer and that each aircraft carried two 250-kg bombs. As escort they had seven Bf 109s. Although No. 32 Squadron[87] had come speeding upon the scene from Biggin Hill and No. 615[88] from Kenley, they arrived too late to prevent the bombing.

At 12:20 the main Stuka force, above cloud and with visibility poor, split into two forces, to attack Hawkinge and Dover. British fighters drove off the Hawkinge raid, then three of the Ju 87s protected by a Gruppe of Bf 109s attacked the Gate Light Vessel, dropping ten HEs and sinking the ship. Two of its crew were killed, one injured and the remainder were strafed as they struggled in the water. Hurricanes of 615 Squadron meanwhile were engaging the Bf 109s of III/JG 2 which claimed two of the defenders, one falling to Adolf Galland. The squadron claimed three Bf 109s, one almost certainly falling to Pilot Officer Lofts (P3161). Pilot Officer E.B. Rogers (L1983) had to belly-land at Hawkinge, the squadron's forward base. Meanwhile, the main bomber force had headed inland to Ashford, spasmodically bombing and being attacked during its withdrawal by the Biggin Hill squadron.

Mid-afternoon saw Raid H5 consisting of Do 17s heading towards Pevensey. Upon being engaged it jettisoned its bombs in the Fairlight area at 16:15. The enemy did not however give up that easily. At 17:37 Raid H44 mounted by a Dornier ran up on Pevensey RDF station at 7,000 feet to place four HEs in the compound but caused no damage. The Dornier was apparently hit by AA fire and as it came lower was fired upon by the crew of searchlight 51733. The pilot baled out before the Dornier crashed, and was taken to Hayward's Heath police station.

Between 15:30 and 21:00 many small groups of unescorted bombers operated over a 100-mile front with aerodromes and rail centres as targets. Radar stations this time accurately identified the strength of each raid, which allowed small, accurate responses. Six raiders were destroyed during 11 engagements. On the outskirts of Swindon 20 HEs fell. Of eight RAF stations attacked only three reported much damage. Andover's W/T station was hit, Kemble too, and at Hullavington there were 13 casualties. At Middle Wallop 609 Squadron's hangar received a direct hit and offices were destroyed at 17:00 by three He 111Ps of KG 55. Three airmen, Corporal R.W. Smith and Leading Aircraftmen H. Thorley and K. Wilson, were killed attempting to close a giant door which crashed down upon them. Swift vengeance was wrought after Sergeant Feary (L1065) raced away and brought down the lead[88] He 111

G1+AA carrying senior personnel. Other Heinkel 111s dropped 14 large bombs on Portland, damaging roads, and KG 27 produced slight damage at Colerne ASU. A trio reached Sealand and three staff pilots of No. 7 OTU Hawarden set off in pursuit, their Spitfires downing Heinkel 111 1G+FS near Chester. At least 17 German aircraft fell variously to the defences during 14 August. Fighter Command lost eight fighters.

The Luftwaffe had gravely underestimated the strength, ability and clever leadership of Fighter Command. The successes claimed by the Germans were prodigious — 40,000 tons of merchant shipping sunk, 300 British fighters destroyed, over 30 aerodromes and major factories wiped out — all in a week. There is little doubt that many in the enemy camp believed these claims, but those in the fight knew that the opposition remained strong, skilfully mounted, and that their own losses were higher than predicted. Göring was quick to apportion blame, citing as foolish the small-scale raids on the 14th needing picked crews. He condemned the choice of targets, many having no bearing on Fighter Command's ability to survive. He reckoned that the RAF was particularly singling out Ju 87s for attack and ordered that each Stuka be protected by three Bf 109s. He also expressed concern about Bf 110 wastage.

Poor liaison was apparent between senior officers and units, to which the British could have added 'Your bombing accuracy is lousy!' Luckily the enemy seems not to have realized that.

August 15 began with the usual reconnaissance sorties, a Do 17 of 3(F)/31 being picked off south of Ventnor by Spitfires, and Medway guns firing at a Ju 88. Clouds over the north and west were breaking by mid-morning. As the general improvement set in, fighter squadrons dispersed to forward bases. Their serviceability rate had risen during the pause and once more they stood at readiness. It seems certain that the British knew of intended widespread operations with aerodromes — some strangely selected — as primary targets.

A 64 Squadron pilot races to his Spitfire on 15 August 1940.
(IWM)

Fighter sweeps over the Channel between 09:00 and 11:00 prompted 11 Group to mount precautionary patrols over two Thames convoys. Soon came the first inkling of big trouble when at 10:45 a large force — Ju 87s of IV/LG 1 and II/StG 1 escorted by Bf 109s began assembling over the Pas de Calais. Four 11 Group squadrons were ordered to patrol Manston-Dungeness and at 11:25 40 strongly escorted Ju 87s reached the coast on their way to bomb Lympne and Hawkinge. Twenty-four of the Stukas then turned abruptly towards Folkestone as British fighters engaged them and claimed their leader. Some bombs fell on Folkestone town and others caused damage to a hangar and barrack block at Hawkinge.

The other Stuka formation which bombed Lympne at 11:36 was engaged from out of the sun by fighters which claimed two Stukas.

Nevertheless, they and the two other squadrons soon involved were unable to prevent StG 1 from putting Lympne out of action for two days.

Just after midday a totally new feature of the campaign began unfolding when northern radar stations detected unidentified aircraft approaching from far east of the Firth of Forth. Their progress was extremely slow and they were eventually to be identified as He 115 floatplanes of KflGr 506 flying a feint towards Montrose. The number of raiders was soon seen to be gradually increasing to well over 30, so No. 13 Group was ordered to respond to the first large-scale day raid on its territory. By 12:35 Spitfires of 41[89] Squadron now back at Catterick were heading to meet what turned out of be a second enemy force off the Farne Islands. Hurricanes of 605[90] Squadron had meanwhile left Drem in order to protect Tyneside. No. 79 Squadron and 607 Squadron, Usworth, were also scrambled. A formidable force manned by resting, combat experienced pilots was eager to show its prowess. The Luftwaffe's belief that the

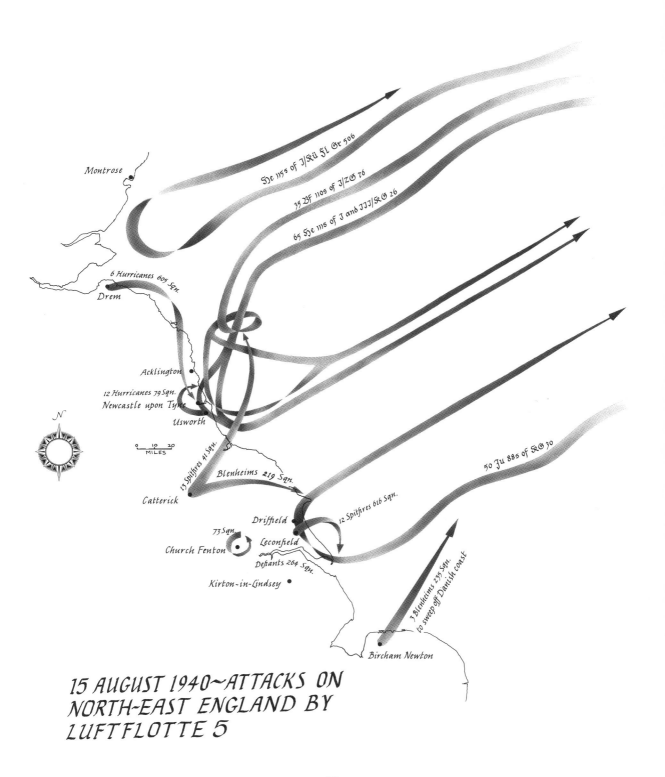

Montrose

He 115s of 1/Kü Fl Gr 506

35 Bf 110s of I/ZG 76

65 He 111s of I and III/KG 26

6 Hurricanes 605 Sqn.

Drem

Acklington

12 Hurricanes 79 Sqn.

Newcastle upon Tyne

Usworth

N

0 10 20
MILES

15 Spitfires 41 Sqn.

Blenheims 219 Sqn.

50 Ju 88s of KG 30

Catterick

Driffield

12 Spitfires 616 Sqn.

73 Sqn.

Church Fenton

Leconfield

Defiants 264 Sqn.

Kirton-in-Lindsey

3 Blenheims 235 Sqn. to sweep off Danish coast

Bircham Newton

15 AUGUST 1940~ATTACKS ON NORTH-EAST ENGLAND BY LUFTFLOTTE 5

north was poorly defended, that all our fighters were in the south, was about to be disproved.

As many as 72 He 111s of Stavanger's KG 26 are believed to have set forth, although only 65 are thought to have completed the North Sea crossing with bomber bases at Driffield and Linton-on-Ouse their designated targets. Newcastle-upon-Tyne, Sunderland and Middlesbrough were secondary aiming points. Flying above the Heinkels were about 35 Bf 110s of I/ZG 76.

A serious navigation error was taking the bombers well north of their prescribed track, which gave defenders ample time for positioning. When the Heinkels were 30 miles out to sea from the Farne Islands 41 Squadron, amazed at the number of bombers, pounced upon them. Packed in threes, the Heinkels were at 18,000 feet, the escort 1,000 feet above and in two groups; the Spitfires from 3,000 feet higher and up sun, bore down upon the raiders who were clearly taken by surprise. Some jettisoned their loads, others ran for cloud cover, and the '110s quickly adopted their usual strange defensive circle forsaking the bombers to their fate. The Spitfires claimed 11 enemy aircraft destroyed — Luftwaffe records suggest two 110s

and a He 111, although yet again the truth could well rest between these figures.

Confusion certainly gripped the German force, part of which headed for Tyneside, there meeting 79 Squadron whilst leaving the remainder heading south. After engaging the Bf 110s, No. 79 reformed to tackle Heinkels approaching Newcastle or Usworth. Tyne guns greeted those, also 605 Squadron which destroyed four He 111s. Most bombs fell in the sea. The other force, engaged by 41 and 607 Squadrons, as well as Teeside guns, unloaded mainly near Seaham Harbour. The Bf 110s, seven already lost, had fled. As for the Heinkels, eight of which are known to have been shot down, they made for home in groups, one of which unfortunately met Coastal Command Blenheim IV fighters of 235 Squadron[91] whose Pilot Officer Jackson-Smith destroyed yet another Heinkel. Debriefing reports acquired years later showed that on their return the crews stated that the results of their 'attacks on Linton-on-Ouse and another airfield to the north were not

My wife said, 'If you meet Churchill, grab hold of him — hard'. In truth, a confident crew of KG 30's Ju 88A WNr. 4021 alongside another, 4D+LS. (Bundesarchiv)

observed'! In actuality, 10 bombs fell on South Shields, 27 at Cleadon and seven houses were destroyed in Seaham Harbour. At Dawdon 12 houses were damaged, and 15 at Easington, where 15 people were injured. Sunderland, where 24 houses were damaged, bore the brunt of the bombing. The Germans claimed to have shot down at least 20 British fighters — the truth, none lost, was presumably too hard to bear.

As the day's operation had evolved, radar stations detected another threat heading in from Denmark towards Spurn Head. It resolved itself as about 50 Ju 88s of KG 30 including a sprinkling of Ju 88C long-range fighters to ward off opposition. It was a matter for 12 Group, and at 13:00 Air Vice-Marshal T. Leigh-Mallory ordered Leconfield's 616 Squadron (12 Spitfires) to patrol over Hornsea and 264 Squadron Defiants to guard a Humber convoy. No. 73 Squadron left Church Fenton to protect its base and a second convoy. Blenheim 1fs of 219 Squadron were contributed by 13 Group.

First to soar into action was 616 Squadron, which forced the Ju 88s to hurry into cloud. Then six Hurricanes of 73 Squadron fell upon them as they crossed the coast. Although mauled, the Ju 88 force courageously pressed on to Driffield, there at 13:20 seriously damaging a dozen Whitleys, four hangars and three blocks of buildings. Onto the fields around rained 46 × 250-kg bombs. More bombs were unloaded onto Bridlington and by chance an ammunition truck six miles away at Burton Agnes was hit.

Now it was the turn of 219 Squadron[92] Blenheims to pester the '88s up to 100 miles out to sea. When KG 30 reached home it was short of eight aircraft. Sergeant Dube flying Blenheim L8698 had been injured by return fire, so his air gunner, Sergeant Bannister, skilfully nursed his new charge to Driffield, where he had to execute a wheels-up landing. No mean achievement. Both were awarded DFMs for their efforts. Apart from that, Fighter Command had lost neither aircraft nor crews whereas General Stumpff had sacrificed an eighth of his bomber and a fifth of his long-range fighter forces.

The implications for the Luftwaffe were serious. Unescorted bomber raids in daylight over half of Britain, and where much of its industry was sited, were clearly out of the question and never repeated by Luftflotte 5. Small-scale daylight cloud-cover precision attacks were effectively mounted, but Göring and the management were more attuned to often less destructive spectaculars.

Around 14:00 a complex operation was launched, featuring Dorniers of KG 3 in league with three Jagdeschwaderen of Bf 109s ahead of which 60 '109s of JG 26 provided forward support. Erpro 210 was also on the move, and only detected moments before its Bf 110s raced in low across Martlesham Heath at 15:10 to give it the 'Manston treatment'. Both official and private reports differ in their accounts of this raid. Some, including Martlesham's anti-aircraft gunners and two very keen local aviation enthusiasts, emphatically agree that nine Ju 87s in two vics, one of four the other of five, dived from about 5,000 to 2,000 feet and dropped eight 250-kg HEs. It seems possible that they had been ordered to attack Bawdsey radar, for reports often speak of them aiming for a 'radio station' east of Martlesham aerodrome. As for the Bf 110s at least six, and possibly nine, bombed and strafed Martlesham Heath including at least one oil bomb in their assault. Above them at 15,000 to 20,000 feet and awaiting any RAF response flew the Bf 109 top cover. Three Hurricanes of 17[93] Squadron had managed to evade the bombs just in time, whereas a visiting Battle of 12 Squadron was blown apart and the nearby watch office was wrecked. Two hangars suffered badly, also Station Workshops and the Officers' Mess, from 11 HEs. The Hurricanes of No. 17 Squadron, quickly reinforced by nine Hurricanes of 1[94] Squadron, chased after the top cover, which responded by picking off three British fighters.

As that fast raid had progressed 24 Hurricanes of 111 and 151[95] Squadrons and Spitfires of 64[96] Squadron were over Kent tangling with a Bf 109 forward sweep while four squa-

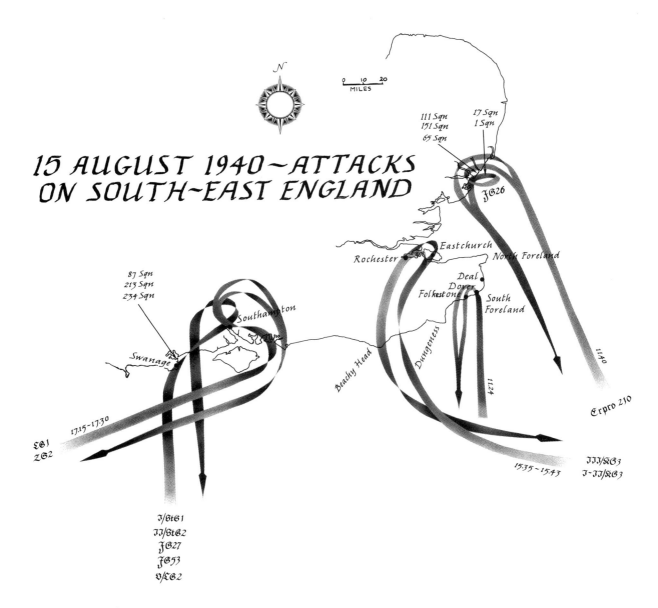

15 AUGUST 1940~ATTACKS ON SOUTH~EAST ENGLAND

drons were positioned between Manston and Hawkinge to disrupt the approaching bomber force. Massive protection by Bf 109s made that task tough, only two Do 17s being destroyed while freelancing JG 26 claimed to destroy at least eight British fighters. KG 3 pressed on, to split over the Thames Estuary. Gruppen I and II in two waves between 15:35 and 15:43 aimed over 30 HEs at the Short and Pubjoy

Rochester factories while gunners in that area fired 231 rounds at the Dorniers. Only eight bombs fell anywhere near the works, and III/KG 3 did little better around Eastchurch.

Maintaining the pressure, about 80 bombers and many fighters challenged 10 Group which, between 17:00 and 17:20, scrambled the largest number of fighters it had yet fielded. Three squadrons made for Swanage to engage about

A cross-Channel chase ended disastrously for Pilot Officer R. Hardy flying N3277 AZ:H of 234 Squadron. At 17:30 on 15 August 1940 he had to force-land near Cherbourg.

40 Ju 87s of I/StG 1 and II/StG 2 protected by Bf 109s of JG 27 and JG 53 and BF 110s of V/LG 2 and all heading for Portland. Nos. 87[97] and 213 Squadron tackled the bombers and the '110s, leaving 14 Spitfires of 234[98] Squadron to engage first the Bf 110s and then the Bf 109s, which in overwhelming their interceptors shot down four. Nevertheless, the Stukas had been forced to jettison their loads before heading home cheated of attacking their airfield targets.

Patrolling off the Isle of Wight 43[99] Squadron was vectored to 60 Ju 88s of LG 1 escorted by about 40 Bf 110s of ZG 2 and battled with raiders heading towards Southampton. Successively, five Hurricane squadrons including Nos. 601[100] and 249[101] fought them, not to mention the Solent and Southampton gunners who joined in. That did not prevent the Ju 88s from reaching Middle Wallop fighter station, where two hangars were hit, an aircraft was destroyed and five were damaged. At Worthy Down little damage was done and seven of the 15 would-be destroyers soon lay shattered. Only three crews even claimed to have reached their target. A few bombed Odiham, and five bombers fell to 601 Squadron alone. The entire operation cost Luftflotte 3 eight bombers, four dive-bombers and 13 Bf 110s. Fighter Command lost 16 aircraft.

Just after 6 o'clock Park faced one of his most difficult moments so far. Dorniers of KG 1 and KG 2 escorted by Bf 109s of I/LG 1 were approaching, and many of his pilots recently landed had already flown two or three operations during the day. No. 501 Squadron had been airborne for 45 minutes, and twice been in action, but Park retained it in position. He called upon four more squadrons to assist and reinforced those with another four and a half. Maybe he had been advised of, or expected, an attack on inland aerodromes. The raiders were intercepted at the coast by three squadrons, 501 included, which spoilt their operation so much that those bound for Biggin Hill unloaded upon West Malling and intended Redhill entirely escaped. At 18:50 anti-aircraft gunners of Site S25 claimed a direct hit with a 3-inch shell on the aircraft leading the West Malling raid and recorded that their prize fell at Burrough Green (Ref. R050760).

There remained just one spectacular event to unfold before darkness fell, the bombing of Croydon. 'Croydon'. Everyone in those times knew of Croydon, home of Imperial Airways, starting point for Amy Johnson and many more record breakers. Few had ever flown from it due to the expense, but most could recognise Croydon Airport's distinctive terminal and well-known tower from many a cinema newsreel. Would a foreigner be so well acquainted? Concurrent with that last big raid of the day Erpro 210 was hell-bent on ruining Kenley. Maybe a navigation error or mistaken identity allowed that station to escape. Whatever the reason, the Bf 110s instead blitzed Croydon moments after nine Hurricanes of 'Treble One' had taken off, just in time to escape the bombing which wrecked hangars, ammunition stores — for Croydon was now a fighter base — damaged Rollason's aircraft repair section, killed 68 people (only six Service personnel) and injured 192, for no civilian warning had wailed in time. As the Bf 110s and some Bf 109s climbed away, 111 Squadron and some of 32 Squadron tackled them, Squadron Leader J. Thompson of 111 Squadron despatching a Bf 110 to its doom over Rotherfield. His was a spectacular, fiery victory: his victim Swiss-born Hauptmann Walter Rubensdorffer, leader of Erpro 210. Six Bf 110s were shot down in the skirmish which deprived the Luftwaffe of much more than very brave and skilful warriors.

Barely had the remaining raiders departed our shores when an amazing newsflash on the wireless announced that the Germans had dive-bombed Croydon. Initially the raid was attributed to Stukas, which encouraged an image of merciless, screaming Nazi butchers. It was some time before bomb-carrying Me 110s, or 'Jaguars', were blamed.

Somehow, hitting Croydon seemed a highly immoral act. Mind you, its use as a fighter station was being quietly overlooked. The Ministry of Information was undoubtedly orchestrating a skilful campaign, strengthening our will by suggesting ultimate certain victory. Without having lived through those days it would be difficult to appreciate the boost to the will to succeed that the raid achieved.

By the late evening it was being suggested that during 15 August the Luftwaffe had flown over 2,000 sorties against which Fighter Command had despatched 974 during an outstanding day of aerial conflict. Claims abounded suggesting that over 150 German aircraft had been destroyed for a loss of 29 fighters and around a score of other aircraft wrecked by bombing. The Luftwaffe reckoned it lost 69 aircraft. What remains certain is that, after a day of bitter conflict between two of the world's most cultured nations, neither side was a winner. Both had lost brave men — and Fighter Command, and its aerodromes, were still very much going concerns.

In the 24 hours ended 06:00 on 16 August it was reckoned that 867 HEs and 1,566 incendiaries had fallen on Britain, killing 79 civilians, seriously injuring 196 and variously hurting another 175.

German fighter pilots form a reception committee for one of their number, safely back. (Bundesarchiv)

Spitfires and Hurricanes in Aircraft Storage Units

	number outstanding 18:00	despatched since 18:00 yesterday	in hand during the day	ready for despatch	likely to be ready by noon next day	additional but still deficient in equipment
Spitfires						
31.7.40	3	1	79 + 17 Mk II	22	33 + 9 Mk II	2
12.8.40	3	3	105 + 34 Mk II	22	33 + 9 Mk II	6
15.8.40	2	10	98 + 34 Mk II	22	20 + 2 Mk II	7
24.8.40	—	6	51 + 31 Mk II	19	21 + 11 Mk II	—
Hurricanes						
31.7.40	12	2	140 + 15 for Middle East**	45	133	11
13.8.40	4	24	152 + 3 for Middle East	45	136	21
24.8.40	—	11	88 + 3 Mk II*	56	18 + 5 Mk II	—

* first Hurricane Mk II received by ASUs
** between 1 July and 30 September 84 Hurricanes were shipped to the Middle East

Across the Channel the German Air Staff had been doing its sums, concluding that Fighter Command's losses since the start of July left it with about 300 aircraft.

Despite such an encouraging picture, the stored reserve of Hurricanes and Spitfires had by 16 August fallen during the previous week. Current output and loss rates meant that a necessary reserve could exist for only two months. If loss rates rose, if factories were destroyed... Each squadron currently held an average of 19 pilots, barely enough to replace casualties, allow essential rest. To equate listed establishment nearly 350 more pilots were needed, but only about 80 would complete operational training during the next week.

There was no let-up. Even as the morning haze was late rising on 16 August fighters were engaging escorted Dornier raids. Around noon a two-pronged operation was mounted by KG 2. I/KG 2 entered over Dover and soon faced Spitfires of Nos. 64[103], 65[104] and 266[105] Squadrons, and Hurricanes of 32[106] and 111[107] Squadrons — over 50 RAF fighters all told. Head on Hurricane attacks forcing open the bomber force brought disaster to Flight Lieutenant H. Ferris (R4193) of 111 Squadron who careered into a Do 17, the combined wreckage

falling at Marden, Kent. The Dorniers pressed on and at 12:25 during a high level pass delivered 80 bombs onto West Malling, 66 of them exploding in surrounding farmland. Four No. 266 Squadron Spitfires were shot down in a bitter struggle with II/JG 26 over Deal.

II/KG 2 swung in over the North Foreland where a dozen anti-aircraft gun sites greeted its 24 Dornier 17s. Prevented by fighters over the Thames Estuary from attacking Hornchurch, and while Spitfires of 54 Squadron tangled with accompanying fuel-short Bf 109s, the Dorniers dropped seven bombs upon Tilbury before crossing the river to Northfleet's Pepper Hill and Hazels districts and giving the town its biggest punishment of the war. Included was an horrific incident at Bowaters Paper Mill where ten bombs started a fire and casualties amounted to 25 workers killed and 32 injured.

The third, and most damaging intrusion, evolved east of the Isle of Wight at around 12:30. It comprised Ju 87s of StG 2 supported by Bf 109s of JG 2, and Ju 88s of KG 54 shepherded by Bf 110s of III/ZG 76. Eight defending fighter squadrons were airborne as the approaching force split into four groups. Stukas almost immediately bore down upon

Controlling the Battle

Vital to Fighter Command's success was its fighter control system, whose layout was basically this:

1. All aircraft plots obtained by radar stations, Observer Corps and searchlight detachments were notified to the Filter Room at HQ Fighter Command.

2. These were analysed, identified and plotted on HQ Operations table.

3. Relevant Fighter Group HQ were notified of approaching raids.

4. Group Commander decided which Sector should meet the enemy, and the number of aircraft it should deploy.

5. Sector Commander detailed squadron(s) to intercept and the means by which they should operate.

6. Sector Commander maintained control of his fighters by R/T (Radio Telephony) D/F (Direction Finding).

R/T signals were transmitted automatically for 15 seconds each minute by selected fighters and picked up by two or three D/F stations and passed by direct telephone link to Sector HQ where a mechanical plotting device gave an almost instant plot of the fighters' position. Where no D/F station was available, pilots had to be given speed and direction orders — acceptable if the wind at various altitudes was accurately known.

During 1940 IFF (Identification Friend and Foe) was slowly introduced. It modified the 'echo' received by a radar station from a friendly aircraft, greatly easing the problem of identity.

Simple voice instructions and terms:
'Scramble' = take off   'Orbit' = circle
'Vector 180' = fly on course 180°
'Pancake' = land   'Angels 21' = fly at 21,000 feet (sometimes a secret addition could mean, say, add 3,000 — so that Angels 21 meant fly at 24,000 feet)
'Released' = Not to be called upon for action
'Available' = to be ready to operate in 20 minutes   'Readiness' = ready to operate in 5 minutes   'Stand-by' = available for take off in 2 minutes time

Tangmere, challenged by Hurricanes of Nos. 1[108], 43[109] and 601[110] Squadrons, while 602[111] Squadron Spitfires tackled their escort. The fighters were unable to prevent Tangmere's mutilation by 20 accurately aimed bombs that disposed of its hangars, Station Workshops, sick quarters and the Officers' Mess. The Blenheim-equipped Fighter Interception Unit — developing AI radar and operational techniques — was mauled. Five Hurricanes blazed in hangar fires, 15 Tangmere aircraft in all being smashed. Six civilians and 12 Servicemen were killed, and 41 injured. In the midst of the attack Pilot Officer W. Fiske force-landed Hurricane P3358, which was then strafed and burnt. Next day Fiske became the first volunteer American pilot to die in the Battle. Losses were not one-sided, for No. 43 Squadron alone claimed 17 Ju 87s — Luftwaffe records reckon nine were lost.

Soon after the raid other Ju 87s rained 22 bombs onto Ventnor radar. No. 152 Squadron engaged their escorting Bf 109s and No. 213 Squadron was, by then, trying unsuccessfully to prevent other Stukas from attacking Lee-on-Solent, where three hangars were hit and naval aircraft left burning.

Gosport was the target for Ju 88s which distributed 53 bombs onto the town and Gosport/Fort Grange aerodrome, where a hangar was fired and seven were killed and 15 injured. Three Hurricanes of 249 Squadron[112] came from the Ringwood area to deal with escorting Bf 110s, then became embroiled with rescuing Bf 109s. Flight Lieutenant J.B. Nicolson, his Hurricane P3576 hit, courageously continued fighting, the aircraft burning furiously by the time he baled out. Both he and companion Pilot Officer M.A. King (P3616), also forced to parachute to safety, were in error subjected to ground fire. King died and Nicolson, further injured, was awarded the first Victoria Cross given to a Fighter Command pilot.

A further operation developed in the late afternoon, He 111s of KG 27 escorted by Bf 110s crossing the coast near Brighton and heading for Brooklands. They were met by Nos. 1[113], 64[114] and 615[115] Squadrons, which successfully thwarted the bombers' intent. Instead, HEs and incendiaries fell on Wimbledon station and a factory, killing 18 and injuring 57. Others fell on Merton, Mitcham and on shops at Esher. Ten minutes later bombs were bursting on the railway near Basingstoke. At Eastbourne 18 HEs had earlier killed three and injured one person. Defending fighters, in trying hard to prevent all this, destroyed four He 111s and two Bf 110s. One He 111 was brought down at Steyning by Pilot Officer K.T. Lofts (P3111), Pilot Officer C.R. Young (L2075), also of 615 Squadron, destroying another off Bognor. Squadron Leader Macdonnell (P9554) of 64 Squadron helped destroy a third and Pilot Officer Simpson shared another before his Spitfire L1068 was damaged by cannon fire.

Raid B simultaneously heading along the Thames Estuary and bound for Biggin Hill was also driven off track, by Nos. 32[116], 501[117] and 610[118] Squadrons. No. 56 Squadron, scrambled at 16:50, engaged near Eastchurch a third element comprising 27 Do 17s, claiming two Dorniers and two Bf 109s for the loss of a Hurricane burnt out at Whitstable.

Around 18:00 single aircraft attacks delivered against inland airfields again proved stunningly effective. Four bombs at Harwell set fire to petrol bowsers, one of which was courageously driven away to open ground. Three Welling-

tons were also destroyed and two men were killed. Ten bombs at RAF Farnborough destroyed wooden structures, but the highlight of these attacks was at Brize Norton. At 18:05 two hitherto unnoticed wheels-down Ju 88s in the circuit suddenly switched to attack profile, promptly gutted two hangars and left furious fires engulfing no less than 46 fully-fuelled wooden Airspeed Oxford trainers of No. 2 Service Flying Training School. Six more were badly damaged, also 11 Hurricanes at adjacent 6 MU, an ASU. As a gigantic pall of black smoke billowed over Oxfordshire, BF 109s were strafing Manston. How easily, cheaply, more safely, a handful of intruders achieved far more than a clumsy fleet. Shades of future Mosquito raids!

After dark, KG 27 returned to attack South Wales where 15 HEs (and 5 UX) hit central Cardiff. KG 4 operating from Schiphol interfered with aerodromes in East Anglia. In the 24 hours ending 06:00 on the 17th ground casualties in Britain totalled 88 killed, 192 injured. In the 24 hours of the 16th the Luftwaffe's 1,700 sorties cost it 45 aircraft, and the RAF 25 fighters.

Producing replacement aircraft was easier

NCO pilots of 610 Squadron. Mae Wests on, clearly weary on a hot summer day at Hawkinge. (IWM)

than replacing fighter pilots. Dowding, realizing the seriousness of that aspect, requested the Air Staff to agree to releasing pilots from Merlin-engined Fairey Battle bomber squadrons despite their anti-E-Boat and invasion attack roles. Losing 94 fighter pilots killed and 65 wounded since 8 August was acutely alarming — especially as Fighter Command had entered the Battle far below pilot establishment. The Air Staff, accepting Dowding's proposal, asked for 20 Battle pilots to volunteer for transfer and 33 from 22 Group whose Lysander army co-operation squadrons (already administered by Fighter Command) also had a major anti-invasion role. Thus, 53 fighter pilots additional to about 80 still expected from fighter OTUs would become available.

Fighting for freedom meant, for the Poles and Czechs, a long difficult trek, language problems, adjustment to strange food and ways. At Duxford Czech pilots formed No. 310 (Czech) Squadron. One of its Hurricanes NN:D — P3143 — forms a backdrop. It joined '310' on 24 July and was destroyed on 16 October in a crash near Ely. (IWM)

Waiting to avenge the misappropriation of their homelands were experienced Czech and Polish pilots. Air Ministry had sanctioned formation of one Czech and three Polish squadrons at half strength — on the understanding that they trained more of their pilots. Although the first squadron, No. 302 (Polish), was formed on 13 July none could be completed and operational for some time. In any case, shortage of aircraft and operational stations for them would retard their progress.

August 17, a day of reduced activity, was limited to single aircraft seeking coastal shipping. Around 17:00 a photo-reconnaissance aircraft lingered ominously high over London before another, at 35,000 feet and flying even higher, surveyed the Thames and its Estuary.

During night attacks, which commenced around midnight, homes were destroyed in Aberavon. Bombs also fell south-west of Coventry, and a dozen on Liverpool. By the end of October 893 HE bombs had been dropped there, nearly 150 on Birkenhead and 70 or so on Wallasey. Liverpool County Borough was assessed by the time of its last raid, on 10/11

January 1942, as having received 2,345 HEs, 117 parachute mines and 50 oil bombs, which gives some idea of its ultimate punishment and a guide against which to measure the August attacks. The 17 HEs dropped on the Hodge Hill Common area of Birmingham 17/18 August certainly look few in comparison although Birmingham was ultimately listed as receiving 4,429 known HEs, 86 oil bombs and 50 mines. By 06:00 on 18 August, however, 23 more civilians had died in Britain and 80 seriously injured, 1,000 incendiaries having been recorded.

Pilot Officer R.A. Rhodes and Sergeant Gregory had notched up a notable night success. Operating a Mersey Blue Line patrol from Ternhill in Blenheim 1 fighter L6741 of 29 Squadron, they were vectored at 02:28 onto a

Mid-August saw sharp, low-level and effective attacks on Sector aerodromes. This famous shot taken on 18 August from a Do 17 of 9/KG 76 during a raid on Kenley shows Spitfire SH:G of 64 Squadron in a protective earth revetment doubling as an air raid shelter. Extensive hard taxiways are in evidence. (Bundesarchiv)

raider discovered 15 miles south-west of Chester. After locating it by aid of lights in its rear position, they followed it over Hucknall, Newark and Lincoln before catching it out to sea. Rhodes fired from 400 yards, then his gunner opened up towards the starboard beam. The Heinkel He 111 of II/KG 53 slowly spiralled, eventually ditching ten miles west of Cromer Knoll Light Vessel. Killed in the encounter was KG 53's Gruppenkommandeur.

Daylight on 18 August saw the Luftwaffe again busy trying to destroy Fighter Command. First came six high snoopers including a Bf 110 of LG 2 shot down from 31,000 feet over Manston. Come midday and an enormous force 350-strong was assembling. Nos. 10 and 11 Groups' squadrons were called to readiness. Three waves of raiders crossed the coast between North Foreland and Dungeness eager to reach targets south and south-east of London. Their first challenge came from veteran 54[120] Squadron scrambled at 12:40 from its Manston advanced base, and soon joined by another 70 fighters from nine other squadrons. Forces now responding were frequently having to be larger

Parachute and Cable

By February 1940 arrangements were complete for the installation of a novel rocket defence system for the aerodromes at Manston and Wattisham, and Great Bromley radar station. The weapon consisted of a standard Schermuly rocket carrying a 37-inch diameter parachute in a small metal container. The bottom of a second metal container also contained a parachute, the two being connected by 480 feet of one-ton cable. Propelled to 600 feet (later 1,000 feet) the rocket was fired from a tube set in the ground, or at radar stations from a 23-foot-square platform carrying rocket tubes mounted in batches of fours, and sited on the top of a high tower.

The tubes at aerodromes were arranged in groups of 25, each 60 feet from the next, and in three rows set 20 feet apart. Each bank of rockets could be fired independently. The fire controller was given the best possible view of aircraft approaching the airfield.

The intention was that batteries of the small rockets would be positioned at both French and British airfields to prohibit the types of low-level attack experienced by the Poles. Then, on 30 April, all the units built were suddenly ordered to Norway — and lost.

Training to use 'PAC' began at Exeter on 6 May 1940. On 25 May it was decided to initially instal the system at eight aircraft and engine factories, and then at airfields in this order: Manston, Hornchurch, North Weald, Biggin Hill, Kenley, Tangmere, Debden. Installation, by No. 1 PAC Rocket Unit, was to be completed by 5 June.

On 21 June the scheme was extended to 27 airfields, 13 of them bomber airfields and all manned by personnel from PAC Pool Uxbridge. Concern about rockets possibly landing on dispersed aircraft was brushed aside by the supporters who stated that 'when they come down they only weigh 15 lb.' By 15 July installation was complete at 26 sites (8 of them factories) and another 22 sites were chosen. Biggin Hill had four sets, North Weald four — roughly in each corner of the aerodrome — and Northolt six sets. Hawkinge's five sets, installed on 14 June, were controlled from the Station Commander's house.

The first suitable low attack for engagement was reckoned to have been against Manston on 17 August, although the aircraft might have been out of range. The firing staff were officially rated 'not proficient', for they took shelter instead of opening fire. 'Unreliable people', claimed the higher echelons! On 20 August 12 Bf 109s shot up Manston in two waves, diving in from 5,000 to 400 feet. Since they approached over buildings PAC engagement was not then practicable.

By then some success had been achieved. On 18 August nine Do 17Zs ran in at 500 feet to attack Kenley, the Observer Corps stating that near Hartfield these aircraft had laid a smoke screen for cover. As the Dorniers approached Kenley, 914844 AC2 Roberts of 1 PACU Post B Line quickly checked the circuitry of his equipment and found three units ready. He saw a twin-engined aircraft 50 feet above a hangar release its bombs, then the bombers flew in a straight line in vic across the airfield machine-gunning ground defences and gathering height, three of them heading directly for his line of rockets. When the leading aircraft was within range he released his first line of nine rockets and watched the aircraft fly directly into a mass of cables and release a bomb which exploded beneath it. By then the other two were within range of No. 2 line so he pressed the firing button. Both this and Line 3 were out of use, their circuits having been concussed by the bombing. He looked up and saw about 100 yards away smoke rising above trees from a crashed aircraft, which he and Wing Commander England inspected. The wrecked Dornier had cable caught around one of its mainplanes. By then the station had been dive-bombed, against which PAC was of little use because the attackers pulled out quite high. PAC Mk II with a 1,500 foot range was later developed to help cope with that. Two other units of the

Oberleutnant Lamberty's Do 17Z-2 F1+DT leading 9/KG 76 was shot down near Biggin Hill on Sunday 18 August. Few raiders landed as intact as this. (IWM)

Kenley barrages had been fired inefficiently due to miscalculation of the speed of the aircraft.

Lord Beaverbrook thought the weapons very effective as factory defences. Over 50 were fired when North Weald was under threat on 30 August, and by mid-September they were installed at 72 sites. In October, the Navy asked for its aerodromes to have them and by the end of that month Castletown, Skaebrae and Skitten in Scotland had them. They were a feature of very many operational airfields until well into the war. Phase-out started from bomber stations in July 1942, by which time ample light machine-guns were available.

than hitherto to achieve much success. One raid unleashed 33 bombs on Deal, and the others pressed on.

It was at this time that another complex high- and low-level raid heavily fighter-protected was injected into the action, its aiming points the vitally important Fighter Sector Stations at Biggin Hill and Kenley. A major diversion was provided by two bomber formations flying at 15,000 feet, the first of which bombed West Malling at 12:52 and the second at 13:20. Local gunners, who took on the attackers before defending fighters arrived, claimed hits on two aircraft, from one of which two men baled out. Fifty HEs fell on West Malling, scoring two direct hits on hangars and wrecking three Lysanders. Meanwhile, nine Do 17Zs of 9/KG 76 had raced in extremely low over Kent, confusing ground trackers and penetrating to Big-gin Hill where, at 13:30, they strafed and released short- and long-delay mixed bombs. Such activity demanded faster aircraft than the Do 17, and Nos. 32[121] and 111 Squadrons shot down two Dorniers including the leader's. A further two crashed in the Channel and three force-landed in France. Just as the Dorniers quit Biggin Hill, three waves of Ju 88s of KG 76 heading easterly at 12,000, 15,000 and 18,000 feet cratered the station's landing ground. About 150 HEs were dropped, but only 60 hit the aerodrome, the remainder falling on the nearby golf course. Some small anti-personnel bombs were dropped on gun sites, killing two men by a Bofors gun. Two of the Ju 88s were destroyed, one by Flight Lieutenant Stanford Tuck, forced by return fire to bale out of his 92 Squadron Spitfire (N3040).

MAINWARING'S MEN?

Among many claims as to who shot down enemy aircraft was one by the Home Guard. The Captain involved who had served in France in World War 1 said 'I gave the order for rapid fire and my second in command directed the distance and the height of the firing. We saw the machine stagger and lose height. Although some of my men were of the younger generation they all behaved splendidly. Their discipline was beyond praise.'

Kenley had been similarly dealt with shortly before. Slipping in very low over Newhaven, another nine Do 17Zs of KG 76 attacked the aerodrome at 13:22 from between 50 and 100 feet. The leading three bomber crews machine-gunned the station's anti-aircraft defences before dropping their bombs on the north-east side of the camp, leaving their colleagues to deal with the hangars and sick quarters. Five minutes later came the high-level force, arriving by way of Dungeness and flying at 10,000 feet. They scored hits on the Station Armoury, Station Sick Quarters, variously damaged eight aircraft (including six of 615 Squadron's Hurricanes) and dropped many delayed action HEs. No. 111 Squadron again tackled the low-flying element, two of which were brought down by Parachute and Cable rocket defences (see page 106). About 100 bombs were dropped. Twelve personnel died, 20 were injured. No. 615 Squadron[122], responding as quickly as possible to the raid, was caught by the rear support Bf 109s. As a result Flight Lieutenant Gaunce (P2966) was forced to bale out near Sevenoaks, Pilot Officer Hugo (R4221), wounded, crash landed; Pilot Officer Looker's Hurricane (L1592), which caught fire, was landed at Croydon, Flight Lieutenant Sanders (P3111) was shot down near Kenley and Sergeant Walley (P2768), who crashed at Morden, Kent, was killed. Such was Kenley's state that 615 Squadron's remaining aircraft had to divert to Croydon. Conditions there were also extremely bad, for more bombs had caused a serious fire, there was devastation in Purley Way and at the Rollason works. In Coulsdon there was widespread civilian damage, a gasometer was burning at Sevenoaks and a dozen goods waggons at Paddock Wood station. No. 64 Squadron[123], which laid many claims, managed later to land at Kenley on a narrow flag-marked track and found fires still raging there six hours after the raid. Phone lines were generally disrupting 11 Group activity at both vital Sector Stations — and the day was still young.

The afternoon phase began with six raids approaching east of the Isle of Wight shortly after 14:00. About 70 Ju 87s of StG 77 accompanied by 24 Ju 88s of KG 54, delivered four sharp strikes upon 1) Poling CH radar station, where 44 HEs from screeching Stukas brought down two pylons and disabled the installation for a week and another 43 bombs exploded outside its perimeter; 2) Ford naval air station, where dive-bombing mutilated two hangars, destroyed a third of the quarters, killed 14 and started a huge petroleum fire; 3) Gosport, where Ju 88s caused further damage; and 4) Thorney Island, where at 14:30 a handful of Ju 87s bombed a hangar and started a fire. German fighters were giving extensive top cover when 43 Squadron[124] latched on to the Poling Stukas, attacking them in both dive and recovery phases. Much worse followed as, after regrouping, the dive-bombers were furiously engaged by Nos. 152, 601[125] and 602[126] Squadrons while 234 Squadron[127] challenged the top cover. The Stuka formation was devastated, no less than 16 Ju 87s being shot down. Two more crash-landed and another four were badly damaged, in addition to a surprising eight escorting Bf 109s shot down — all for the loss of four Spitfires and two Hurricanes. During 14 main raids within two weeks 39 Ju 87s had been destroyed in action; and now just one Stuka Geschwader had lost another 17. Clearly the reign of the dive-bomber had been cut short by Fighter Command, the aircraft's role in future resting with the fast strike fighter. Proof of that came at 15:30 when a dozen Bf 109s strafing Manston destroyed two Spitfires, killing one man and injuring 15.

A new development in the Battle came two hours later when eight raids crossed in mainly over the Essex coast via the Blackwater and Thames estuaries. That brought Nos. 54[128] and 151[129] Squadrons into action and prevented much of the bombing of North Weald and Hornchurch. Some of the bombers turned away, jettisoning 150 HEs on Shoebury at 17:45, another 69 near Strood and 77 in the countryside beyond. Unexpected bombing by the Medway caused numerous casualties, for no sirens had sounded.

Shot down German aircraft were often displayed in a drive to increase War Savings. Outside the Market Inn at Salisbury, a rare Do 17P, 5D+JL of 3(F)/31 Aufkl shot down on 27 August by 238 Squadron Hurricanes near Tavistock, Devon.

About 70 German bombers operated next night, 40 over South Wales. Sealand was bombed and a considerable number of delayed action HEs fell at Birmingham and Wolverhampton. Another, at Hook, Hampshire, exploded killing five members of a bomb disposal squad dealing with it. Grim as all the incidents were, they could not eclipse the main event of the day, the defeat of the Stuka, on what proved to be one of the toughest of the Battle. Although the Luftwaffe had lost 69 aircraft, 68 RAF fighters had been destroyed.

Little wonder Göring was enraged and ranted that, since his fighters were incapable of defending them, the Stukas must now be held back for their designated invasion tasks. He must have been equally furious when presented with the news of the losses of the last week which, on three days, exceeded 50 aircraft. Luftflotte 5's bombers operating beyond Bf 109 range in daytime proved so vulnerable that he ordered

them to switch to prepare for night raids on Glasgow and only daylight cloud-cover precision attacks. Despite the poor combat showing of the Bf 110 it retained Göring's confidence although he hedged his bets by ordering that Bf 109 fighters must now protect the 110 fighters! Even more restricting was his instruction that Bf 109s must stay close to bombers, shielding them instead of breaking away to fight the enemy. That had profound consequences, particularly as the Luftwaffe's prime task remained the destruction of Fighter Command.

Whilst cloudy conditions on 19 August limited operations, one small-scale attack unleashed success out of all proportion to the effort when two Ju 88s of KG 51 at 15:15 scored

Spitfire QJ:P N3245 reputedly of 92 Squadron and wearing the markings of 616 Squadron is officially recorded as being with 266 Squadron, in whose hands it was when badly damaged at Manston on 24 August 1940! (RAF Museum)

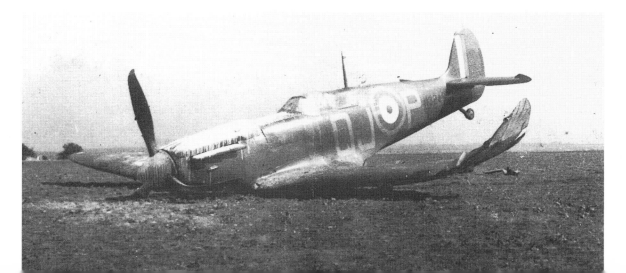

hits with eight bombs on the Llanreith oil farm, Pembroke, instantly causing a huge conflagration which blazed for many days. Another III/KG 51 Ju 88 struck at Bibury grass airfield, killing an airman and damaging two Spitfires of newly-arrived 92 Squadron. Flight Lieutenant T.S. Wade, later Hawker's Chief Test Pilot, and Pilot Officer J.A. Paterson quickly climbed aboard Spitfires R6703 and P9368, gave chase and eventually disposed of the cheeky raider in the Solent. In a crash-landing, Wade had to get away fast from his exploding aircraft. East Anglia was also subjected to a host of afternoon intrusions directed mainly at aerodromes. Some 23 bombs fell on residential property at Chelmsford, killing two and injuring five, and other incidents occurred at Dover Castle, Shoeburyness, Canterbury and Deal Royal Marine Infirmary. No. 19 Squadron's cannon Spitfires R6882, R6897 and R6911 destroyed a 7/KG 2 Do 17Z off Essex, but scores reflected a quieter day — three raiders destroyed, four RAF fighters lost.

After dusk, He 111s of KG 27 exploiting Göring's recent instruction aimed a few bombs towards Liverpool and Birkenhead. KGr 100 dropped 43 HEs in an attempted beam-guided precision attack on Derby, after which three He 111s crashed on return due to fuel shortages. In a low-level strike on Driffield a hangar was damaged, also two Whitleys, and bombing also took place at Hull, Leicester, Nottingham and Sheffield, with 23 dying and 74 injured by dawn.

Attempts were made on 20 August to stoke the Llanreith fire, and Erpro 210 interfered with a convoy off Aldeburgh before striking sharply at Southwold's coastal defences. Early afternoon brought in 27 Do 17s of KG 3 escorted by Bf 109s of I/JG 51 via Dover and Canterbury to the Thames Estuary, and in the process they faced six squadrons — 40 fighters. No. 615 Squadron[130] claimed two bombers and a Bf 109, heading again for Coastal Command's Eastchurch. No. 65 Squadron[131] claimed another, and in engaging the escort destroyed two Bf 109s. Smaller-scale activities included

a convoy attack off Dunwich. A Do 17 was shot down off Southwold by 257 Squadron; a Ju 88 of KG 30 which came down near Withernsea provided the eager members of 302 (Polish) Squadron, declared operational only the previous day, with their first victory. Next night, among the 60 raids plotted was a repeat attack directed at Rolls-Royce Derby. Casualties for the 24 hours ending 06:00 on the 21st were 46 civilians killed, 108 injured.

The great air battle which had been in progress over this island for the last few weeks has recently attained a high intensity. It is too soon to attempt to assign limits either to its scale or to its duration... It is quite plain that Herr Hitler could not admit defeat in his air attack on Great Britain without sustaining most serious injury... The gratitude of every home in our island, in our Empire, and indeed throughout the world, except in the abodes of the guilty, goes out to the British airmen who, undaunted by odds, unwearied in their constant challenge and mortal danger, are turning the tide of the world war by their prowess and by their devotion. Never in the field of human conflict was so much owed by so many to so few. All our hearts go out to the fighter pilots, whose brilliant action we see with our own eyes day after day... I hope — indeed I pray — that we shall not be found unworthy of our victory if after toil and tribulation it is granted to us.

Winston Churchill, 20 August 1940

Widespread operations, again mainly by individual bombers, continued on 21 August, one of a KG 3 Dornier trio penetrating Norfolk being destroyed at Burnham Market by 611 Squadron using the new Spitfire IIs (P7290, P7303, P7304) before another three of the squadron's Spitfires (P7314, P7292, P7305) destroyed two more off Mablethorpe. Airfields came under attack, plentiful damage at Bircham Newton affecting both buildings and aircraft, there being 22 casualties. No. 242 Squadron downed a Do 17 near Harlesden soon after midday and 56 Squadron another near Ipswich. In Southwold three houses were wrecked, and seven at Leicester, where five died and 13 were injured during the city's first bombing episode. Trains were strafed at Umberleigh and Guildford, civilian property hit in Canterbury and Hastings, three trawlers damaged at Falmouth, and balloons shot down at Southampton, where a dredger was sunk. Bombing at St Eval damaged six 236 Squadron Blenheims.

Convoy CE9 had left Plymouth on the 20th and embarked kite protection at Southampton and was running the Dover Straits by 09:30 on the 21st when shelling commenced. Around 10:55 high-level bombing was added. Between 11:20 and 12:07 every salvo of four to six shells straddled the convoy. By that time 134 rounds had been hurled at the ships, the worst problem being five feet of water accumulated aboard the SS *Eddystone*. Soon after, 16 bombers trying in vain to sink the ships were driven off by their intense AA fire. Low-level attack was prevented by kite flying, but these eventually had to be close hauled, being very unstable in afternoon rain squalls. Cost to the Luftwaffe of the day's activity, 13 aircraft; to the RAF, four fighters.

Southern and eastern airfield targets on 22 August generated about 120 sorties. 'B' Flight of 54 Squadron[132], ordered to bring down an aircraft range-spotting for guns shelling trawlers in the Dover Straits, arrived simultaneously with 30 Bf 110s and 20 Bf 109s of Erpro 210. Driving them off resulted in one of each destroyed and a Spitfire lost. Erpro 210's Bf 110s mounted an evening strike upon Manston, 616 Squadron dealing with accompanying Bf 109s while other intruders swept Kent's skies. Some 30 shells damaged houses and a church at Dover. Off Scotland, Ju 88s of KG 30 bombarded a convoy and in the south-west St Eval endured more fire bombs. Night bombing included the dropping of 33 HEs at Bristol, Fil-

ton's aero engine No. 4 works attracting 10 HEs, 5 oil bombs and 200 incendiaries. Others fell on nearby Patchway and Almondsbury. Other attacks involved Aberdeen, Swindon (14 HEs), Harrow, Pontefract, a convoy off Kinnaird's Head, Bradford, Middlesbrough and Liverpool, at all of which there was minimal damage. A notable event occurred at 03:10 when a 250-kg HE exploding in a boiler house demolished Edmonton's Alcazar Cinema. Another three bombs fell at Willesden Green, Middlesex, one hitting a large house, and these incidents again raised concern that London was about to be heavily bombed.

Poor weather continued restricting daytime operations whereas at night activity continued apace. Manston received 30 more bombs at 01:25 on the 23rd, and three Ju 88s attacked Thorney Island. Other incidents involved the Scillies, where 15 HEs fell on and around the radio station. At Colchester there were 40 casualties and Cromer, Harwich, Maidstone, Portsmouth and Tangmere were all bombed. Darkness on the 23/24th concealed He 111s bombing Cardiff, Pembroke Dock and Birmingham's Fort Dunlop factory, the latter attracting specialists of KGr 100. There was by now an improvement in the weather, HEs and fire bombs falling widely over Wiltshire, Somerset, Dorset, Devon and more precisely at Westbury, Shepton Mallet, Camerton, Yeovil, Crewkerne, Wareham and near Exeter.

FROM THE PAPERS:

23 August: 'For the first time since the war started Londoners were aroused from their beds by the crashing of AA guns, wailing of sirens and distant thud of bombs. Gunfire was described as tremendous and heard miles from the scene of the attack. Three areas on the outskirts are reported to have had bombs.'

For almost a week activity had been restricted by the weather, but the lull was about to end, for a huge anti-cyclone was creeping in from the Atlantic to greatly improve Britain's weather. Not surprisingly, dawn on 24 August saw the Luftwaffe commence operations in great strength and by evening, perhaps more by carelessness than certain intent, it had delivered two brutal attacks. Early morning saw one squadron advance to Manston, another to Hawkinge and parts of two more to Martlesham Heath and Tangmere, for information suggested that the day ahead would involve heavy attacks.

Following fighter feints between 06:00 and 08:00 came 40 bombers and 60 fighters intent upon caning Dover. Although Hurricanes were concentrating upon destroying bombers, leaving fighters to the nimble Spitfires, penetrating the bombers' tight escort was difficult. Only two squadrons managed it, No. 85[133] being well placed just as Dover's AA guns began firing. That probably caused the bombers to unload onto the town's residential areas before their rear support unsuccessfully interrupted British fighters returning to forward stations. Pressure upon Dover was resumed when at 09:55 long-range guns put three shells into the town and two more nearby.

With only three Defiants on guard while its other fighters refuelled, the murder of Manston began, heralded by 30 Ju 88s in three vics. Three minutes later 25 He 111s arrived for a follow-up attack from 4,000 feet, a dozen watchful Bf 109s patrolling almost four miles above

them. Intense anti-aircraft fire greeted this second wave, in combination with clouds of chalk dust and smoke which brought welcome protection to what was left of the station. The Heinkel crews, unable to aim through the chaos, continued on track and unleashed their loads on to tiny Ramsgate airport and the town, wrecking 78 houses, making 300 uninhabitable and seriously damaging another 700. Fierce flames engulfed the gas works and its sulphur plant; ARP workers and other civilians were machine-gunned; a military HQ and the fish market and customs house were all wrecked. Over 60 bombs also fell on Broadstairs. Two serious and 30 minor fires raged at Ramsgate, where 17 UXBs needed attention. Casualties — fewer than expected — totalled 20 killed outright in the relatively heaviest daylight bombing of any population centre (apart from London) during the Battle. Official assessment of the total jettisoned load was at one time quoted as 500 HEs, later reduced, although an uncertain number of bombs fell in the sea.

Manston's Defiants had scrambled and escaped the bombing only just in time. Dowding, despite his lack of confidence in the turret fighter, had No. 264 Defiant Squadron moved

Narrow outer yellow rings to fuselage roundels were also featured by 264 Squadron Defiants including PS:H and 'L photographed on 25 July 1940. Both have the combing fore and aft of the turret retracted, permitting gun traverse. (IWM)

A medium-level bombing attack carried out on 24 August on a permanent RAF station, possibly St Athan. (Bundesarchiv)

to Hornchurch on 22 August in case massed bomber raids expected at any time on London allowed deployment of the aircraft in their intended formation. The squadron then advanced to Manston and faced tasks for which it was never intended. Before '264' could adopt battle formation three Defiants were shot down, and Squadron Leader P.A. Hunter, their leader (N1535), was last seen heading out across the Channel chasing a Ju 88. The sad remnants of the squadron were ordered back to Hornchurch.

Throughout the morning Luftwaffe fighters patrolled over the Channel, their presence intended to confuse British radar and disguise various ventures. Until late afternoon only minor threats were apparent. Their activity caused some worrying scrambles and brought varying fuel states to formations on patrol. Between 13:00 and 14:00 about 30 enemy aircraft were active between North Foreland and Deal — Manston being dive-bombed yet again between 13:11 and 13:30. The station's ordeal still wasn't over, for at 14:47 20 Bf 109s/110s strafed and bombed it, wrecking a hangar, airmen's quarters and cutting remaining phone links. One freakish event was the hurling onto a wrecked hangar roof of a searchlight, which rested there swaying.

Principal afternoon activity opened at 15:20 when four large raids this time crossed Kent, two bound for Hornchurch and North Weald.

One of the others bombed Manston, yet again, the station being hit because its defenders were too low on fuel to prevent it. Manston was now all but evacuated due to the presence of many UXBs, and did not re-open until 26 August.

As Hornchurch came under attack by He 111s and Ju 88s, No. 264 Squadron[134] was again in the throes of scrambling. Heinkel 111s of Raid H8 flying in formation at 15,000 feet aimed their bombs at the aerodrome, which in total was hit only by six. Predicted AA fire proved accurate, the fourth salvo from battery N11 scoring at 15:41 a direct hit on a He 111, knocking out its port engine. As it curled away to the north-west a fighter finished it off and it crashed at North Ockenden. Battery N20 seriously damaged the wing of another He 111. Most of the bomb salvoes fell around Dagenham and Upminster not long after at 16:00, and in the Rainham area about ten minutes later, with many single bombs falling widely. After swinging left, the enemy formation progressed along the Thames Estuary to the accompaniment of riverside gunfire. Cost of the raid to III/KG 53, five He 111s.

North Weald was bombed at the same time as Hornchurch, about 15 He 111s entering from the east at 12,500 feet, and following the main road to the aerodrome. Spirited action by 111 and 151 Squadrons prevented other raiders from reaching their objective, 111 Squadron making head-on attacks and leaving 151 Squadron[135]

to then deal with the Heinkels. Covering Bf 109s, fuel shortage looming and too high to intervene, left bomber protection to supporting Bf 110s which, for once, guarded their charge well against some 50 RAF fighters by then active. Although there were many casualties at North Weald, restricted damage was caused to the radio station and huts, a nearby woodland fire producing a deceiving huge pall of smoke after 300 incendiaries ignited.

The extent of the afternoon raids was such that nearly all of 11 Group's serviceable aircraft had operated, for intelligence sources had indicated that London was about to be bombed. Warned of the potential development, Keith Park at around 16:00 asked 12 Group's Commander, Leigh Mallory, to provide cover for 11 Group stations north of London. No. 12 Group responded by attempting to marshal a large group of fighters over Duxford to defend Lon-

don, but that took too long to assemble. Without ample practice the scheme was impracticable and instead six cannon-armed Spitfires of 19 Squadron[136], ordered to North Weald, arrived in time to see smoke rising from there and around Hornchurch. Before gun stoppages occurred (caused by spent cartridges jamming in breeches because the cannon had to lie on their sides in the thin wings), the Spitfires claimed three Bf 110s. All told, five bombers were destroyed and four fighters. Fighter Command lost eight aircraft and three pilots.

While the London area was under threat, Ventnor radar, barely working again, detected many raiders approaching from Cherbourg and the Channel Islands at between 13,000 and 18,000 feet. They turned out to be about 50 Ju 88s of LG 1 escorted by Bf 110s of Luftflotte 3 mounting one of its last major day raids prior to unit re-arrangement for the coming invasion.

Unaware of the withdrawal of the '87s, some fighters scrambled by Middle Wallop and Tangmere to the east and west of the Isle of Wight patrolled low to dispose of the expected Stukas,

which let in Ju 88s to deliver a devastating four minute deluge on Portsmouth soon after 16:00. Around 100 HEs (reckoned to be 80 250-kg and 20 50-kg) caused widespread damage, killing 118 civilians and injuring 230 and 191 slightly. Three Anderson shelters received direct hits, all their occupants dying. Naval casualties at Victoria Barracks totalled another 50. A direct hit on a cinema, the Princes Theatre, produced a most ghastly incident in which eight out of 35 people in the balcony died, and another 84 in the building — many children — were grievously injured. Three workmen repairing a fractured water main were killed when a UXB exploded. A 250-kg bomb on a shelter killed 20 occupants, and another 25 sheltering in a trench were killed when a bomb exploded within it. Bombing of houses claimed another 31 killed and 98 badly injured, for there were many direct hits on domestic property. Another

Scene of a major incident on 24 August, the Princes Theatre, Lake Road, Portsmouth. (Courtesy: The News, Portsmouth)

eight were killed in shops, five more in the open, with 21 injured. As a result of this, the heaviest and sharpest daylight raid on a city so far, 700 were made homeless and a fuel oil store hit burned for 36 hours. Two naval ships were damaged and rail links cut. The Battle of Britain was certainly no glamorous event, with worse coming almost daily.

The 11 Solent anti-aircraft batteries fired intensively between 16:19 and 17:30, and shot off 384 heavy rounds, Site 1 destroying a Ju 88 which fell at Q 079188. Five enemy aircraft were claimed between 16:20 and 16:50 and two RAF fighters were shot down. In a diversionary raid on Warmwell a hangar roof was damaged, the station sick quarters burnt out, a Battle and a Wellington ravaged, but luckily there were no casualties.

Enemy activity around Portsmouth led to a most serious example of mistaken identity when at 16:15 over Thorney Island three Blenheim IVs[137] — not unlike Ju 88s at first glance — were set upon by Hurricanes of the freshly arrived No. 1 Squadron, Royal Canadian Air Force. Despite firing off the colours of the day, Blenheim T1804-E was shot down off Wittering. Six Hurricanes then attacked a second

Blenheim, getting hits in its mainplanes and starboard engine despite repeated firing of the colours of the day. It was forced to crash-land. The other Blenheim was also damaged. Soon after that tragic event a further eight heavy shells were ineffectively fired towards Dover and Hawkinge, then came the day's final major incursion by over 100 fighters over Kent. By dusk 32 enemy aircraft had been destroyed, and 23 RAF fighters.

All through the day expectation rose concerning an imminent attack upon London, and when darkness came it was soon apparent that the developing activity was on a greater scale than ever before. Over 150 bombers were counted, and they made over 350 intrusions and lost two of their number, He 111 G1+TC of KG 55 shot down by Flight Lieutenant J.G. Sanders of 615 Squadron (V7314) and another which succumbed to Swansea AA. Those two events would have marked the night as unusual, it

Oberleutnant Priller (centre), Staffelkapitan of 6/JG 51, with his pilots at Wissant. Behind, his Ace of Hearts marked aircraft. Possibly taken on 24 August when Fritz Beeck (hands behind his back) was shot down by Flying Officer Wicks of 56 Squadron. (Michael Payne)

being besmirched with the heaviest night bombing of the country so far. Most significantly of all it included the expected, extensive bombing of Greater London and the first bombing of the City of London. Whilst the latter might have been in error, intelligence sources *did* know of a listed attack on London, which had provoked the extensive reception given to the afternoon's raiders. Peripheral targets also listed for attack included Hawker's Kingston works and, further out, Shorts at Rochester, and the Thameshaven oil installations, at all of which th aim was poor. It is untrue that London was not widely and intentionally bombed before September 1940. Hitler thought that raids on London would lower morale during the run up to the September invasion.

The night of the 24/25 was alarming for the defenders because they began experiencing round-the-clock heavy raids. In Bethnal Green alone nine were killed, 58 injured and 100 made homeless. Early on the 25 August bombs fell in Millwall, Tottenham, Highbury, Islington, Leyton, Enfield, Stepney, Canonbury, Wood Green, Hampton, Kingston as well as Banstead, Watford, Feltham, Maldon, Coulsdon and Feltham. Nos. 3, 4 and No. 11 Warehouses, West India Dock, were soon blazing. Other incendiaries on Canary Wharf, West India Dock, luckily burnt themselves out on the roof and three on the SS *Boka* did no damage. The worst incident was at Bethnal Green, where at 00:16 the LNER Hackney viaduct north of Cambridge Heath was hit. Only by a stroke of luck did a derailed train not fall into the crater on the crown of a 35-foot span bridge, although seven casualties were caused. A second bomb, on a curbstone in Wadeson Street, blasted two houses, injuring five occupants.

Twenty minutes later three bombs set Stepney's Dundee Wharf ablaze, also a house in Phoebe Street; in Garford Street a single storey factory was burnt out, and next the Imperial Tobacco factory. Carter Paterson works in Goswell road also suffered slight fire damage.

Most portentous of all was the first bombing of the City, brought about by a high-flying

Heinkel 111 of KG 53 which released four bombs. The first fell in Fore Street, the second at St Giles in Cripplegate, the third in Castle Street and a fourth on the Aldersgate Street/Manchester Avenue junction. A large fire was caused which gutted a four-storey wooden-floored building in Fore Street and spread to London Wall, starting another blaze among straw and wax. The St Giles bomb exploded at the base of the stone turret, while the Aldersgate bomb dealt a blow at a five-storey building.

South of the line Northumberland to Lancashire indiscriminate raiders were rampaging, facing little opposition. Over Kent, Sussex, Surrey, Reading, Oxford, Devon, Gloucestershire, Cardiff (where the main railway line was hit and a train bombed), Liverpool, Sheffield, Bradford, Hull (where eight 250-kg HEs fell), Middlesbrough, near Tadcaster, Hedomb, Withernsea (12), Hartlepool, and South Shields, the Midlands, East Anglia and Surrey in particular the Luftwaffe roamed. Birmingham received spasmodic attacks over a four-hour period, bombs falling at Fort Dunlop and Castle Bromwich without causing much damage. Elsewhere six HEs fell on Plymouth docks, a fire was started at ICI's Billingham works, UXBs nestled into Swan Hunter at Newcastle, and at Coventry a theatre was hit. More serious was a fire at Rootes No. 2 Ruyton engine factory. At RAF St Athan the hospital received a direct hit, likewise the Sergeants Mess at Driffield, from where the Whitley squadrons were two days later evacuated for safety. Aerodromes at Acklington, Catterick and White Waltham were also raided and coastal waters extensively mined. In the 24 hours ending 06:00 on the 25th 102 civilians had died and 335 had been injured in operations carried out by 13 Kampfgeschwaderen. London reported 76 bombing incidents, 11 of them needing attention from a dozen or more fire pumps.

By contrast the morning of 25 August was unnaturally quiet. Apart from feints, Channel patrols, no large raids appeared until about 16:00, when a strong force headed for Weymouth. Nos. 10 and 11 Groups faced it with all available aircraft, between Tangmere and Exeter, Nos. 87[138] and 609[139] Squadrons defending Portland and 17 Squadron protecting Warmwell. Before they could engage them, the Ju 88s of II/KG 51 and II/KG 54 protected by many Bf 110s split into three groups to raid Portland, Weymouth and Warmwell. No. 87 Squadron took on the Portland bombers, leaving the Bf 110s to 609 Squadron, the latter rapidly coming under attack by Bf 109s of JG 53. Although Warmwell's attackers were assaulted, 17 Squadron[140] found the bombers impossible to reach through the dense fighter screen. Accordingly, Warmwell succumbed. As that group withdrew they were short of a Ju 88, fighters from Nos. 92, 152, 213 and 602 Squadrons having reinforced No. 17. In the fight the RAF lost 12 fighters and had eight pilot casualties.

The only other sizeable raid of the day developed over Kent around 18:00. Six 11 Group squadrons were in action, 32 Squadron[141] operating from Hawkinge and engaging a dozen Do 17s until Bf 109s drove them off and destroyed a Hurricane. By then more squadrons were airborne and the enemy had gone home. The day's scoreboard showed 14 RAF fighters lost, and 20 German aircraft.

RAF losses during operations, 13-25 August 1940

a indicates failed to return/shot down *b* written off — battle casualty *c* seriously damaged.

August	13			14			15			16			17			18			19		
Type	a	b	c	a	b	c	a	b	c	a	b	c	a	b	c	a	b	c	a	b	c
Blenheim F	—	—	—	—	3	—	—	—	—	—	6	1	—	—	—	—	—	—	—	—	—
Defiant	—	—	—	—	—	—	—	—	—	—	—	—	—	—	—	—	—	—	—	—	—
Hurricane	12	—	4	3	—	4	—	—	—	7	4	2	—	—	—	26	10	4	—	—	—
Spitfire	1	1	1	1	—	—	—	—	—	11	2	—	—	—	—	4	1	—	3	1	—
Blenheim B	13	—	—	—	—	—	2	—	—	2	—	—	—	—	—	—	—	—	1	—	—
Hampden	4	—	—	1	—	—	1	—	—	—	—	—	—	—	—	—	—	—	1	—	—
Wellington	—	—	—	—	—	—	—	—	—	3	—	—	1	—	—	—	—	—	3	—	—
Whitley	1	—	—	2	—	—	1	—	—	1	—	—	3	—	—	—	—	—	1	—	—
Coastal Cmd	10	—	—	1	—	—	1	—	—	3	—	—	1	—	—	8	—	—	1	—	—
TOTALS	41	1	5	8	3	4	5	—	—	27	12	3	5	—	—	38	11	4	10	1	—

August	20			21			22			23			24			25			TOTAL LOSS IN PERIOD		
Type	a	b	c	a	b	c	a	b	c	a	b	c	a	b	c	a	b	c	a	b	c
Blenheim F	—	—	1	—	—	—	—	2	—	—	—	—	—	—	—	—	2	—	0	13	2
Defiant	—	—	—	—	—	—	—	—	—	—	—	—	4	1	1	—	—	—	4	1	1
Hurricane	—	1	—	1	—	—	—	—	1	—	1	1	—	2	2	7	—	—	56	18	18
Spitfire	1	—	—	—	—	—	4	—	—	1	—	—	6	—	1	7	1	2	39	6	4
Blenheim B	2	—	—	—	—	—	—	—	—	—	—	—	—	—	—	—	—	—	20	0	0
Hampden	—	—	—	1	—	—	—	—	—	—	—	—	2	—	—	—	1	—	10	1	0
Wellington	—	—	—	—	—	—	—	—	—	1	—	—	—	—	—	—	—	—	8	0	0
Whitley	—	—	—	—	—	—	—	—	—	—	—	—	1	—	—	—	1	—	10	1	0
Coastal Cmd	2	—	—	3	—	—	2	—	—	2	—	—	4	—	—	—	—	—	38	0	0
TOTALS	5	1	1	5	—	—	6	2	1	4	1	1	17	3	4	14	5	2	185	40	25

Luftwaffe losses during operations 1-12 August 1940

a indicates shot down *b* crashed after action *c* seriously damaged

August	1			2			3			4			5			6			7		
Type	a	b	c	a	b	c	a	b	c	a	b	c	a	b	c	a	b	c	a	b	c
Do 17Z	—	1	—	—	—	—	—	—	—	—	—	—	—	—	—	—	1	—	—	—	—
He 59	—	1	—	—	—	—	—	—	—	—	—	—	—	—	—	—	—	—	—	—	—
He 111H	—	—	1	2	—	—	—	—	—	—	—	—	—	—	—	—	—	—	—	—	—
He 111P	—	—	—	—	—	—	1	—	—	—	—	—	—	—	—	—	—	—	—	—	—
He 115	—	2	—	—	—	—	1	—	—	—	—	—	—	—	—	—	—	—	—	—	—
Hs 126	1	—	—	—	—	—	—	—	—	—	—	—	—	—	—	—	—	—	—	—	—
Ju 87B	—	—	—	—	—	—	—	—	—	—	—	—	—	—	—	—	—	—	—	—	—
Ju 88A	2	2	—	—	1	—	—	—	—	—	—	—	—	—	—	—	—	—	2	—	—
Bf 109	—	1	1	—	—	—	—	—	—	1	—	1	1	—	—	—	—	—	—	—	—
Bf 110	—	—	—	—	—	—	—	—	—	—	—	—	—	—	—	—	—	—	—	2	—
TOTALS	3	7	2	2	1	1	2	0	0	1	0	1	1	0	0	1	0	0	2	2	0

August	8			9			10			11			12			GRAND TOTALS		
Type	a	b	c	a	b	c	a	b	c	a	b	c	a	b	c	a	b	c
Do 17Z	—	—	—	—	—	—	3	—	—	—	—	—	—	—	—	4	1	0
He 59	1	—	—	—	—	—	—	—	—	—	—	—	—	—	—	2	1	0
He 111H	1	—	—	2	—	—	—	—	—	1	—	1	—	1	—	6	1	2
He 111P	—	—	—	—	—	—	—	—	—	—	—	—	—	—	—	1	0	0
He 115	—	—	—	—	—	—	—	—	—	—	—	—	—	—	—	1	2	0
Hs 126	—	—	—	—	—	—	—	—	—	—	—	—	—	—	—	1	0	0
Ju 87B	8	—	3	—	—	—	—	—	—	1	1	—	—	—	—	9	1	3
Ju 88A	—	—	—	1	1	—	—	—	—	5	—	—	10	—	1	20	4	1
Bf 109	10	—	1	—	—	—	—	—	—	10	2	1	11	1	1	33	4	5
Bf 110	1	—	3	—	—	—	—	—	—	10	—	1	5	1	—	16	3	4
TOTALS	21	0	7	3	1	0	0	0	0	30	3	3	26	3	1	90	17	15

Luftwaffe losses during operations, 13-25 August 1940

a indicates shot down *b* crashed during course of sortie *c* seriously damaged.

August	13			14			15			16			17			18			19		
Type	a	b	c	a	b	c	a	b	c	a	b	c	a	b	c	a	b	c	a	b	c
Do 17P	1	—	—	—	—	—	1	—	—	—	—	—	—	—	—	—	—	—	—	—	—
Do 17Z	5	—	1	—	—	—	2	—	1	4	1	—	—	—	—	5	1	4	1	—	—
He 59	—	—	—	—	—	—	1	—	—	—	—	—	—	—	—	—	—	—	—	—	—
He 111H	—	1	—	—	—	2	13	2	1	1	—	—	—	—	—	4	1	—	—	1	2
He 111P	1	—	—	7	2	—	—	—	—	4	—	1	—	—	—	1	2	1	1	—	—
He 115	—	—	—	—	—	—	1	—	—	—	—	—	—	—	—	—	—	—	—	—	—
Ju 87B	—	—	1	4	—	—	2	—	—	9	—	—	—	—	—	14	2	2	—	—	—
Ju 87R	5	1	—	—	—	—	5	—	—	—	—	—	—	—	—	—	—	—	—	—	—

August	13			14			15			16			17			18			19		
Type	a	b	c	a	b	c	a	b	c	a	b	c	a	b	c	a	b	c	a	b	c
Ju 88A	6	1	4	2	—	—	12	—	—	1	—	2	—	—	—	2	—	1	1	—	1
Ju 88C	—	—	—	—	—	—	5	—	1	—	—	—	1	—	—	—	—	—	—	—	—
Bf 109	5	1	4	6	—	—	6	2	—	11	5	3	—	—	—	15	1	3	—	—	—
Bf 110	8	1	6	2	—	—	25	2	1	7	—	1	—	—	—	12	1	1	—	—	—
TOTALS	31	5	16	19	0	0	73	6	4	37	6	7	1	0	0	53	8	12	4	1	3

August	20			21			22			23			24			25			GRAND TOTALS		
Type	a	b	c	a	b	c	a	b	c	a	b	c	a	b	c	a	b	c	a	b	c
Do 17P	—	—	—	—	—	—	—	—	—	—	—	—	—	—	—	—	—	—	2	0	0
Do 17Z	2	—	—	6	—	—	—	—	—	1	—	1	—	—	—	1	—	—	27	2	7
He 59	—	—	—	—	—	—	—	—	—	—	—	—	—	—	—	—	—	—	1	0	0
He 111H	—	—	—	1	—	—	—	—	—	1	—	—	5	—	—	—	1	—	25	6	5
He 111P	—	—	—	—	—	—	—	—	—	—	—	—	—	—	—	—	1	—	14	5	2
He 115	—	—	—	—	—	—	—	—	—	—	—	—	—	—	—	—	—	—	1	0	0
Ju 87B	—	—	—	—	—	—	—	—	—	—	—	—	—	—	—	—	—	—	29	2	3
Ju 87R	—	—	—	—	—	—	—	—	—	—	—	—	—	—	—	—	—	—	10	1	0
Ju 88A	1	—	—	6	—	—	2	1	—	1	—	—	5	2	1	—	1	—	39	5	9
JU 88C	—	—	—	—	—	—	—	—	—	—	—	—	—	—	—	—	—	—	6	0	1
Bf 109	1	—	1	—	—	—	—	—	—	—	—	—	12	7	—	7	—	3	63	16	14
Bf 110	1	—	—	—	—	—	—	—	—	—	—	—	2	—	—	7	2	1	64	6	10
TOTALS	5	0	1	13	0	0	2	1	0	3	0	1	24	9	1	15	5	4	281	43	51

CHAPTER 9

IF YOU BOMB US, WE'LL
BOMB YOU!

'RAF aircraft continued their attacks on military objectives in Germany last night. Targets in North-West Germany and the Ruhr were bombed, as well as armament factories in the Berlin area.' With those last two words appearing almost as an afterthought the Air Ministry communiqué of 26 August gave the nation a tonic it needed. Propaganda reply to the bombing of London it may primarily have been, its significance soon transcended that, for it undoubtedly encouraged Hitler to order huge attacks on London, thereby relieving fighter stations from attack. Bomber Command, none too keen to raid the capital, considering there were more worthwhile targets closer at hand, had bowed to political power.

It was 17:00 on 25 August when Operations Orders detailing targets in Berlin reached bomber stations, and when crews attended late briefings few could have much relished the long flight. True, Berlin was packed with worthwhile industrial targets, but reaching them entailed a round trip of over 1,300 miles — about ten hours flying, most of the time over hostile areas and, on this first occasion, during a very cloudy night. Yet they knew that bombing Berlin would bring delight to the suffering British civilians who knew little or nothing of the traumas Bomber Command crews were experiencing. In summer 1940 such ventures as the latest were always questionable excursions.

Accurate weather forecasting was essential for night operations, its accuracy at distant targets conjectural without deep reconnaissance flights. Target photographs, if they existed, were ancient. Lacking navigation aids and target marking items, bombing accuracy depended upon perfect timing, excellent map reading and radio fixes supported by visual and astro navigation — and luck. After bombing and passing through searchlight and flak areas came the tricky task of getting home, sometimes with low fuel state, on a breezy night — in the rain — and having to land on a poorly lit aerodrome with the ever increasing possibility of German intruders present. All quite hazardous.

Whitley and Wellington crews were told on the 25th, 'Your main target is the Siemens & Halske factory in Siemensdadt, producing 85 per cent of the electrical equipment used by the German forces'. Hampden crews were briefed to demolish Berlin's Klingenberg power station, output 200,000 kw. Other objectives for destruction were the Henschel Aircraft Factory (one of whose Hs 126s had fallen foul of Fighter Command), the Bucker training aircraft factory at Rangsdorf, Templehof aerodrome, used by the Nazi mighty, and Tegel's gasworks. By dawn next morning all were still intact.

Finding them even in moonlight and the guidance of Berlin's lakes would have been difficult. When the crews arrived around midnight they discovered cloud 9/10 down to 2,000 feet, lit below by searchlights, which ruined aiming. Heavy flak — luckily inaccurate — had to be faced along with trios of balloons in and above the clouds. Such discouragements to the night tour of Germany were nothing new and had been spasmodically encountered en route.

Ultimate analysis suggested that only one Wellington and two Whitleys had dropped their loads — a total of 25 × 500-lb GPs and 400 × 4-lb incendiaries — on or near Siemens. Two Wellington and six Whitley crews claimed to have bombed their designated factory areas and 14 Hampden crews reckoned to have put 36 × 500-lb and 32 × 250-lb GPs around Klingenberg. Another Hampden attacked the Henschel works, one the Bucker factory, three Templehof, one Tegel, and seven others vaguely bombed Berlin.

Elsewhere five out of eight Wellingtons dispatched were, as instructed, dropping their bombs around Hamm, Schwerte and Cologne marshalling yards, while Whitleys attacked Bremen docks and the Oranienburg Heinkel works. Seven out of 12 Blenheims tried to disrupt night life on aerodromes at St Inglevert, Ploescat, Lisieux, Le Tréport and among searchlight campers at Hardelot. A returning Hampden of 83 Squadron ditched off Grimsby, its crew spending seven hours in their dinghy prior to rescue. Next night 83 Squadron lost another two Hampdens, one of which crashed on the north Norfolk coast, the other in the sea off Lincolnshire.

Neutrals in revealing some of the bombing angered the Nazis, and particularly when Berlin was bombed. 'Unprovoked', 'indiscriminate', 'attacks on women and children' chorused the enemy. 'Unprovoked'?! And how many of these civilian women readily encouraged their regime when it was doing well, willingly aided its war machine? Complex, cynical attitudes to such activities will always remain controversial, but for the British, heavily under attack, the bombing of Germany was a morale booster when it was most needed, and very much a part of the Battle of Britain. 'To ignore Bomber Command's part is like having a Christmas dinner without the pudding', a senior officer once commented. For Hitler, every bomb on German soil was galling, but although the Berlin raids angered him they did not by themselves provoke the impending bombing of London. The capital was to be reduced to chaos just ahead of the invasion.

Bomber Command was dropping mainly 250-lb and 500-lb general purpose high explosive bombs, and 4-lb incendiaries delivered from SBCs (Small Bomb Containers) which shed their contents indiscriminately, because that was the only practicable means of deliv-

Left *Frequently attacked was the Schellinwoulde seaplane station near Amsterdam, where this Dutch-built Fokker T8-W/20 was photographed,* (via G.J. Zwanenburg)

Right *Roundels, according to the Germans, were ideal firing targets. Blenheim IV VE:G of Wattisham's 110 Squadron has been duly peppered.* (IWM)

ery. Unlike the German 1-kg basic cylindrical incendiary the British used a 2-kg bomb of hexagonal section thus shaped to induce it to lodge more easily on buildings. Use was also made of the 25-lb incendiary, relying upon its weight for penetration.

On 1/2 July from Hampden L4070 of 83 Squadron flown by a very handsome Flying Officer G.P. Gibson, later of 'dam buster' fame, fell the first large weapon, a 2,000-lb SAP (Semi-Armour Piercing) bomb dropped on Kiel. Although the four-man Hampden gave the impression of being the poor relation of the Whitley and Wellington and was unsuitable for much development, its weapons bay readily accommodated large sea mines and the lengthy 2,000-pounder. Under each wing a 250-lb GP was at this period sometimes carried. Hampdens outnumbered other medium bomber types in the summer of 1940.

On 18/19 July three Wellingtons of 15 OTU dropped leaflets over the French coast, and on 25/26 July a few Hampdens of 16 OTU similarly operated. The use of crews of training units for such purposes showed a level of desperation emphasized when on 28 July the Air Council decided that operations must now take

precedence over training. Bomber Command ordered on 8 August that each OTU must fly up to eight operational sorties a week.

In a class of their own were the Blenheim IVs of supremely courageous 2 Group. During June 1940 each Blenheim station was ordered to make 24 aircraft available once in three days to carry out cloud-covered attacks on oil targets and marshalling yards in Germany, thereby encouraging daytime German home defence. Other Groups bombed these and aircraft production resources at night.

On 19 June Blenheims began daylight formation raids on airfields in France, supplemented by moon period night raids. As fear of invasion mounted, Bomber Command's Blenheims assisted Coastal Command in observing activity in Channel ports. On 21 June the cloud-cover raiding commenced, Blenheims proceeding only when at least 7/10 cloud-cover offered protection. Although 90 per cent of all such attempts had to be abandoned in July, very courageous deep sorties were flown. That month saw ports and shipping elevated into No. 1 priority targets; but until Channel ports filled with invasion craft, airfields and factories were particularly raided. Steadily, listing widened to

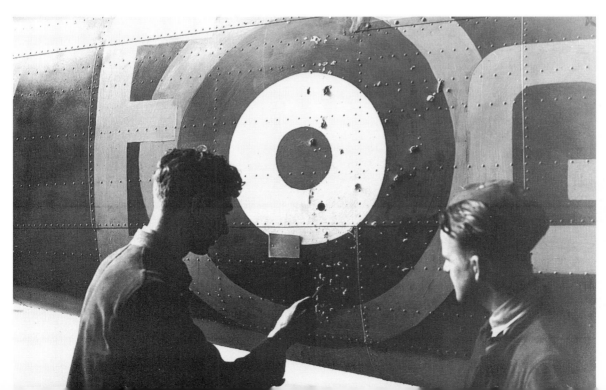

include oil installations, railway centres, canals and power stations.

From early June discussion concerned the employment of Bomber Command in the event of the sailing of an enemy invasion force. About 120 Ansons, Audaxes and Blenheims from training units would have immediately joined 2 Group forces, Bomber Command concentrating upon sinking ships at sea and vessels directly participating in the landings. Troops ashore would be dealt with by other forces. On 30 June a decision was made to keep, from the following night and thereafter nightly, a minimum of three bombers per squadron bombed up with 250-lb/500-lb GP HE bombs in case the enemy launched a surprise invasion force. The move was timely, for on 9 July the first few ships for the invasion reached the Channel ports, their destruction receiving high priority. Blenheim crews were then told to reconnoitre and attack 'Rhine barges' in canals leading to Zwolle, and to strike at coastal shipping.

Fear of seaborne raids mounted from Norway was sufficient for Nos. 21 and 57 Blenheim

Total numbers of aircraft available on bomber squadrons at 18:00 on given dates.

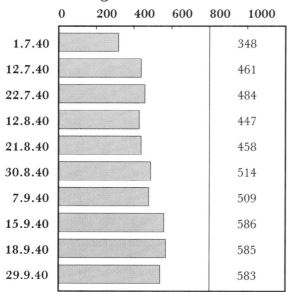

Date	Number
1.7.40	348
12.7.40	461
22.7.40	484
12.8.40	447
21.8.40	458
30.8.40	514
7.9.40	509
15.9.40	586
18.9.40	585
29.9.40	583

squadrons to fly daily sea searches from Lossiemouth. On 9 July, when 12 Blenheims attempted to bomb Stavanger/Sola airfield, flak broke the formation apart and Bf 109s swept in, destroying half the force. Next day No. 107 Squadron, ordered to destroy grounded aircraft near Amiens, barely escaped destruction. Heavy losses, common in 2 Group, prompted more night employment for its Blenheims and on 17/18 July Squadron Leader Webster of XV Squadron made the first night intruder attack on any airfield mounted as such by the RAF when he attacked Caen/Carpiquet. Several night raids on airfields were exceptionally effective.

Although over 400 aerodromes had by August been listed for attack, the Air Staff showed little inclination to concentrate on the task, mainly because insufficient fragmentation bombs were available. Standard GP weapons, they argued, were often wasted on such ventures. Fighter strikes against aircraft massed on French aerodromes would undoubtedly have been effective, but Dowding had none to spare for such hazardous operations. On all except three nights in July and August 1940 Bomber Command's Main Force operated, fielding 100 or more bombers only twice in that period, when the nightly average was 60. On 25/26 July 122 medium bombers — 57 Wellingtons, 24 Whitleys and 41 Hampdens — operated, and typically, for nowhere did they concentrate their effort. Well over 100 crews claimed to have completed effective sorties. July 13/14 was the second busiest night.

Particularly long flights were mostly undertaken by the Whitleys, and included raids on Augsburg (27/28 August), four attacks on Berlin by the end of August and six on Italy. About 30 per cent of the crews dispatched on night raids did not complete their primary tasks, but many of those attempted to find and bomb secondary or alternative targets.

Hampdens additionally undertook two more specialized tasks. In April 1940 they commenced mining enemy shipping lanes. Drops had to be made from between 400 and about

Above *High-flying bomber crews wore thick clothing and thick-lined boots. They flew trussed in thick webbing parachute harnesses, worn by these men of 83 Squadron boldly striding by Hampden OL:D at Scampton.* (IWM)

Below *Hampden P1333 of 49 Squadron, here being loaded at Scampton with 500-lb GPs, joined the squadron in May 1940. The aircraft flew 11 sorties between 1 July and 16 August, when it was missing from a raid on Merseburg. No hard dispersals yet, the aircraft standing on perimeter grass.* (IWM)

800 feet — dangerous activity, for a glassy sea could seem deceptively distant, and mines were laid where enemy shipping and flakships were present. The Hampdens each carried one sea mine and often a few 250-lb GP bombs to deal with annoying defenders or coastal aerodromes. Both these types of target were also the prime objects of interest to the 'Special Reconnaissance' Hampden force which gave support to the minelayers and also sought enemy minelayers at their bases.

The most spectacular of the night raids was executed on 12/13 August. Five Hampden crews drawn from Scampton's 49 and 83 Squadrons attacked the Ladbergen aqueduct on the Dortmund Ems Canal, which called for very accurate bombing. That in turn meant low flying and the use of special M bombs. Two of the

Left *Flight Lieutenant Roderick Learoyd, awarded the Victoria Cross for his gallantry when he made a low-level attack on the Dortmund-Ems Canal on 12 August.* (IWM)

Below *Blenheim IVs of 82 Squadron along Watton's apron. Some have under-nose gun cupolas. UX-K, N and O are visible; nearest is UX:A P6915, which was shot down on 7 June 1940 after seven sorties. Others survived longer.* (RAF Museum)

Aalborg photographed during 82 Squadron's tragic raid in August 1940.

first four Hampdens to attack were shot down, the others seriously damaged. Then came Flight Lieutenant R.A.B. Learoyd flying hazardously in fifth place. He dived through searchlight beams and flak to score a very near miss, then nursed P4403 home, where he circled until day light before landing. His courage, and indeed that of all who bravely operated that night, was marked by his being awarded the Victoria Cross. The raid blocked the notorious canal for ten days, delaying the progress of barges sailing from inland waterways to the Channel ports, and was claimed to have forced back the projected invasion date by several days.

One of Bomber Command's heaviest one-raid losses was then but hours away. A dozen Blenheims of 82 Squadron led by Wing Commander E.C. Lart set off from Watton in brilliant weather for Aalborg airfield in Denmark. Nearing the enemy coast a pilot broke radio silence claiming his fuel state to be low and signalling that he was turning back. That message denied the raid any element of surprise, alerting gunners and fighters of 6/JG 77. All held their fire until the Blenheims were near Aalborg. Then they massacred them all.

CHAPTER 10

NEARING THE CLIMAX

Although it had no immediate effect upon the campaign, the bombing of Berlin certainly annoyed the enemy. Throughout the last week of August, with increasing intensity, the Luftwaffe attempted deeper daylight penetrations and frequently used the Thames as a line of approach. Fighters of 11 Group therefore mainly operated from their inland stations. Heavy raids had in any case rendered Manston and Hawkinge barely tenable.

Night raids continued unabated, 25/26 August seeing factories on Croydon's Whaddon Estate hit, railway shops and Dorman Long steel works at Stockton-on-Tees bombed and three Cottesmore Hampdens damaged. At Birmingham the Electric Furnace Co., British Timken and the Birdlee Works at Erdington were hit.

Then came early reconnaissances between Harwich and Land's End on 26 August preceding three major operations. The first, embrac-

ing five distinct raids over Kent, commenced at 11:37 with intrusions by around 50 bombers and 80 fighters, some of which strafed east Kent targets. Some 40 11 Group Hurricanes and 30 Spitfires rose to protect their bases, a battle ensuing between Canterbury and Maidstone. He 111s which bombed Folkestone damaged the railway and a laundry, killed two and injured 22. Seven No. 616 Squadron Spitfires which arrived too late to prevent that ran into a host of Bf 109s. Five more Spitfires soon joined them, but against so many German fighters there was little the few could do. The Yorkshire squadron, which lost seven aircraft, had two pilots killed and four injured.

Dornier Do 17Zs of KG 77 (which converted to Ju 88s during the Battle) were responsible for some of the earliest 1940 reconnaissance flights over eastern England. The nearest example being primitively refuelled stands by 3Z+CM, right. (IWM)

Much had been expected, by both sides, from the Messersch-mitt Bf 110 long-range fighter. Instead, it proved a disappointment. (Bundesarchiv)

Warned of an intended attack on its base, Hornchurch, 264 Squadron[142] hastened away to engage KG 3s Do 17s over Herne Bay. Although the Defiants assembled in their specified battle formation for bomber interception they were no match for the Bf 109s which roared in to destroy three. No. 264 Squadron claimed six Do 17s and a fighter. The bitter struggle reduced the Bf 109s fuel state, forcing them home and making it unwise for the unprotected Dorniers to proceed, and the bomber crews jettisoned their loads, particularly over Swale Rural District. As the defenders were landing, more Bf 109s arrived seeking easy kills and Dover's balloons.

A number of lone 'pirates' penetrated deeply during the day, one placing four HEs on Harwell, killing six and injuring ten, and damaging buildings and two Wellingtons. Whitleys which later landed at Harwell to refuel for a long flight to Fiat Torino seem to have been a possible target.

Shortly after 13:00 eight raids, the second major operation, developed. Assembled near Lille, its two bomber formations comprised 78 Do 17s of II/KG 2 and III/KG 3 escorted by Bf 110s of ZG 26 and ZG 76 and Bf 109s. Intel-ligence sources had already discovered their targets to be Debden, North Weald and Hornchurch so it was not surprising to the well informed when, over the mouth of the River Crouch, half the bombers turned west. Seven 11 Group squadrons scrambled just in case a London raid developed and thwarted the attack by engaging escorting '109s which quickly became short of fuel. Once again, bombs fell widely over Kent, including 32 on Broadstairs and more on Manston.

Other Dorniers (believed now to number 39) escorted by long-range tanked Bf 110s, continued to the River Blackwater estuary, there turning towards Debden. Colchester's AA guns caused several Dorniers to turn away. Two 11 Group squadrons unable to break through to the bombers included No. 1 Squadron. RCAF, operational since 17 August and now participating in its first combat. By reckoning to destroy six Dorniers near Braintree, the Canadians were over optimistic, their true successes probably being two Bf 110s and one Do 17. A second

Left *The British made consider-able use of the Swedish 40-mm Bofors gun. Fast firing and mobile it was ideal for defence of KPs and VPs (key and vulnerable points).* (IWM)

Below right *Life jackets on, briefcase and maps ready, a He 111 crew awaits the action call.* (IWM)

Dornier which fell at Whepstead, Suffolk, may have been theirs although the situation was soon so confusing that certainty is not possible. The Canadians very usefully drove the Bf 110s away from the bombers and harried them.

Debden, an 11 Group station and the most northerly yet raided in daylight, was close to the 12 Group boundary so Park urgently asked Leigh Mallory for assistance. It arrived too late to prevent Debden — its protection in the hands of the local Bofors gunners — from being bombed at 15:20. Site M3 scored a direct hit on a Do 17, 160 bombs rained over the area, and a score of Bf 110s raced low across the aerodrome before No. 310 (Czech) Squadron[143], scrambled from 12 Group's Duxford, tackled

the retreating raiders near Little Hallenbury. Many bombs had been jettisoned over a wide area. The operation by this time was chaotic, with some Czechs fighting lone battles. Sergeant Pilot Prchal who chased a Dornier out to sea had the wing nearly blown off his Hurricane by cannon fire from a Bf 109 before he baled out near Upminster. Squadron Leader G.D.M. Blackwood, the leader, was shot down and Pilot Officer Bergman baled out near Southminster only to land a few yards from his blazing Hurricane.

Some idea of the day's events can be gleaned from the intelligence summary prepared late on 26 August at HQ Fighter Command, and reproduced below.

No. of aircraft	Squadron	Time up/down	Combat area	Losses	Claims
12	615	14:45-15:45	Thames Estuary	3 FTR	4 x BF 109 damaged
12	85	14:45-15:56	Thames Estuary	1 FTR	3 x Do 17 claimed 1 probable '109
11	1 RCAF	14:45-17:00	Essex-Eastchurch	1 FTR	2 x Do 17 destroyed 2 x Do 17 damaged
9	111	15:00-15:50	off Clacton	1 FTR	1 x Do 17 destroyed 1 x BF 109 destroyed
12	56	15:02-?	Colchester	—	2 x BF 110, and 1 probable
12	310	15:30-?	E. of North Weald	3 FTR	1 x Do 17, 1 x BF 110

Debden had suffered considerable damage including hits on a hangar, the NAAFI, MT Section and one Hurricane burnt out. At 15:40 an estimated 250 enemy aircraft were operating between Bury St Edmunds and Dungeness. In a costly afternoon No. 1 RCAF Squadron had lost its leader, Squadron Leader N.E. McNab.

The third operation, directed against Portsmouth and Southampton, and which materialized in the late afternoon, was the final large-scale day raid mounted by Luftflotte 3. It consisted of about 50 He 111s of I and II/KG 55 escorted by Bf 109s and 110s. Of eight fighter squadrons ordered to engage, Nos. 43[144], 602[145], and 234 Squadrons[146] went into action, preventing the bombing of Southampton and shooting down four He 111s and four Bf 109s, for the loss of four fighters and three pilots wounded. Bombs released at 16:00, partly through cloud, fell on the outskirts of Portsmouth, in Langstone Harbour, demolished Fort Cumberland, caused a small fire at Hilsea gas works and fell well short of the dockyard target. Later, an escorted rescue He 59 was shot down south of the Isle of Wight.

By the end of the day Fighter Command had lost 31 aircraft and 16 pilots — heavy losses indeed. The enemy lost 41 aircraft, 19 of them bombers. Further indicative of the trend, KG 55 was switched to night raids, the extent of which was again considerable on 26/27 August. About 200 German aircraft operated, mainly singly, to bomb Greater London's Tottenham, Wood Green, Wormwood Scrubs and Southgate, where there was major damage. Also hit were Dartford, Tilbury, Bournemouth, Coventry, Middlesbrough, Newcastle, RAF North Coates (one of six airfields attacked) and the Plymouth area, where over 50 HEs fell and damaged Millbay Dock. Birmingham suffered the most damage when between 21:25 and 03:00 a score of He 111s attacked industrial targets, including the Castle Bromwich Spitfire factory, which was little damaged; not so Small Heath goods and timber yard, where a large fire was started. Bordesley Junction GWR station was badly damaged, and fierce fires gutted George Jones foundry in Lionel Street. Other incidents involved Dunlop, Humber, Daimler and Smith's Stamping Works. Over 60 fires in all were caused, and one consumed the Old City Market Hall. Low cloud handicapped both searchlights and gunners. In the 24 hours to dawn on the 27th 37 civilians had been killed, 102 injured.

On 27 August early drizzle and low cloud over southern England were soon replaced by clear, warm weather. Six reconnaissance flights overflew the Portsmouth-Southampton areas;

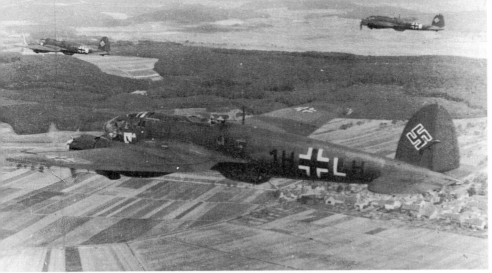

A trio of He 111s of KG 26, a unit which frequently raided the north of Britain. 1H+GH is leading, 1H+LH nearest and possibly 1H+BP furthest away. They wear typical zig zag camouflage patterning although I can vouch for He 111s being dark green overall on upper surfaces. (Bundesarchiv)

Impressive formation of He 111s reputedly heading for London and engagement by fighters. (IWM)

small formations operated over Kent and single aircraft with little success attacked airfields, among them Edzell, Montrose, Gravesend, Cranfield, Biggin Hill, Cottesmore, Kirton-in-Lindsey and Catfoss as well as RAF Bentley Priory. Two squadrons which had borne much of the fighting, Nos. 32 and 65, were about to be withdrawn for rest.

When such changes were made they often involved the use of air transport for ground crews. Suitable aircraft being in very short supply, the RAF made use of a handful of converted pre-war Handley Page Harrow bombers operated from mid-placed Doncaster by 271 Squa-dron. They were supported by a few Bristol Bombays, several impressed HP 42 air liners and, most exotic of all, a Ford Tri-Motor whose service life was brief. The Harrows were busy most days shifting men and materials and played a very useful part in the Battle without, apparently, ever being set upon by enemy fighters. Harrows were not the only pre-war bombers still flying; it was at this time that the remaining Heyfords serving as trainers were retired. Indeed, I caught my last glimpse of one of these aircraft during the Red Alert at Cambridge while Debden was being bombed on 26 August.

Fighter squadrons' movements 1 July-31 October 1940

Throughout the campaign RAF fighter squadrons were moved for tactical reasons or to rest them from front line action. These movements occurred:

Sqn. No.	Base on/from 1 July 1940	Movement/date
1	Tangmere	Northolt 1 August, Wittering 9 September
3	Wick	Castletown 2 September, Turnhouse 14 September, Dyce 9 October, Castletown 12 October
19	Fowlmere	Duxford 3 July, Fowlmere 24 July, Duxford 30 October
25	Martlesham	North Weald 1 September, Debden 8 October
29	Digby	Wellingore 8 July
32	Biggin Hill	Acklington 28 August
41	Catterick	Hornchurch 26 July, Catterick 8 August, Hornchurch 3 September
43	Tangmere	(Northolt detached 23 July-1 August, Usworth 8 September
46	Digby	Stapleford Tawney 1 September
54	Rochford	Hornchurch 24 July, Catterick 28 July, Hornchurch 8 August, Catterick 3 September
56	North Weald	Boscombe Down 1 September
64	Kenley	Leconfield 19 August, Biggin Hill 13 October, Coltishall 15 October
65	Hornchurch	Turnhouse 28 August
66	Coltishall	Kenley 3 September, Gravesend 11 September, West Malling 30 October
72	Acklington	Biggin Hill 31 August, Croydon 1 September, Biggin Hill 14 September, Coltishall 13 October, Matlask 30 October
73	Church Fenton	Castle Camps 5 September
74	Hornchurch	Wittering 14 August, Kirton-in-Lindsey 21 August, Coltishall 9 September, Biggin Hill 15 October
79	Hawkinge	Acklington 11 July via Sealand, Biggin Hill 27 August, Pembrey 8 September
85	Debden	Croydon 19 August, Castle Camps 3 September, Church Fenton 5 September, Kirton-in-Lindsey 23 October
87	Church Fenton	Exeter 5 July
92	Pembrey	Biggin Hill 8 September
111	Croydon	Debden 19 August, Croydon 3 September, Drem 8 September, Dyce 12 October
141	Turnhouse	West Malling 12 July, Prestwick 21 July, Turnhouse 30 August (Biggin Hill detached 13 September-22 October), Drem 15 October
145	Tangmere	Westhampnett 31 July, Drem 14 August, Dyce 31 August, Tangmere 9 October
151	North Weald	Stapleford Tawney 29 August, Digby 1 September
152	Acklington	Warmwell 12 July
213	Exeter	Tangmere 7 September
219	Catterick	Redhill 12 October
222	Kirton-in-Lindsey	Hornchurch 29 August
234	St Eval	Middle Wallop 13 August, St Eval 11 September

Sqn. No.	Base on/from 1 July 1940	Movement/date
236	Middle Wallop	Using Thorney Island as advanced base, where squadron consolidated on 4 July on leaving Fighter Command
238	Middle Wallop	St Eval 14 August, Middle Wallop 10 September, Chilbolton 30 September
242	Coltishall	Duxford 26 October
245	Turnhouse	Aldergrove 20 July
247		Roborough — not formed until 1 August
249	Leconfield	Church Fenton 8 July, Boscombe Down 14 August, North Weald 1 September
253	Kirton-in-Lindsey	Turnhouse 21 July, Prestwick 23 August, Kenley 29 August
257	Hendon	Northolt 4 July, Debden 15 August, Martlesham 5 September, North Weald 8 October
263	Grangemouth	Drem 2 September for work up on Whirlwind
264	Duxford	Kirton-in-Lindsey 23 July, Hornchurch 22 August, Rochford 27 August, Kirton-in-Lindsey 28 August, Rochford 29 October
266	Wittering	Tangmere 9 August, Eastchurch 12 August, Hornchurch 14 August, Wittering 21 August
302		Leconfield — formed 13 July, Northolt 11 October
303		Northolt — formed 2 August, Leconfield 11 October
306		Church Fenton — formed 28 August, became operational 8 September
307		Kirton-in-Lindsey — formed 5 September
310		Duxford — formed 10 July, operational 18 August
501	Croydon	Middle Wallop 4 July, Gravesend 25 July, Kenley 10 September
504	Castletown	Catterick 1 September, Hendon 5 September, Exeter 26 September
600	Manston	Hornchurch 22 August, Redhill 12 September, Catterick 12 October
601	Tangmere	Debden 19 August, Tangmere 2 September, Exeter 7 September
602	Drem	Westhampnett 13 August
603	Turnhouse	Hornchurch 27 August
604	Manston	Gravesend 3 July, Middle Wallop 26 July
605	Drem	Croydon 7 September
607	Usworth	Tangmere 1 September, Turnhouse 10 October
609	Northolt	Middle Wallop 5 July
610	Gravesend	Biggin Hill 2 July, Acklington 13 September
611	Digby	
615	Kenley	Prestwick 29 August, Northolt 10 October
616	Leconfield	Kenley 19 August. Coltishall 3 September, Kirton-in-Lindsey 9 September

Across the Channel, the switch of Luftflotte 3 to mainly night operations released fighters for Luftflotte 2, but Dowding still resisted the temptation to bring more squadrons into 11 Group for fear of that permitting attacks in other Group areas. Instead, he decided to rotate six squadrons. From 24 August about a third of 11 Group squadrons were manned by inexperienced pilots, many but recently trained at OTUs. That may have accounted for increased losses and fewer successes, although additional enemy fighters were now operating over the south-east. Dowding's only alternative would have been to keep experienced pilots in 11 Group until they were exhausted.

Large bomber formations splitting to attack several targets were presenting difficult tasks for the defenders, for precise positions of enemy groups, once scattered, were hard to locate however much the Observer Corps tried. Fighter squadron leaders were therefore told to give their positions upon entering combat so that reinforcement could readily be sent. As soon as it was realized that Luftflotte 3 had halted large-scale day raids and passed its fighters to Luftflotte 2, both Nos. 10 and 12 Groups could be used to reinforce No. 11 Group. Nos. 10 and 12 Groups were also steadily switched to night fighting.

...this loyal and public-spirited body of men [the Observer Corps] had maintained their watch with admirable efficiency since the beginning of the war... at this time they constituted the sole means of tracking enemy raids once they had crossed the coastline. The country was divided into about 130 'Warning Districts' the boundaries of which were determined by the layout of the public telephone system.

Air Chief Marshal Sir Hugh Dowding,
Commander-in-Chief Fighter Command

Birmingham was again bombed on the 27/28, a water main to the Castle Bromwich Spitfire factory being shattered and fires started at BSA Tools, Mongomery Street, around which area 46 HEs fell. In the early hours of

28 August Gillingham, Kent, received its third attack within a few hours when it was dive-bombed — a very frightening experience at night — and again probably in error for another Medway target. Hundreds of incendiaries were released, 20 houses were damaged, 16 fires caused and 16 people killed in a sombre overture to another day's tough fighting.

Reconnaissance flights including three along the south-east coast at dawn preceded a large build-up of forces over France. He 111s and Do 17s escorted by Bf 109s of I and III/JG 51 proceeding north near Sandwich and preceded by fighter sweeps were met by squadrons of Hurricanes including Nos. 501[147] and 615[148], along with a dozen 264 Squadron Defiants[149]. They were unable to prevent the Dorniers of I/KG 3 from reaching Eastchurch and He 111s of II and III/KG 53 from raiding Rochford. The enemy fighters engaged Defiants trying to deal with the He 111s, No. 264 Squadron destroying a Heinkel, and the leader's gunner damaging another before his Defiant (L7021) was shot down. Two more Defiants (L7026 and N1574) were destroyed, N1569 forced-landed and out of eight that returned to Hornchurch five were damaged. Some 15 Heinkels broke through to Rochford — despite the ferocity of its AA defences — and cratered its turf with 15 tons of bombs. The 18 Dorniers by dropping 44 HEs from 15,000 feet seriously damaged Eastchurch, where two Battles were destroyed and another pair damaged. Eight RAF fighters and six pilots were lost, and five enemy aircraft brought down.

Rochford was attacked again at 12:40 by Raid 13H which headed in from the south-east and left some buildings damaged. Carried out by 27 Do 17s of II and III/KG 3 attacking from 18,000 feet, it was delivered just too late to prevent 264 Squadron[150] yet again managing to get away just before bombs began bursting on their flying field. Spitfires of 54 Squadron[151] positioned at 30,000 feet dived upon the escort, Flight Lieutenant Deere claiming a Bf 109, Flight Lieutenant George Gribble another at the end of an 11-aircraft line, and Squadron

Leader Leathart a Dornier. In a quite astonishing chase of a Bf 109 Gribble (R6899) and Norwell (R6898) ended the fight so low that Gribble's shooting killed a cow. After landing he discovered pieces of a tree lodged in his Spitfire. Deere (R6832) was less fortunate; he had to bale out. As the raiders were approaching Rochford, Hurricanes of No. 1 Squadron[152] downed a Do 17 of 6/KG 3 on Rochford aerodrome, its crew becoming PoWs.

Afternoon fighting exposed a disturbing feature, the success of a Bf 109 and 110 seven-element excursion over Kent. Fighters from seven squadrons responded in case bombers were included, which led to a wasting high-level battle observed by Mr Churchill viewing coastal defences at Dover. At between 25,000 and 30,000 feet over the Canterbury-Dungeness-Margate area a fierce battle developed exclusively between fighters, with 11 Hurricanes of Squadron Leader Peter Townsend's 85 Squadron opening for the defence. Attacking 20 Bf 109s out of the sun over Dungeness Flying Officer Woods-Scawen (P3150) shot down one, and another fell in the sea two-thirds of a mile off Folkestone and to the great satisfaction of Mr Churchill. Eight Bf 109s of JG 51 and JG 53 are thought to have been variously destroyed during this phase, one of I/JG 53 crashing on land at a site visited by the Prime Minister. Nos. 56[154] and 151 Squadrons each lost two Hurricanes, and 54 Squadron[155] Spitfire X4053 flown by Squadron Leader Donald Finlay, who baled out and was injured. By the end of the day 16 British fighters had been destroyed, the same as the number of Bf 109s believed lost by five Geschwaderen. Dowding expressed his feelings very strongly over precious fighters being committed to pointless fighter-versus-fighter engagements, issuing clear orders that such activity must not be repeated.

Night operations spearheaded by beam-riding He 111s of KGr 100 were certainly increasing. On the 28/29 the first major attack directed at one target was mounted, 150 crews being briefed to bomb Merseyside. Although pathfinders led the main force in from Selsey

to Liverpool and Sealand, and some houses were destroyed and fires started in Liverpool, the bombing went so badly astray that the recipients were convinced that, despite intelligence indications, the Midlands and the London area were instead main targets. London, under Red Alert for 7 hours, the longest yet, reported incidents in many suburbs, the most damaging being at Cricklewood, at Enfield, where a gas main was ruptured, and Lambeth. Bombing was also recorded at Birmingham, Bournemouth, Derby, Manchester and Sheffield. At Avonmouth the Shell Mex installations and the National Smelting Co. works were hit, and in Coventry 13 houses and shops were damaged and 11 fires started. At Altringham a 50,000-gallon oil tank at the Anglo-American oil depot caught fire, incendiaries being suspected. Despite the extent of enemy activities, patrolling night fighters had only one glimpse of the foe.

Concentration on night raids may well have reduced the daylight effort on 29 August, for it was mid-afternoon before, in clear conditions and using Do 17s and He 111s as bait, a small Channel sweep was flown between Beachy Head and Hastings, as high overhead Bf 109s and Bf 110s waited to pounce. No. 85 Squadron[156] patrolling Hawkinge nibbled — claimed two Bf 109s and lost two Hurricanes. Sergeant Walker's was hit by cannon fire which deprived him of throttle and rudder control and forced him down at Hawkhurst. Sergeant Ellis, his Hurricane hit in the engine, cockpit and soon blazing, crashed a hundred yards offshore 12 miles west of Battle after he had baled out. By then Nos. 603[157] and 610[158] Squadrons were on hand, 610 sweeping into action over Mayfield carrying a cautionary warning from Command. A Bf 110 was destroyed and several Dorniers damaged, but Sergeant Manton was shot down. Pevensey guns claimed a Bf 109. About 170 tempting enemy aircraft are thought to have swept inland towards Biggin Hill during the afternoon, which earlier included a small attack on Warmwell and at 15:58 one on Tresco Radio, Scilly Isles.

Around 18:00 a 20-aircraft provocation flight to the Rochester area ended with Hurricanes of 501 Squadron battling over Hawkinge with Bf 109s and losing two of their number. Other Bf 109s, some of which strafed gunsites at Dover, tangled with Nos. 85[159], 603[160] and 610[161] Squadrons. During a day which had seen only two bombing raids aimed at the Kent coast seven Bf 109s had been shot down and nine RAF fighters lost.

At dusk single-bomber sorties struck at Debden, Duxford and other East Anglian aerodromes before the Luftwaffe arrived in strength, about 200 raiders heading for Merseyside, target for four-fifths of the force. From a cloudless sky they released incendiaries intended for warehouses packed with food, but of an intended 130 tons of HE they managed to deliver

Photographed on 25 July wearing unusual markings, Hurricane P2923:VY-R joined 85 Squadron on 11 June 1940, and was last seen — whilst being flown by Flying Officer R.H.A. Lee on 18 August — engaging Bf 109s 30 miles out from Foulness. Credited with 110 hours 20 minutes flying. (IWM)

only 50 tons to Merseyside. Rootes factory and Speke industrial estate were hit, but most effected were domestic property and public utilities. Bombs also fell on Manchester, the Midlands, South Wales, Carlisle, Tees and Tyne region and Scotland. Little wonder the British were once more doubting that Merseyside really was the target, particularly since many raiders had concentrated over Portsmouth. There was no doubt by dawn that night bombing was increasing.

Some doubts on that score might have been entertained on 30 August when a period of hot, excellent weather arrived, morning cloud at 7,000 feet over Kent putting the Observer Corps at a disadvantage. With signs of invasion preparations under way across the Channel the Bat-

tle was undoubtedly proceeding towards a climax. By nightfall the day had seen the greatest number of sorties so far flown on one day, the biggest enemy effort since the middle of August — 36 enemy destroyed and 26 RAF fighters lost.

Leading the assault, 100-plus aircraft arrived in the Deal-Dungeness area at 07:06, Do 17s escorted by Bf 110s of ZG 76 and heading for a convoy sailing from the Thames for Methil. Then at 10:30 the first element of phase one of a three-part operation revealed itself as three Gruppen of Bf 109s coming in over the Kent coast to pave the way for 40 He 111s, 30 Do 17s and another 90 fighters. No. 151 Squadron[162] engaged the Heinkels, claiming three for the loss of two Hurricanes before 85[163] Squadron made head-on attacks, widely splitting the bomber formation. Two escorting Bf 110s were then shot down, and another Hurricane lost. Scattered groups of bombers produced another confusing and dangerous situation, prompting Park to order part of 253 Squadron (new to the campaign and patrolling over Maidstone) to guard Kenley, whose fighters were scrambled. At about this time a small, hitherto undetected, formation of Ju 88s over Biggin Hill at 18,000 feet unloaded their wares, most of which luckily fell wide. They were able to bomb mainly because Biggin's guard sent to patrol over Maidstone believed their base to be in 12 Group's care. Upon retiring, the three formations, each of nine Ju 88s with 30 fighters providing top cover, were met by No. 253 Squadron[164] vectored from Kenley, for that station had not come under the expected attack. 'B' Flight set about the bombers and soon had the help of 43 Squadron near Brighton. Other newcomers soon in action were Spitfires of 222 Squadron[165] whose 'B' Flight north-west of Dover contacted '109s. Destruction of six enemy aircraft during the operation cost Fighter Command ten aircraft and five pilots.

The pressure was building, and before the squadrons completed their turn-rounds Kesselring dispatched small groups of bombers protected by many fighters and crossing the Kent coast from 13:00 at around 15,000 feet at 20-minute intervals, and largely unplotted because power supplies to radar stations had been cut during morning raids. For over two hours the enemy roamed over south-east England. Five fighter squadrons responded, among them 222 Squadron, which was to operate three times during the day, have eight of its Spitfires put out of use, lose five, have a pilot killed and two injured. Twelve of 222 Squadron's Spitfires on patrol at 16,000 feet over Lympne sighted 15 escorted He 111s near Canterbury and as they attacked were set upon by the Messerschmitts. They claimed a Bf 110 damaged but Pilot Officer Asheton was forced to land on the obstructed Bekesbourne airfield, Sergeant Baxter had to put down at Eastchurch and Pilot

Officer Carpenter baled out of P9378 near Rochford.

Early in the afternoon another squadron strode boldly into the main arena. Since the start of the Battle 12 Group's Coltishall-based 242 Squadron, led by Squadron Leader Douglas Bader, had been flying convoy patrols off the East Anglian coast and seen little fighting. Around midday of 30 August 242 Squadron was ordered to Duxford, from where 14 Hurricanes[166] set off to police the North Weald area, and led by Douglas Bader (P3061) they tackled Raid X33, a diamond formation of KG 1s He 111s which had already braved 54 rounds of heavy AA fire, and shot down two. Before returning to Coltishall that evening '242' operated on two occasions.

By 16:00 a huge force of enemy aircraft, probably over 300, was crossing the Kent coast, some heading for distant inland targets. Thirteen squadron were scrambled to deal with them. Over Kent and the Thames Estuary proceeded over the ensuing two hours a mighty array drawn from 19 Gruppen, which split into smaller groups heading for Hawker's at Slough, the Hurricane and Spitfire repair centres at Oxford, for Luton and three vital airfields — North Weald, Kenley and Biggin Hill. One small formation, intercepted by only one squadron, managed to put Detling out of use for 15 hours. The biggest, potentially most damaging operation so far, had to be ferociously dealt with using as many aircraft as possible.

The first bombing incidents came at Lambeth. Soon after, a group of fewer than ten Ju 88s made low and fast for Sheppey, suddenly veered south, then delivered a devastating 15-ton blow on Biggin Hill smashing a hangar, the workshops, armoury, barrack blocks, MT Section, WAAF quarters, killing 39 and injuring 26. Too late, six Hurricanes of the recently arrived 79 Squadron chased after the '88s claiming two of them. By then other raids were well inland, that directed at Oxford being intercepted and forced back over Surrey.

It was around 16:10 that 20 He 111s of II/KG 1 escorted by Bf 110s flew across Southend and

Biggin Hill, under attack from high flying Ju 88s, despite the attempt to camouflage its surface with painted hedgerows. Bombs are bursting mainly among buildings. (Bundesarchiv)

then North Weald bound for Luton's industrial area. Despite spirited efforts by Hurricanes of 1, 56, 242 and 501 Squadrons — Nos. 1 and 56 each destroying a Heinkel — the raiders reached Luton, where at 16:40 they carried out five minutes of bombing during which 207 HEs fell, many on Vauxhall Motors factory. No public warning had sounded and horrific scenes followed the destruction of the factory's main internal stairway. Casualties totalled 59 killed and 141 injured. Over 60 bombs fell very wide of the target, 18 of them in Whipsnade Zoo.

During daylight 1,054 sorties had been flown by the 22 fighter squadrons involved. In some cases they had seen action as many as four times, a rate not long sustainable. Nine Hurricanes and eleven Spitfires had been destroyed and the enemy had lost eight bombers and fourteen fighters.

Throughout the hours of darkness Fighter Command licked and tried hard to heal its wounds. The Luftwaffe was preparing to worsen them — and soon — with an even larger effort in the most crucial week which saw heavy onslaughts on Sector Stations vital to the defence of London. Losses over the period were to prove about equal, Fighter Command losing 161 aircraft between 31 August and 6 September and the Luftwaffe 189, of which 154 were shot down. The brunt of the battle was to be borne by a score of 11 Group squadrons and 400 pilots, for Dowding still refused to reduce 10 and 12 Groups, making it imperative that Park's squadrons avoided wasted effort. Larger formations, attractive in principle, wasted precious moments assembling, but Park on 2 September, gave instructions for squadrons to commence operating in pairs, and when practicable to formate on other couples. Like

Castle Camps, Debden's spartan satellite, complete with painted hedgerows, photographed on 31 August by a passing Dornier. (via P.H.T. Green)

Dowding, he stressed the advisability of this only when targets were well inland. With Manston lost, and Biggin Hill and Kenley seriously damaged, the need to protect other main fighter stations was now the paramount one.

I must disclaim any exact accuracy in the estimates of enemy losses. All that I can say is that the utmost care was taken to arrive at the closest possible approximation. Special intelligence officers examined pilots individually after their combats, and the figures claimed are those recorded as 'certain'.
Air Chief Marshal Sir Hugh Dowding,
Commander-in-Chief Fighter Command

At 08:05 on Saturday 31 August the first of the day's four huge onslaughts began crossing the Kent coast. Within the four-wave array flying at between 15,000 and 20,000 feet were formations soon swinging in over the Thames Estuary, and Park ordered ten squadrons to intercept.

One raid heading north crossed into Essex, there to divide. Protecting its western flank were long-range tanked Bf 110s which Hurricanes of 257 Squadron[167] led by Flight Lieutenant Beresford (P3705) tackled soon after they crossed the coast south of Clacton and formed a defensive circle. Pilot Officer Henderson claimed two before his aircraft was shot down in flames and he was plucked from the water by the Navy, along with a German airman. Pilot Officer Gundry (P3704) chased a Bf 110 as far as Deal and then facing a huge enemy force decided to turn back, and Pilot Officer Moffat was shot down and killed. Near Colchester it was the turn of 56 Squadron[168] to engage, the squadron losing a pilot killed and four Hurricanes while attempting in vain to force back the invaders, Dorniers of KG 2 mainly heading for Debden. Nine Hurricanes of No. 1 Squad-

ron[169] next tackled the Bf 110s near Chelmsford, claiming one for the loss of two aircraft. No. 111 Squadron also in the battle destroyed a Dornier and a Bf 110 but lost yet another Hurricane — V7375, flown by Sergeant H.J. Merchant.

The bombing of Debden caused 18 casualties, the hundred 250-kg bombs damaging 14 Hurricanes on the airfield. As the raiders turned for home, the remainder of KG 2 headed for 12 Group's Duxford, whose AA defences very effectively forced the raid off track. Soon after 08:30 they jettisoned their load in one enormous salvo, about 215 HEs, which exploded almost simultaneously in a narrow line across open country between Fowlmere and Shepreth villages and sent an earthquake-like shudder miles around. Cannon-armed Spitfires of 19 Squadron[170] scrambled at the last minute from Fowlmere were vectored on to the retreating bombers, but had little success in preventing them from getting home. They were, however, credited with two Bf 110s shot down as the escort was rejoining its charge.

While that engagement took place other Dorniers were again battering Eastchurch and Bf 109s and 110s strafing other airfields, Detling among them. Strange, the persistent preoccupation afforded Eastchurch. More purposeful the activity over Kent by rear support and diversionary Bf 109s some of which at 08:45 shot down no less than 23 of Dover's balloons. At 09:40 a high-flying reconnoitring Dornier overflew Debden and Duxford and left via Bircham Newton, by which time a second major intrusion over Kent and the Thames Estuary was about to begin.

Shortly after noon the large operation unfolded, raiders approaching along two corridors over Dungeness heading for Croydon or Biggin Hill and opposed by 13 RAF squadrons. The former aerodrome came under attack at 12:55, Do 17s placing bombs along one edge and upon a hangar as a dozen Hurricanes of 85 Squadron[171] took off to deal with them. Launching their attack over Tunbridge they were soon in the sights of Bf 109s which shot down Squadron Leader Townsend's VY-Q:P3166 and Pilot Officer P.A. Worrall's Hurricane V6581 in exchange for which 85 Squadron claimed two Bf 109s and a '110.

Close by, two Staffeln of He 111s were running in at 12,000 feet to deal Biggin Hill another mighty blow, blasting its two remaining hangars, messes and quarters and setting fire to its operations block. Most of the station's aircraft had now to be withdrawn to adjacent Sectors. No. 253 Squadron[172] managed to punish decisively one Heinkel, but another casualty was well-known 253's Squadron Leader Tom Gleave (P3115), who was wounded and shot down by a Bf 109.

And still there was more blasting to come, from a portion of the II/KG 3 Dornier force which broke through to Hornchurch where Spitfires of 54 Squadron were taking off as the bombs fell. Flight Lieutenant Deere (R6895) and Sergeant J. Davis (X4235) had amazing escapes, their aircraft being written off, and Pilot Officer E.F. Edsall's Spitfire (X4236) faired little better. AA gunners claimed one of the three Do 17s shot down generally credited to 151 Squadron[173] and 310 Czech Squadron[174], and which at 13:25 fell near Canewdon. Reconnaissance aircraft once more began seeking evidence of raid effectiveness, a spying Do 17 being destroyed 20 miles off Bawdsey.

Afternoon activity included fighter-bombing Erpro 210 attacks on several radar stations in Kent and Sussex, but insufficiently effective to prevent them operating. Later the same unit and a few hand-picked Ju 88 crews made small-scale attacks on Hornchurch and Biggin Hill.

Then between 17:30 and 19:15 came another giant blow. Over 300 enemy aircraft mounted six raids against airfields in Kent and near London, opposed this time by 20 squadrons. In ferocious fighting around Hornchurch Spitfires of 54[175] and 603[176] Squadrons claimed two Bf 109s and lost three of their number. Medway guns too made claims before, to round off their daylight adventures, four Bf 109s again assaulted Dover's balloons, disposing of another 15. Defending gunners insisted that they had

During air attacks only non-essential personnel took cover; aircraft crews and the staff of the Operations Room remained at their posts. At Kenley and Biggin Hill direct hits were sustained on shelter trenches, at the latter place by a bomb of 500 kilogrammes or more. The trench and its 40 occupants were annihilated. The trenches in use were lined with concrete and covered with earth. They had to be within a short distance of the hangars and offices. Wooden hangars were generally set on fire by a bombing attack, and everything in them destroyed. Steel, brick and concrete hangars, on the other hand, stood up well against attack, though, of course, acres of glass were broken. Hangars were generally empty, or near so. Damage to aerodrome surface was not a major difficulty.

The main safeguard for aircraft against air attack was dispersal. Experiments on Salisbury Plain in Summer 1938 had shown that dispersal alone, without any form of splinter-proof protection, afforded a reasonable safeguard against the forms of attack practised by our own Bomber Command. Thirty unserviceable fighters were dispersed in a ring of about 1,000 yards diameter and Bomber Command attacked them for a week. The result was three were destroyed, one damaged beyond repair, eleven seriously damaged. I therefore asked that small splinter-proof pens for single aircraft should be provided at all fighter aerodromes. This was not approved, but I was offered pens for groups of three. I think they were too big, they had a large open face to the front and a concrete area the size of two tennis courts which made an ideal surface for the bursting of direct action bombs. Eventually, splinter-proof partitions were made inside the pens, and till then some aircraft were parked in the open. As for aircraft damaged in battle any returning to its base was capable of another 15 minutes straight flight to a Repair Depot. Two were improvised about 30 miles west of London.

Air Chief Marshal Sir Hugh Dowding,
Commander-in-Chief Fighter Command

destroyed three attackers!

By the end of the day, 25 Hurricanes and nine Spitfires had been written off, German losses amounting to nine bombers and 29 fighters, a totally insufficient tally to prevent 160 night bombers mainly heading for Merseyside. Up to 03:00 raids streamed across the south coast to the Midlands and Leeds, with some crossing central London as attempts were also made to bomb Hornchurch, Debden, Biggin Hill and, incredibly, Eastchurch!

Merseyside had now been subjected, theoretically, to more heavy bombing than any other British target. Over four nights 70 per cent of the crews involved claimed they bombed the area, dropping on each night an average of 114 tons of HE and 257 BSK 36 incendiary containers. The quartet of raids were probably Luftflotte 3's biggest effort so far and included naval crews of KGr 606 and Fw 200 Condors of KG 40, with the first and third attacks being the most effective. On 29/30 August 137 crews out of 176 dispatched to Merseyside claimed to have bombed their targets, using 130 tons and 313 incendiary containers; most of the 180 aircraft dispatched on the second raid bombed elsewhere. The 112 sent on the 30/31 dropped 40 tons, mainly on houses and suburbs, and missed the docks. On the fourth night Liverpool was badly hit although the bombing drifted. In the commercial area of Liverpool 160 fires were started and Birkenhead was bombed yet again although few bombs found its dock areas. For a loss of seven aircraft, one per cent of the whole force, these Liverpool raids were a moderately successful investment.

With invasion definitely being prepared there was no let-up in the day raids on 1 September. Very heavily screened by fighters, Göring's fliers violated Kent over a five mile wide front mid-morning before splitting into two groups and then into another two, providing the defenders with four huge forces to grapple with, each heavily wrapped in fighter protection. Despite its need to destroy Sector Stations the Luftwaffe was still fascinated by Detling, Eastchurch and more sensibly Biggin Hill. Some success was achieved at Tilbury, raided at 11:05 by a diversionary force which damaged Riverside Station,

Ill-prepared briefing for many German bombing raids was often an open-air event, in much contrast to the highly sophisticated briefing of RAF crews prior to bombing operations. (IWM)

NIGHT BOMBING
29 AUGUST 1940 ~ 30 AUGUST 1940
1800 hrs ~ 0600 hrs   119 Incidents

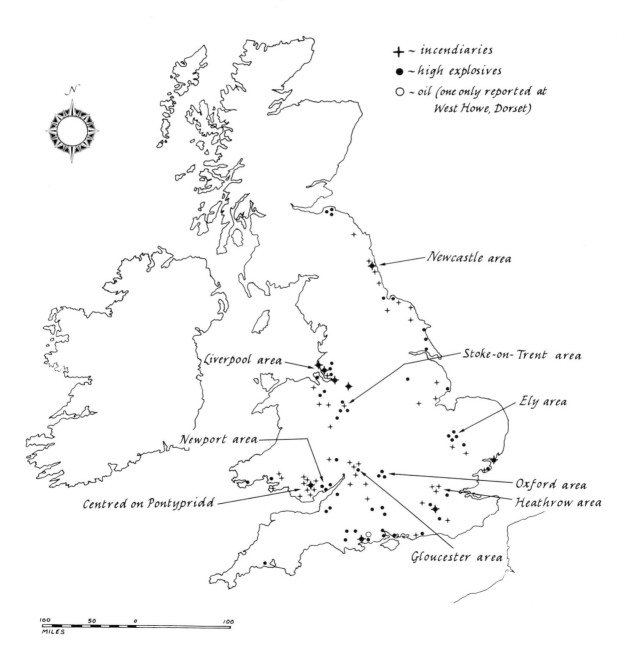

+ ~ *incendiaries*

● ~ *high explosives*

○ ~ *oil (one only reported at West Howe, Dorset)*

N

Newcastle area

Liverpool area

Stoke-on-Trent area

Ely area

Newport area

Oxford area

Centred on Pontypridd

Heathrow area

Gloucester area

100   50   0   100

MILES

dock buildings, workshops, Harland and Wolff, killed five workers and injured 28.

Around 13:45 a second, similar operation was mounted against aerodromes, but it was during the third operation that one of the most notorious raids of the Battle occurred. Large groups of fighters attempted yet again to distract the British into wasteful combat and, failing to do so, contented themselves by bombing and mainly strafing Hawkinge and Lympne aerodromes. Meanwhile, a clutch of very low-flying Dorniers penetrated to Biggin Hill, delivering the third and most damaging bombing of the day when one scored a direct hit with a 250-kg HE on its Sector Operations Room whose reinforced concrete ceiling collapsed into the building where two WAAF's remained at their posts. Such devotion to duty won both Sergeant Helen Turner and Corporal Elspeth Henderson a Military Medal. A new, temporary, operations room was established in a village shop. At night, over 100 bombers operated mainly individually over much of the country.

The first of four major daylight operations on 2 September was carried out by KG 3 Dorniers heavily escorted by many Bf 109s which approached Kent at 07:00. Although Park scrambled five squadrons few contacted the enemy, for close protection of Sector Stations was now prescribed. The Dornier formations parted near Maidstone and headed for Rochford, North Weald, Biggin Hill and Gravesend; at the latter 11 bombs fell around the airfield at 08:00. At the same time 48 bombs caused considerable damage to houses at Rochester and 20 minutes later Chatham received ten HEs. At the initial division point No. 72 Squadron[177] had been busy dealing with some Dorniers and Bf 110s at around 13,000 feet as another nine Do 17s, contour hugging, again struck Biggin Hill. No. 603 Squadron, patrolling over Hornchurch was vectored to withdrawing Bf 109s and bagged one which fell to Pilot Officer Richard Hillary (X4277) later to become famous as the author of the book *The Last Enemy*.

Around noon, with about 250 enemy aircraft approaching, Park decided this time to order his squadrons forward. While resultant scores were not high, the tactic diminished the military effectiveness of the operation although it caused the bombing of Maidstone, where many houses suffered and 15 casualties resulted. More raids in similar strength followed, taxing the defenders to the extreme, and at 16:40 Maidstone endured a second onslaught. Soon after 17:00 a tremendous battle resulted when about 90 RAF fighters took on 160 Bf 109s. By then seven aerodromes had been bombed — including, yes — Eastchurch, where this time the bomb dump exploded. Detling, Kenley, Biggin Hill, Hornchurch were hit, also Brooklands, where Hawker and Vickers-Armstrongs factories were sited. At night four civilians died during incidents at Bristol/Knowle.

The war was now a year old. True, there had been some terrible disasters and for many deep grief even from the start, after the *Athenia* had

The guns and lights of London's Inner Artillery Zone

Ready for Action on	31.8.40	30.9.40	31.10.40
4.5 in	48	48	60
3.7 in static	32	32	40
3.7 in mobile	14	113	127
3 in	34	6	6
40mm Bofors	36	55	47
Vickers Twin Mk 8	3	5	9
Vickers .5 in Single	—	1	1
Vickers .5 in Twin	—	1	1
Searchlights	240	265	265

been torpedoed on day one. But there had been euphoria too! Such as when the *Graf Spee* was sunk, and at the time of the stirring boarding of the *Altmark*, trapped in a Norwegian fiord. Every hour seemed packed with tremendous excitement and one was constantly aware of the traumatic days through which all were passing. Rumours included amazing tales of secret weapons — death beams, wire coils and springs to ensnare the raiders, and of course gigantic German bombs and booby traps — none of them, surprisingly, doing much to dent astonishingly high morale. 'Careless talk costs lives' we were for ever being told, but the ease with which one could build up a fairly accurate picture of the events and forces of the day remains surprising. By autumn 1940 Cambridge residents were even talking (privately) of a strange thing called an atom bomb! It's amazing that spies parachuted into this country discovered so little.

Air Marshal Trafford Leigh Mallory, whose 'Big Wing' idea won some official favour to the detriment, said some, of the generally better concepts of Dowding and Park. (IWM)

The largest bombing attack on 3 September was the first, made by 50 Do 17s preceded by many fighters and which threaded its way westerly along the Thames Estuary. Again, fear that London would soon be in their sights caused Park by 09:40 to place 16 squadrons (122 fighters) over Kent and Essex. Instead, the bombers turned north near Southend, swung westerly, then 'carpet bombed' North Weald before the fighters could stop them. Most bombs fell on the aerodrome, killing four men, gutting two hangars, hitting the operations block and damaging many other buildings. Three Blenheim crews of 25 Squadron scrambled, intent upon fighting the Dorniers, but this unusual injection proved disastrous when surprised Hurricane pilots erroneously attacked them. Sergeant Powell, gunner in Pilot Officer Hogg's aircraft, crawled to the nose, only to find his pilot slumped dead over the controls. He then baled out, leaving L1512 to crash near Greenstead Green, Essex. Squadron Leader Loxton landed safely but Pilot Officer Cassidy had to force-land his damaged Blenheim L1409 at Hatfield Heath. As the enemy was making for home, cannon Spitfires of 19 Squadron[178] tried to dispose of the Bf 110s, only to have the usual gun stoppages. Hurricanes of Nos. 1, 17[179], 46[180], 257[181] and 310[182] Squadrons were soon on hand to force escorting Bf 110s into combat. Despite the sharp raid the airfield remained operational.

For persevering, No. 19 — the first Spitfire squadron — received a reward next day, replacements in the form of 8-gun Spitfires. Time expired 'heaps', they were kindly donated by No. 7 OTU! Fate was also unkind to 25 Squadron, for when Pilot Officer Rofe made a night patrol and engaged three raiders heavy AA guns fired upon his Blenheim, twice putting it into dangerous spins. But all was not failure: Pilot Officer Herrick in another Blenheim shot down two night raiders.

Their main target again was Merseyside, to reach which He 111s of Luftflotte 3 overflew Dorset performing their distinctive signature tunes. For a night fighter to catch one was a

rare event, even when searchlights illuminated it. Mounting an interception without radar remained difficult until 2 September when the Beaufighter entered squadron service.

The first Beaufighters to serve RAF units were R2066, delivered to Tangmere Special Flight on 12 August 1940, and R2055 which joined AFDU Northolt next day. On 2 September R2073 reached 604 Squadron and R2072, the first squadron aircraft to operate, came on the strength of 29 Squadron at Wellingore. R2057 went next day to 25 Squadron, North Weald, the squadron which had been originally chosen to develop the aircraft. Nos. 23 and 600 Squadrons each received a Beaufighter on 8 September. The first operational patrol was flown over Hoylake by Squadron Leader S.C. Widows on 17/18 September.

Trials with early production Beaufighters revealed top speeds of between 312 and 325 mph at 15,000 feet — and German bombers persistently operated higher than that. Early Beaufighters carried four cannon, and whilst such examples did not have AI radar their capacious fuselages had ample room for it.

Purely by chance a new version of the Hurricane, the eight-gun Mk IIa also entered squadron service on 2 September, with No. 111 Squadron. A dozen had been delivered to ASUs

Below *A well-dressed man in 1940 — if he was a 19 Squadron 'Big Wing' Spitfire pilot.* (IWM)

in the last week of August, ten of which were on hand when on 3 September, from Croydon, they first and briefly operated. With a Merlin XX engine the Mk II's top speed was around 335 mph at 21,000 feet, but only with full super-charger running. Mid-September saw these Mk IIs withdrawn for modifications, re-issue coming in October to No. 421 Flight for special observation duties.

More immediately successful was the Spitfire Mk II (Merlin XII), first flown from Castle Bromwich in June 1940. The first to receive them was No. 611 Squadron at Digby, and a few days later No. 266 at Wittering began re-arming with the new Spitfire, whose ceiling and rate of climb showed improvement over the Mk 1. As it turned out, placing the Mk IIs in 12 Group allowed last minute snags to be cleared in time before 611 Squadron flew as part of the 12 Group Wing. Not all the fighters were in the pristine condition of the Mk IIs. After two months of fighting, many Spitfires and Hurricanes were so obviously battle weary, oil stained, much patched and in need of considerable attention. Both those and aircraft suffering from serious battle damage beyond unit capacity to repair were placed in the hands of the civilian repair organization. Hurricanes and Spitfires were taken to Oxford and Witney for rebuilding and modification, Rolls-Royce helping too — mainly with engines. After test flying, the aircraft were passed to MUs for final modifications and checks before being placed in ASUs, particularly at Little Rissington and Brize Norton.

The entry into the Battle of new, superior fighters was very encouraging to the defenders. Incredible as it now seems the Luftwaffe never made a really determined attempt to destroy Britain's aircraft and engine factories and storage depots, and by this stage of the Battle clearly appreciated such folly. On 4 September, after further morning raids particularly on irrelevant airfields, heavily protected Do 17s and He 111s headed for targets in Kent including Short's Rochester aerodrome. A small group of low-flying, bomb-carrying Bf 110s of ZG 76

crossed the coast at Littlehampton, then made for Brooklands Hurricane factory. Hurricanes of 253 Squadron[183] patrolling near Guildford and using Observer Corps information swooped upon the '110s, destroying six. Confusion overtook the remainder at their target as they hurled 500-kg bombs onto the Vickers Wellington factory, killing 88 and causing over 700 casualties as a result of heavy machinery, materials and glass being hurled around factory shops. The intention was that Bf 110s and '109s of Erpo 210, after attacking Poling CH Station, would provide withdrawal cover for ZG 76. Instead, RAF fighters also dealt effectively with the escort, picking off its Gruppenkommandeur and forcing ZG 76 to find its own way home.

There were two main raids on the south-east on 5 September, the first between 10:15 and 10:45 directed at targets in the suburbs of southeast London. In a second and more serious phase, between 15:15 and 16:30, Detling aerodrome was bombed and five oil tanks at Thameshaven set on fire, which came to serve as a useful beacon despite the efforts of 43 and 303 Squadrons to prevent the bombing. During the engagement Flight Lieutenant A. Rabagliati of 46 Squadron took a four-cannon Hurricane, V7360, into action for the first time. Operating alongside 249 Squadron, No. 46[184] encountered Bf 109s over the Thames Estuary, one being blown apart by cannon fire. The day's engagements cost Fighter Command 23 aircraft written off and the Luftwaffe 3 bombers and 16 Bf 109s.

At night the Luftwaffe roamed almost with impunity over a wide area, many single aircraft overflying London's IAZ (Inner Artillery Zone). The only encouragement for the defenders rested in the first night patrol by an AI-armed FIU Beaufighter. That was of little consequence to the people of Greenwich, where fires were started at the Green & Silley Weir buildings. Shops and buildings in Clifton, Bristol, were hit and four people killed, while at Liverpool bombs found the docks, Dunlop's Walton works, domestic buildings and shops in Bootle, Lime Street Station and Rainhill Men-

tal Hospital. At Prescot, St Helens, four died, and others in incidents at Birkenhead, Wallasey and Wigan.

In the last few days five forward airfields and six 11 Group Sector Stations had been damaged. Another week of such activity and London would be laid bare for destruction. There were still surprises, one occurring at 18:00 on 6 September when a few Ju 87s — two of which were claimed by Wing Commander Victor Beamish — helped stoke the beacon fires at Shell Mex, Thameshaven. There were two main operations that day, the first coming between 09:00 and 10:00 when No. 303 Polish Squadron[185], tackling Ju 88s and Do 17s over Kent, along with 249 Squadron[186], was set upon by Bf 109s which quickly disposed of five Hurricanes. Such heavy losses meant replacement by completely new, inexperienced squadrons whose losses would certainly rapidly mount. The alternative was to briefly rest the remainder of a fractured squadron before posting its more experienced fliers into squadrons in the thick of a fight that showed no sign of abatement that day and cost the RAF 23 fighters, the Luftwaffe losing 33 aircraft, 8 of them bombers. Main rail lines at Oxten and Caterham had been damaged slightly, also

Above *Bombs fall on Rochester in September. The aerodrome is on the other side of the road to the explosions.* (Bundesarchiv)

Below *Before the first heavy London raid of 7 September a giant fire was caused among oil tanks nearer the mouth of the Thames.* (Bundesarchiv)

Hawkers at Brooklands and Pobjoy's Rochester works. While the intensity of attacks had eased, relentless pressure over many weeks had produced battle weariness throughout 11 Group. Only a respite could cure it, and that seemed most unlikely.

Double Summer Time — surely a splendid idea — meant that it was just dark when at 20:43 bombs fell on West Ham; others that followed damaged houses, railway lines, the Victoria Docks and caused 55 casualties. More bombing involved Woolwich, Southwark and London's south-east suburbs, where over 70

Bf 110 U8+CL Nr 2146, of I/ZG 26 which ended its days at 09:30 on Cannons Hill Golf Course, Coulsdon, Surrey, on 6 September 1940. U8+FL is in the distance, and the tail of a Fw 58 may be glimpsed. (Bundesarchiv)

casualties were caused before the night's bombing petered out. There was not the slightest clear indication that London was on the threshold of what had so long been dreaded, and probably nobody yet realized that it would provide a miraculous turning point. Incredible that salvation would be brought by what was most feared.

RAF losses during operations 26 August-31 August 1940

a indicates failed to return/shot down, *b* written off — battle casualty, *c* seriously damaged

Aug/Sept	26			27			28			29			30			31			Totals		
	a	*b*	*c*	*a*	*b*	*c*	*a*	*b*	*c*	*a*	*b*	*c*	*a*	*b*	*c*	*a*	*b*	*c*	*a*	*b*	*c*
Type																					
Blenheim F	—	—	—	—	—	—	—	—	—	—	—	—	—	—	—	—	—	—	1	0	0
Defiant	3	—	—	—	—	—	4	—	1	—	—	—	—	—	—	—	—	—	7	0	1
Hurricane	14	—	1	—	1	—	6	—	1	6	—	—	10	—	1	24	1	—	60	2	3
Spitfire	7	2	3	1	—	—	7	—	—	3	—	—	10	4	2	6	3	2	34	9	7
Blenheim B	—	—	—	—	—	—	—	—	—	—	—	—	2	—	—	3	—	—	5	0	0
Hampden	2	—	—	—	1	—	1	—	—	1	—	—	1	—	—	1	—	—	6	1	0
Wellington	—	—	—	1	—	—	—	—	—	—	—	—	1	1	—	—	—	—	2	1	0
Whitley	1	—	—	—	—	—	—	—	—	—	—	—	1	—	—	—	—	—	2	0	0
Coastal Cmd	—	—	—	2	—	—	3	—	—	1	—	—	—	—	—	2	—	—	8	0	0
TOTALS	27	2	4	4	2	—	21	—	2	10	—	—	25	5	3	36	4	2	125	13	11

Luftwaffe losses during operations 26 August-31 August 1940

a indicates shot down, *b* crashed during sortie, *c* seriously damaged.

August	26			27			28			29			30			31			GRAND TOTAL AUGUST		
Type	a	b	c	a	b	c	a	b	c	a	b	c	a	b	c	a	b	c	a	b	c
Do 17P	1	—	—	1	—	—	—	—	—	—	—	—	1	—	—	1	—	—	5	0	0
Do 17Z	4	7	3	—	1	—	2	2	—	2	2	—	—	1	—	4	2	1	48	7	7
Do 215	—	—	—	—	—	—	—	—	—	—	—	—	1	—	—	—	—	—	1	0	0
He 59	1	—	—	—	—	—	2	—	—	—	—	—	—	—	—	—	—	—	5	1	0
He 111H	—	1	—	1	—	—	—	5	2	1	1	1	11	—	—	—	—	—	35	11	4
He 111P	4	1	—	—	—	—	—	1	—	—	1	—	—	1	—	—	—	—	20	4	2
He 115	—	—	—	—	—	—	—	—	—	—	—	2	—	—	—	—	—	—	1	0	2
Ju 88	1	2	—	1	1	—	—	2	—	—	1	—	—	—	—	—	1	1	49	9	13
Bf 109	15	1	—	—	—	1	15	—	—	7	2	—	13	1	1	19	2	—	139	16	15
Bf 110	3	1	—	—	—	—	—	—	—	—	—	—	4	—	—	8	1	2	95	6	18
TOTALS	29	13	3	3	2	1	19	10	2	10	7	3	30	3	1	32	6	4	398	54	61

Luftwaffe losses during operations 1-7 September 1940

a indicates shot down, *b* crashed during sortie, *c* seriously damaged.

September	1			2			3			4			5			6			7		
Type	a	b	c	a	b	c	a	b	c	a	b	c	a	b	c	a	b	c	a	b	c
Do 17Z	1	—	1	1	1	1	1	—	—	—	—	—	—	—	—	—	—	—	3	—	1
Do 18	—	—	—	1	—	—	—	—	—	—	—	—	—	—	—	—	—	—	—	—	—
Do 215	—	—	—	—	—	—	—	—	—	—	—	—	—	—	—	1	—	—	—	—	—
He 59	—	—	—	—	—	—	—	—	—	—	—	—	—	—	—	—	—	—	1	—	—
He 111H	—	1	2	—	—	—	—	—	1	1	—	—	5	1	1	3	4	1	3	2	1
He 111P	—	1	—	—	—	—	—	—	—	—	—	—	—	—	—	—	1	—	1	1	—
He 115	—	—	—	—	1	—	—	—	—	—	—	—	—	—	—	—	—	—	1	—	—
Ju 88	—	1	—	1	1	—	—	—	—	—	1	2	—	—	1	2	—	1	2	1	—
Bf 110	1	—	1	6	1	2	8	1	—	15	—	1	—	—	—	4	—	—	8	—	—
Bf 109	5	1	1	14	6	6	2	2	2	5	2	2	17	1	2	15	2	1	15	1	1
TOTALS	7	4	5	23	10	9	11	3	3	21	3	5	22	2	4	25	7	3	34	5	3

Units, aircraft types, identity letters and bases — Luftwaffe
7 September 1940

Luftflotte 2

BOMBERS:

KG 1	He 111	V4	Stab/Rosieres-en-Santerre I/Montdidier, Clairmont; II/Montdidier, Nijmegen
	Ju 88		III/Rosieres-en-Santerre
Kg 2	Do 17Z	U5	Stab/St Leger, I/Cambrai, II/St leger, III/Cambrai
KG 3	Do 17Z	5K	Stab/Le Culot, I/Le Culot, II/Antwerp-Duerne III/St Trond
KG 4	He 111	5J	Stab and I/Soesterburg, II/Eindhoven
	Ju 88		III/Schiphol
KG 26	He 111	1H	Stab and II/Gilze-Rijen, I/Courtrai and Moerbeke
KG 30	Ju 88	4D	Stab and I/Brussels Evere, II/Gilze-Rijen
KG 40	Ju 88	F8	Stab/Bordeaux-Merignac
KG 53	He 111	A1	Stab/I/II/III Lille complex
KG 76	Do 17Z	F1	Stab and III/Cormeilles, I/Beauvais-Tille, II/Creil
KG 77	Ju 88	3Z	Stab and I/III/Laon, II/Asch
KGr 126	He 111	1T	Minelayers
StG 1	Ju 87/Do 17	I9	Stab/St Pol
	Ju 87		Pas de Calais complex
StG 2	Ju 87/Do 17	T6	Stab/Tramecourt
	Ju 87		II/St Omer, St Trond
LG 1	Ju 87	L1	IV/Tramecourt
	Bf 109E		II/St Omer

FIGHTERS:

JG 1	Bf 109E		Stab/Pas de Calais complex
JG 3	Bf 109 E		Stab, I,II,III/Pas de Calais complex
JG 26	Bf 109E		Stab and I/Pas de Calais II, III/north-east France
JG 27	Bf 109E		Stab and I/Etaples, II/Montreuil, III/Sempy
JG 51	Bf 109E		Stab, I,II/St Omer and St Inglevert, III/Pas de Calais
JG 52	Bf 109E		Stab and I/Laon-Couvron, II and III/Pas de Calais
JG 53	Bf 109E		Stab and III/northern France, II/Wissant
JG 54	Bf 109E		Stab, I,II,III/Netherlands
JG 77	Bf 109E		I/northern France
ZG 2	Bf 110	28	I/Amiens, Caen, II/Guyancourt, Caudran
ZG 26	Bf 110	U8	I/Abbeville, St Omer, II/Crecy, III/Barley, Arques
LG 1	Bf 110	L1	V/Ligescourt, Alencon
Erprobungsgruppe			
210	Bf 109 and 110	S9	Denain

RECONNAISSANCE:

1(F)/22	Do 17/Bf 110	4N	Lille
1(F)/122	Ju 88 F6	S6	Schiphol
2(F)/122	Ju 88/He 111		Melsbroek
3(F)/122	Ju 88/He 111		Eindhoven
4(F)/122	Ju 88/He/111/Bf 110		Melsbroek
5(F)/122	Ju 88/He 111		Haute-Fontaine

COASTAL PATROL/MINELAYER:

1/ and 2/106	He 115	M2	Brest-Poulmiac
3/106	He 115		Borkum

Luftflotte 3

BOMBERS:

LG 1	Ju 88	L1	Stab, I,II/Orleans-Bricy, III/Chateaudun
KG 27	He 111	1G	Stab and I/Tours, II/Dinard, Bourges, III/Rennes
KG 40	Fw 200	F8	I/Bordeaux-Merignac
KG 51	Ju 88	9K	Stab, II/Paris-Orly, I.Melun, III/Etampes
KG 54	Ju 88	B3	Stab and I/Evreux, II/St André
KG 55	He 111	G1	Stab and III/Villacoublay, I/Dreux, II/Chartres
KGr 100	He 111	6N	Vannes
KGr 606	Do 17	7T	Brest, Cherbourg
KGr 806	Ju 88	M7	Nantes, Caen/Carpiquet
StG 3	Do 17/He 111	S7	Brittany
	Ju 87		Brittany

FIGHTERS:

JG 2	Bf 109		Stab, I. II/Beaumont-le-Roger, III/Le Havre
JG 53	Bf 109		I/Brittany
ZG 76	Bf 110		M9/Stab
	Bf 110	2N	II/Le Mans, Abbeville, III/Laval

RECONNAISSANCE:

Aufkläungsgruppen:

7(F)LG 2	Bf 110	L2	
4(F)/14	Bf 110/Do 17	5F	Normandy
3(F)/31	Bf 110/Do 17	5D	St Brieuc
3(F)/121	Ju 88/ He 111	7A	North-west France
4(F)/121	Ju 88/Do 17		Normandy
1(F)/123	Ju 88/Do 17	4U	Buc
2(F)/123	Ju 88/Do 17		Buc
3(F)/123	Ju 88/Do 17		Buc

Luftflotte 5

II/JG 77	Bf 109E		Southern Norway
(F)/22	Do 17	4N	2, 3/Stavanger
1(F)/120	He 111/Ju 88		Stavanger
1(F)/121	He 111/Ju 88	7A	Stavanger, Aalborg
KF1Gr 506	He 115	S4	1/Stavanger, 2/Trondheim, Tromso, 3/Lyst

CHAPTER 11
LONDON'S BURNING

Sooner or later, it was bound to happen to such a close and tempting target. Morning had brought mainly fighter forays to Folkestone and Hastings and Bf 109s dive-bombing Hawkinge in two lines, killing six civilians with a direct hit on a shelter and then striking at Dover. Not until about 16:30 did the big action begin, as six formations, 160 aircraft, passed over Deal and Dover heading north, followed soon by a second wave of more than 200. Act One of the invasion plan was commencing before the overture was completed. London was about to be butchered. A tactical blunder in British minds, the destruction of civilian morale and order in

The tide of battle turned when the enemy shifted his attention to Britain's ports. This reconnaissance photograph shows the Royal Docks, easy to locate in a bold meander of the Thames. (IWM)

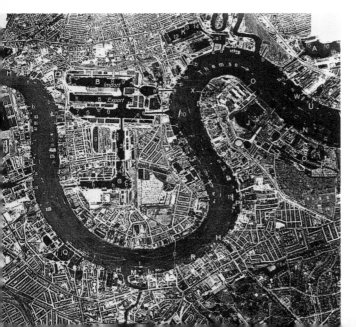

London was considered by the Germans to be an essential invasion pre-requisite. As for the destruction of London's huge dockland, that came to be viewed as an early shot in the Battle of the Atlantic, which it may well have been. London was most certainly neither bombed in error nor pique, but because of its importance as a sea port, industrial and communications centre and seat of government.

Tempestuous, horrific. . . not since the Great Fire had London seen such scenes of destruction. The fires that were started around tea-time on Saturday afternoon, 7 September, were visible 50 miles away. So thick and black was the smoke that it delivered darkness to the East End long before night was due, and soon it smothered the sky over a third of the world's greatest city. Ironically the conflagrations kindled not despair but even greater determination to beat the Nazis, to ultimately achieve victory. Far from lowering morale, it boosted it throughout the land. No cowering, no failure by all to face and tackle horrendous situations, just defiant desire to get to grips with 'that 'itler' and make him pay for the evil being dispensed.

As 11 Group scrambled 14 squadrons, 12 Group another four, the giant German swarm began swinging north-westerly on its approach to London's East End. At 17:15 the first loads began falling, on Beckenham, then Nunhead, hitting three factories and rail links. By 17:30 bombs from another force had smashed into Rochford, Brentwood, then Dartford, and into Stone, where children were imprisoned when a shelter was hit. A few minutes later the Anglo-

American Oil Company installations at Purfleet were rent asunder before a vast petroleum
fire engulfed the site. Nearby, Thamesboard
Mills was soon blazing and more high explosives fired Jurgen's Margarine works, tore apart
Cory's Wharf and battered a berthed vessel.
Shell-Mex and BP oil installations at Shore-
haven were by then flaming furiously, casualties were everywhere mounting fast, and the
Luftwaffe had barely commenced its orgy.

Massed in rectangular formations composed
of vics three abreast, line astern, and protected
by hosts of fighters in two or more layers above
and to the rear, the armada approaching from
north-east and south to bomb both shores of
the Thames was an impregnable force. Neither

*Dornier 17Zs crossing the Thames and heading for Woolwich
Arsenal on 7 September.* (IWM)

Fighter Command nor the 1,026 rounds of
heavy-calibre AA shells fired by the ZE, ZS and
ZW batteries were able to thwart its intent.

At 17:50 bombs by the score began screaming down, tumbling closer to the centre of London, onto Woolwich, lighting an ominous 13
fires at the Arsenal. Siemens' factory too was
soon burning, sewers were torn and Harland

*Try as it might, Fighter Command could not stop the firing
of the docks. No. 615 Squadron is seen returning from an
engagement.* (IWM)

Bombing of the Royal Victoria Dock caused huge fires there and across the Thames. (Bundesarchiv)

& Wolff in North Woolwich battered. In Plumstead Station a train was hit and at Falconwood carriages were derailed. More bombs fell at Crayford, as the Luftwaffe pressed on towards dockland.

Small groups of bombers which had earlier

Seen from the south bank of the Thames, smoke billowing from the Royal Docks, and, right, the Surrey Docks. (IWM)

left the main groups were now bombing Camberwell, Croydon, Putney and Kensington. A feint towards the Solent turned back, as the main force closed in upon the biggest prize.

Before 6 o'clock Göring's bomb-aimers had the warehouses of the Royal Albert Docks, East and West India Docks, London Docks and Surrey Commercial Dock in their sights and unleashed enormous terror among them. Upper Quebec Shed and others in the Surrey Docks erupted into a mass of flame which soon covered a square mile, while mammoth explosions were shattering Millwall Dry Dock. So enormous were the blast storms that huge pieces of masonry floated around and for many hours fragments of glass were wafted about. Serious fires engulfed the East India Dock, Whitechapel's London Docks and Royal Victoria Dock, mercifully killing but four and wounding 58 people. An enemy aircraft was believed to have plunged in to the heart of the South West India Dock, starting an inferno. King George V Dock's vital entry lock gate was battered; within moments the entire dock area embracing many homes was a mass of smoke and fire, and of terrible weeping, for many had died and others were trapped beyond hope of recovery, including some in West Ham's public shelters. That long awaited attack had, in the end, come so suddenly, unexpectedly, and was judged so serious that an hour later the

Army was warned 'invasion is imminent'.

Serious fires had taken hold in Barking, and the major Beckton gas works had received such a heavy pasting that supplies to much of east London were seriously reduced. A potentially highly explosive situation was narrowly averted. Extensive damage had been done to the railway system of east and south-east London. In Bermondsey, where 11 had soon died and 35 were injured, two giant fires were reclassified as 'conflagrations'. Southwark had immediately reported 43 casualties, and there were 46 in the Canal Bridge area of Camberwell. In many parts there was less certainty, but thousands had been injured.

As the fires raged, some consuming mills, many quite out of control as darkness spread over the land, widespread diversionary attacks were being delivered in Kent. Without any doubt this was far worse than anything previously released upon the British Isles — and more was about to follow.

Surviving raiders were homing onto their lairs at around 18:30-19:00. An hour and a half later radar detected fresh activity, this time in the Fécamp-Caen area, Luftflotte 3's region, from which tracks were soon crossing the coast near Shoreham before more were spotted heading for Beachy, Dungeness, Sussex, Kent, Essex — and all bound for Greater London. At 20:50 the first bomber entered the IAZ, whose guns commenced firing at 21:06. Continuously the raiders arrived, three to eight at a time, to deposit their evil upon London's fires in the most intense bombing of any British city so far. They stoked and extended earlier conflagrations, started huge new fires, and brought grotesque and unimaginable horror and grief, shattering lives, homes and livelihoods, particularly in the poorer parts of the East End. In Bethnal Green a large shelter in Columbia Market received a direct hit. A train in Victoria Station was hit too and the driver killed. Silvertown became 'a raging inferno', when it was overtaken by possibly the most horrific event in hours of horror, as at Tate & Lyle, burning furiously, sugar and molasses burst out of their containers and slowly oozed into the streets like molten lava. So terrible was the situation that Silvertown had to be completely evacuated, and mainly by boat, which gave its people a view of their homes being incinerated and an image never to be forgotten.

During the night phase many incendiaries had been dropped and particularly on the docks at West Ham, on Poplar, Liverpool Street Sta-

From 7 and into 8 September huge fires raged in the Royal Docks and by the Thames, where they were fought from the river as much as the land. A burning barge has been towed into mid stream while warehouses not far from Tower Bridge are being gutted. (IWM)

London's defenders 16:00-18:30 7 September 1940

According to the relevant squadron Operations Record Books, the aircraft used were as follows:

No. 1 Squadron Hurricanes: V7379, P2548, V7301, V7258, P3395, V7377, P5199, V7256, P3318 V7376, P3396, P2751, P3406

No. 19 Squadron Spitfires: P9386, P9546, K9967, N3199, P9431, X4059, P9391

No. 41 Squadron Spitfires: X4345, P9500, R6697, N3059, R6756, N3266, X4318, V5346

No. 43 Squadron Hurricanes: V6541, P3466, P3386 — others uncertain

No. 46 Squadron Hurricanes: V7360, V6582, V7438, R4074, P3525, V7409

No. 66 Squadron Spitfires: X4320, N3225, X4321, L1083, X4376, R6925

No. 72 Squadron Spitfires: i) K9847, X4254, K9841, R6710, R7022, X4252, P9460;
ii) second response by R6710, K9841, X4337, P9460, X4252

No. 73 Squadron Hurricanes: identity uncertain

No. 79 Squadron Hurricanes: 6 aircraft of 'A' Flight, identities uncertain

No. 111 Squadron Hurricanes: identity uncertain

No. 222 Squadron Spitfires (with No. 603): N3169, P9364, X4058, P9324, X4024, N3203, X4249, L1031, X4089, P9397, X4275

No. 234 Squadron Spitfires X4009, P9319, R6959, P9320, N3057, N3191, X4251, R6957, X4036, P9466, R6986

No. 242 Squadron Hurricanes: P2967, P3087, P3281, P3090, P3054, V7203, 2884, P3207, P3061, P3715, P3718, P3048

No. 249 Squadron Hurricanes: V6559, V6610, V6574, P3594, V7313, R4230, V6534, R4114, P3579, V6614, V6628, P5206

No. 253 Squadron Hurricanes: i) P5172, P2883, P2865, P5179, V6637, P3551, P3580, P5184, P3537
ii) second response P2883, P5172, P3580, 2686, V6637, P5184, V7441, P2865, V6683, P5179

No. 257 Squadron Hurricanes: P3893, P3620, V7298, V7254, 4088, P3049, P3775, P3776

No. 303 Squadron Hurricanes (with No. 1 Squadron): V7290, V6605, V7242, V7244, R2685, V7235, R4127, P3975, R4173, P3890, V7289

No. 1 Squadron RCAF (with 303 and 1 Squadrons): P3859, L1973, P3670, V6671, P3081, V7228, V6603, P3534, V6609, P3647, P3876, V6670

No. 501 Squadron Hurricanes: P3397, P5193, R4105, V6545, V7403, V7357, P2760, P2329, L1572, V6645, P3605

No. 504 Squadron Hurricanes: P3614, N2481, P3429, P2987, P3774 — all made two sorties. L1945 operated on first response only

No. 602 Squadron Spitfires: L1040, N3198, N3228, R4162, P9515, X4270, P9510, K9839, N3282, P9446, R6965, X4256

No. 603 Squadron Spitfires: X4250, X4259, K9963, X4274, L1057, X4324, P9499, N3267, P9440, X4323, N3196, X4263

No. 609 Squadron Spitfires: X4107, R6915, R6961, N3223, K9841, N3280, L1096, R6691, X4234, K9997, N3113

---

tion, Stepney and other parts on the north side of the river. By dawn, with over 500 HEs reported to have fallen, 600 fire appliances had been in operation, and confirmed casualties totalled 292 killed and 1,285 seriously injured, estimates having been for 320 and 1,349 respectively.

At 22:00 11 Group agreed for the AA gunners to commence firing at fixed azimuth targets and ten minutes later a raider was brought down west of Barking, possibly by Site ZE2 or Cheshunt gunners. A second bomber, a He 111 of KG 4, crashed at 23:18 in the Thames at ref. Q9897 — off Purfleet.

Not until 04:30 did the last bomber leave London, which had endured ten hours of

Night bombing 7/8 September: main incidents

Railways blocked — London Bridge-New Cross; Waterloo-Clapham Junction — blocked by UXBs
Borough High Street — bombs near gunpowder factory
County Hall
Crayford — gas main fired
Dagenham — Ford Co.
Erith — services hit
Edmonton — Grosvenor Bridge
Falconwood railway station
Finsbury
Greenwich — Vacuum Oil Co.
Islington — public shelter
King George V Dock
Lewisham
London Dock No. 10 Warehouse
London Hospital
Minnories
Nine Elms Goods Yard
Plaistow
Royal Albert Dock — No. 25 Shed
Royal Victoria Dock — 3 warehouses gutted
Premier Empire and Vernon Mills
Poplar — LNER bridge and Bow Road
Rotherhithe Tunnel
Stepney
St Thomas's Hospital
Whitechapel Fire Station
Battersea Power Station — major damage
Bermondsey — Bricklayers Arms
 Southern Railway Depot
Bethnal Green — Hackney Road, Columbia Market shelter
Paddington — Harrow Road
Shadwell — Badger's Highway
Twickenham — timber yard fire
Waterloo Bridge
Wapping — Colonial Wharf
Wimbledon — train set on fire
Woolwich — Royal Dockyard
Westminster — Victoria Street, Vauxhall Bridge
 Road, Victoria Station

bombing. Elsewhere a handful of attackers had visited Birmingham, Liverpool and South Wales and mined off Norfolk. At Waddington aerodrome an intruder engaged a landing Hampden bomber before strafing the airfield.

Would the scale, success and low cost of the raid cause the enemy to reduce his daylight effort? Apparently not, for daylight on the 8th witnessed two attacks on south-east England. In the first, one formation attacked the coastal area North Foreland-Rye in an invasion softening-up raid, while small numbers made for Sheppey or the London area. Not until 19:30 was the next raid mounted, by about 30 aircraft which crossed Beachy to London, while reconnaissances were flown to Bedford and Hornchurch. By that time it seemed certain that London was going to suffer another night raid. Around 19:45 the first visitors of Luftflotte 3 were leaving the Le Havre area and an hour later steady streams were overflying Selsey and Shoreham and soon a continuous average of five raiders was over the IAZ until 05:00 — except for a brief lull around 01:00. Every Metropolitan borough and 60 local authority areas reported bomb damage, large fires overtaking Berger Paints in Homerton, Madame Tussauds and Baker Street. Three hospitals were hit, Fulham Power Station was set on fire and many bombs dropped indiscriminately fell close to the Thames. Major incidents occurred at Acton, Leyton, Poplar and at Broad Street Station. The Embankment was flooded at Chelsea.

A new pattern of attacks was clearly evolving. On 9 September there was again little enemy activity until late afternoon, when a large formation bombed London suburbs south of the river as well as targets in Kent, including Canterbury. Behind them they left small fires in Barnes, Epsom, Maldon, Purley and Richmond and blocked roads in Kingston. Wandsworth, Surbiton, Lambeth, Fulham and Chelsea had also been raided.

As dusk settled, London braced itself for what was becoming a nightly event. Clearly, all means of transport were under attack and all communications were prime targets, with pri-

Plan 'Banquet Light' — or, 'How to gently Devour the Invaders'

One of the ideas for utilizing every available resource to counter invading forces was Plan 'Banquet Light', for which the Air Ministry authorized (only) offensive use of Flights of five Tiger Moth and Magister elementary trainers each armed with 8 x 20 lb F (fragmentation) bombs. Each flown by an instructor, these trainers would have given HQ Home Forces an additional strike force whose role was to dive or level bomb troops trying to disembark or land and to attack initial inland penetrations. Attached to and controlled by army co-operation Lysander squadrons, the light aircraft would have operated from their aerodromes or advanced landing grounds. Each pilot would have taken a passenger to his operational base, the latter's task being preparing and bombing-up of the aircraft by drawing upon 4,800 gallons of petrol, 240 gallons of oil and the 2,000 F bombs specially available at each Lysander base.

These unarmed, unarmoured trainers would have depended upon their manoeuvrability to survive. Whilst pilots were authorized to commence their dives at 1,500 feet at up to 60^0, their bombs could not safely be dropped from below 650 feet although plans were for a developed weapon to be delivered from a mere 50 feet! In any case, getaway was, for safety's sake, to be at very low level. Bomb-

ing practice was undertaken at the home training school.

Schools and their designated operational stations as on 13 August 1940 were as follows:-

Command EFTS/Base Southern	No. of Flights*	Lysander Squadron/Base affiliation
No. 2 Staverton	1	No. 225 Tilshead
No. 3 Watchfield	1	No. 225 Tilshead
No. 10 Weston-super-Mare	2	No. 16 Weston Zoyland
No. 13 White Waltham	2	No. 110 Canadian, Odiham
Eastern:		
No. 1 Hatfield	2	No. 239 Hatfield
No. 6 Sywell	2	No. 2 Sawbridgworth
No. 8 Woodley	1	No. 26 Gatwick
No. 18 Fairoaks	1	No. 26 Gatwick
No. 22 Cambridge	2	No. 268 Bury St Edmunds
Northern:		
No. 4 Brough	2	No. 4 York
No. 9 Ansty	2	No. 613 Firbeck
No. 21 Desford	2	No. 4 York
Western:		
No. 14 Elmdon	2	No. 13 Hooton Park
Scottish:		
No. 11 Perth	2	No. 241 Inverness
No. 12 Prestwick	2	No. 614 Grangemouth

* each Flight had a reserve of at least two aircraft

vate houses inevitably suffering badly. Major fires took hold at the Barbican and in warehouses at West Ham, and others occurred at Woolwich Arsenal and Greenwich, where a cordite shop at Batley's exploded. Ludgate Hill, Cheapside, Fenchurch Street, and Cannon street all suffered, along with parts of Bow, Lambeth and Southwark during bombing still particularly directed at the East End. At Charing Cross Station a bomb spectacularly penetrated a platform and closed the Embankment. Others also were acting in unpredicta-

ble ways, often causing damage unrelated to their magnitude, failing to explode for a host of reasons, sometimes detonating prematurely and in most unexpected situations. Some even hurtled through small toilet windows, then bounced downstairs, while others exploded high in trees or low in sewers. Fractured sewers brought health alarms, particularly if water mains were also hit. Luckily, many Londoners had corrugated iron Anderson shelters in their garden, and there were public shelters close by. Some sheltered in basements, which in several

Night bombing of London 8/9 September 1940

Acton marshalling yards
Bank of England
Bushey School
Chelsea Embankment
Deptford Royal Victualling Yard
Hackney — two factories serious damage
Holborn
Homerton — Burger Paints
Poplar — Green, Silley & Wear Ltd; Institution; District Railway
Mansion House
Metal Box Factory
Lindley Aircraft Co.
Shoreditch Road blocked, shelter hit, fires
St Pancras — blocked
Stepney — British Oil Cake Mills, Sutton's Wharf
Stoke Newington — serious flooding
Broad Street Station — all lines cut
Fulham Power Station
Baker Street — Chilton Court, Madame Tussauds
City — Great Arthur Street, King William Street, Lombard Street to Adelaide Place; London Bridge; near Bank of England and Mansion House
Islington — services and sewer cuts
Westminster — Odhams Press
Law Courts
Knightsbridge Barracks
Green Park and St James's
Constitution Hill — UXBs also in Buckingham Palace Gardens
Natural History Museum — fire
Desoutter Co. — fire
Battersea — on the railway Queen's Road-Clapham Junction

Bombing of London 9 and 9/10 September — main incidents

Surbiton — Kingston By-pass
Barnes Station — No. 1 Platform
Stainer Road, Heston — military training centre
Hounslow Heath
Silley Weir Poplar — second fire
Shoreditch — near St Leonards Hospital
West Ham — LNER station
Greenwich — Deptford Bridge
Camberwell — LCC Estate
Bow High Street
Southwark — St George's Road and New Kent Road
Bloomsbury — Guildford Street
Woolwich — Rochester Way and roundabout blocked
Charing Cross — No. 2 track
Stepney — rail bridge
Nine Elms goods yard
Greenwich — Royal Naval College
Crayford — Vickers
East Ham — power station
Somerset House
Fenchurch Street Station
Westminster Embankment

instances, like the shelters, received direct hits, with ghastly consequences. Probably the safest of all places were the underground stations, where increasing numbers spent the night, and then had uncertainties to face at dawn. The bombing of London certainly brought an enormous change to the Battle, and there were other fresh variations, including increased night intruder operations against British bomber bases. On 9/10 September alone intruders fired upon a Blenheim over Alconbury, a Hampden

over Scampton and a Wellington landing at Marham. By Cambridge airport incendiaries burned near squadrons of anti-invasion Lysanders and over the next few weeks night intrusions directed against bomber stations showed a steady increase. Events quite different from conventional ideas of the Battle were occurring.

Daylight operations on the 10th nevertheless followed accepted practice — lone armed reconnaissance flights, convoy attacks off East Anglia, bombing of coastal towns including Great Yarmouth and Hastings, raids on West Malling and Woolwich. The Southern Railway power station at Newhaven was also hit. Then late in the afternoon a build-up over France began, about 300 aircraft crossing in at about 16:55 between Dover and North Foreland. 'Six were reported to be four-engined bombers with

Something to sing about?

Relatively few songs of 1940 have achieved lasting success, and in any case few were recorded in British studios that year. Little of the sheet music, 6d a large format copy, has survived. How many of these songs can you recall?

Let the people sing; It's a lovely day tomorrow; I'm nobody's baby; Memories live longer than dreams; Can't get Indiana off my mind; Arm in arm; My sister and I; Careless; No, mama, no; I hear a dream; Where the blue begins; We'll go smiling along; I'm in love for the last time; You made me care; Get happy; It's a blue world; In a little rocky valley; Sing a round-up song; Too romantic; Moonlight avenue; They call me a dreamer; With the wind and the rain in her hair; The memory of a rose; Faithful, forever; There'll come another day; Our love affair; You gorgeous, dancing doll; If I only had wings; I've got my eyes on you; There goes that song again; I was watching a man paint a fence; Fools rush in.

There was just a handful of lasting songs — Deep Purple, Over the Rainbow, When you wish upon a star, Blueberry Hill, If I should fall in love again — and A nightingale sang in Berkeley Square.

Some 1939 titles were very popular in 1940, among them:
There'll always be an England, We'll meet again, Moonlight Serenade, Little Brown Jug, Stairway to the stars, In the mood, My prayer and Indian summer.

about four raiders being over the capital at any one time. Around 02:30 more began arriving from the Low Countries, and Luftflotte 3 attacked Cardiff. It was 04:55 when the All Clear sounded in London.

This effort of the Germans to secure daylight mastery of the air over England is, of course, the crux of the whole war. So far it has failed conspicuously. . . to try to invade this country without having secured mastery in the air would be a very hazardous undertaking. . . If this invasion is going to be tried at all, it does not seem that it can be long delayed. . . Therefore, we must regard the next week or so as a very important period in our history.

Winston Churchill,
11 September 1940

The events of 11 September brought a reminder of the early days of the Battle, with small-scale attacks being made on Portsmouth, Tangmere, Poling and Weymouth. Port Victoria on the Isle of Grain was attacked mid-afternoon when about 300 enemy aircraft headed in for London, most of them fighters, and only 36 proceeded to bomb the capital before a second, smaller group operated over south-east London. Several serious events occurred, many fires being started once more in Woolwich and the Surrey Docks. A public shelter was hit in Lewisham High Street where 100 casualties resulted, and 50 people were buried by rubble when Deptford Central Hall was hit. UXBs rested at Paddington and Islington. Meanwhile eight Bf 110s dive-bombed the Cunliffe-Owen Aircraft works at Eastleigh, Southampton, where 28 were killed and 70 injured when a shelter was hit.

Another reminder of days long gone was provoked when at 01:20 on the 11th coastal convoy CW11 sailed from Southend. Its seven colliers

strong fighter escort', read the official summary, most swinging west to stream across south London, bombing here and there while a group of about 30 more entered the IAZ and a small diversion was mounted west of Salisbury. Opposing the Kent incursion were 24 RAF fighter squadrons, a far cry from the 'Few' of but a few days before, for Fighter Command was recovering fast. Night brought the usual streams from Cherbourg and the Somme, with

carrying about 10,000 tons of coal and three merchant vessels were being escorted by two destroyers, three armed trawlers and four balloon ships each with its charge flying at around 1,400 feet. By 16:00 the convoy was provocatively in the Straits, which prompted the Cap Gris Nez guns to unsuccessfully blast it, their shells also pounding Dover, where many houses were damaged. At 18:23 three Bf 109s attacked the balloons before a few minutes later bombers attempted a level attack from 4,000 feet and 10 minutes later, near the Goodwins Light Vessel, about 20 enemy aircraft began dive-bombing the escort ships using HE and fire bombs and holing HMS *Atherstone*. The most serious raid came at 19:10 with 34 dive bombers pressing home a daring onslaught on a destroyer and scoring hits amidships on its engine room before RAF fighters arrived in strength. A trawler towed the destroyer safely to port in another episode reminiscent of those now some weeks ago.

Nine hours of night attacks on London by KG 4, KG 27, KG 51, KG 54 and KG 55, although spasmodic, caused more major damage. A blaze at St Katherine's Docks raged out of control and a fire float was sunk at London Dock. Greenwich Telcon Works was set on fire too, and Thomas de la Rue Star Works gutted. At Poplar the Manganese, Bronze & Brass Company wharf was hit, the rail link south from Holborn was cut and there were serious factory blazes in Camberwell. Bombs also fell on Aldgate and Shadwell, where the east end of the Maternity Hospital was hit. At Stepney two warehouses were incinerated and a huge timber fire illuminated Mile End. Over 1,000 incendiaries set fire to Woolworths and a convent in Brentwood — bombing was smashing the lives of many. Many minor raids took place in Lancashire, South Wales, Devon, Cornwall, Buckinghamshire and Hampshire. It was nevertheless obvious that the Luftwaffe was conserving its strength for its part in an invasion expected at any time.

On 12 September around Harrogate's Majestic Hotel HEs exploded injuring 15 during an

The bombing of London 11 and 11/12 September — main incidents

Smithfield Market
Metropolitan Tea Warehouse, India Street
Southwark — Great Dover Street
Borough High Street, Old Kent Road
Shoreditch — Widlock Brewery, Tapton Street
Holborn Viaduct
Islington — rail lines
Woolwich — Commonwealth Buildings, Arsenal
Hackney — Stamford Hill
Tottenham — Haveley Park to High Road
Deptford — Central Hall, cattle market
Greenwich — Telcon Works
Clapham Junction and Battersea
Central Telegraph Office, St Martins le Grand
Thornton Heath — London Road
Thomas de la Rue Ltd in Bunhill Row, also Star Works
City — Littlebrook and adjoining hospital, St Pauls, Blackfriars
Charing Cross Road
Lambeth — Stockwell Road
East Dulwich — Police Station, Camberwell
Lewisham — Park Hospital
West India Dock — Paddington Basin
Beckenham — Burroughes Welcome Ltd
Deptford Wharf, cattle market, supply depot
Finsbury — Allman Engineering Co.
Camberwell — railway arches
Poplar — Manganese, Bronze & Brass Co.
Brickley Station
Crystal Palace Station
London Dock

attack on an area where the Ministry of Aircraft Production had offices. GWR main line services to Reading were interrupted, whereas another attacker failed to hit the Northern Aluminium's Banbury factory. Late afternoon Tunbridge Wells was sharply raided, incendiaries causing house fires and destroying the ambulance station when it was most desperately needed. Seven HEs fell at Hornchurch, damaging the emergency operations room and hitting nearby dwellings. At night, widespread bombing seemed intended to spread alarm preceding the invasion.

Switching to night bombing meant that the Luftwaffe's day raids were often carried out by aircraft with black undersurfaces, like these He 111s including G1+ES of KG 55. (Bundesarchiv)

During the night of the 12/13th, when London had a seven-hour raid and about 120 enemy bombers operated, a Fw 200 attacked a ship off the Isle of Man and KG 54 mounted a small raid on Rugby. As well as many country areas Liverpool was bombed but little damage caused, and Blackpool North station was hit. Fulham's telephone exchange received a direct hit and other bombs hurled a water tank onto the track at West Brompton Station. In the 24 hours to 06:00 on the 13th listed casualties totalled 168 killed, 689 seriously injured.

Shipping in Belfast Loch was attacked at 07:00 on the 13th and incendiaries fell on Bangor. Then over two hours beginning at 07:30 six single aircraft operated over southern England before raiders arrived at about eight-minute intervals over London. At 11:10 bombs fell at Buckingham Palace — on the quadrangle, Chapel, outside the forecourt, injured four and slightly damaged the Victoria Monument. Ten bombs in Eastbourne's centre started large fires and caused 20 casualties. At West Ham the Ravenshill School where homeless were being accommodated was hit mid-morning and 50 casualties caused. Between 13:00 and 15:00 Biggin Hill and Maidstone attracted scattered raids, one bomber later starting a fire in London's Great Titchfield Street, blocking Euston

Road and causing 59 casualties.

The main, eight-hour raid on London commenced at 20:45. Although only five night fighter sorties were flown, Flying Officer M.J. Herrick in ZK-A of 25 Squadron managed to bring down He 111H 5J+BL of 3/KG 4 near North Weald. During the night Lavender Hill GPO sorting office, Wembley's Carrier Engineering Co., Victoria Station, Battersea Public Library and many houses in Hammersmith and Mitcham were among places bombed.

Night operations undoubtedly strained bomber crews, and that became clear when on 14 September after a quiet morning, two main attacks on London were mounted by high-flying escorted fighter bombers. The first developed around 15:30 with waves coming in fast between Dover and Ramsgate. About 100 of Raid 11 concentrated in the Maidstone-Biggin Hill area, leaving about 50 to bomb London. Into the IAZ flew 25 of them, keeping (as Rd 11J) to the south of the river. All had cleared the country by 16:30. To repel these nuisance raids 11 Group fielded 24 squadrons and 12 Group four. While the loads they could drop were not all that great, they were a threat that could not be ignored. After bombing, these aircraft reverted to being fighters — and that was an alarming aspect. A similar, smaller operation developed around 18:00 with about 60 bombing in the IAZ. About 80 bombers, fewer than usual, operated against London that night, suggesting that something big was being prepared.

Luftwaffe losses during operations 1-7 September 1940

a indicates failed to return/shot down, *b* written off, *c* seriously damaged

September	1			2			3			4			5			6			7			TOTAL LOSS IN PERIOD		
Type	a	b	c	a	b	c	a	b	c	a	b	c	a	b	c	a	b	c	a	b	c	a	b	c
Do 17Z	1	—	2	1	1	1	1	—	—	—	—	—	—	—	—	—	—	—	4	—	2	7	1	5
Do 18	—	—	—	1	—	—	—	—	—	—	—	—	—	—	1	—	—	—	—	—	—	1	0	1
He 59	—	—	—	—	—	—	—	—	—	—	—	—	—	—	—	—	—	—	—	1	—	0	1	0
He 111H	—	1	4	—	—	—	—	1	2	1	—	—	5	1	3	4	3	1	3	3	4	13	9	14
He 111P	—	—	—	—	—	—	—	—	—	—	—	—	1	—	—	—	—	—	1	1	—	2	1	0
He 115	—	—	—	1	—	—	—	—	—	—	—	—	—	—	—	—	—	—	—	1	—	1	1	0
Ju 87	—	—	—	—	1	—	—	—	—	—	—	—	—	—	—	—	—	—	—	—	—	0	1	0
Ju 88	—	1	—	1	1	—	—	—	—	—	1	2	—	—	—	2	—	2	2	—	1	5	3	5
Bf 109	5	1	1	16	4	6	2	2	2	4	4	3	14	3	2	15	2	2	14	1	1	70	17	18
Bf 110	1	—	—	6	1	4	6	3	—	15	1	1	—	—	—	4	—	—	8	—	—	40	5	5
TOTALS	7	3	7	25	9	11	9	6	4	20	6	6	20	4	6	25	5	5	33	6	9	139	39	48

RAF losses during operations 1-7 September 1940

September	1			2			3			4			5			6			7			TOTAL LOSS IN PERIOD		
Type	a	b	c	a	b	c	a	b	c	a	b	c	a	b	c	a	b	c	a	b	c	a	b	c
Blenheim F	—	—	—	—	—	—	1	1	1	—	—	1	—	—	—	—	—	—	—	—	—	1	1	2
Defiant	—	—	—	—	—	—	—	—	—	—	—	—	—	—	—	—	—	—	—	—	—	0	0	0
Hurricane	9	—	6	8	1	10	9	1	9	5	1	7	5	2	9	13	2	10	13	2	13	62	9	64
Spitfire	3	2	5	3	2	8	3	1	1	7	2	8	7	6	7	5	—	4	8	—	17	36	13	50
Blenheim B	—	—	—	2	—	1	1	—	1	2	—	—	2	—	—	—	1	—	—	—	—	7	1	2
Hampden	—	—	—	1	—	—	—	—	—	1	1	1	—	1	—	5	1	6	—	—	1	7	3	8
Wellington	—	—	—	2	1	1	—	—	—	—	—	—	—	—	3	1	—	—	—	—	1	3	1	5
Whitley	—	—	—	1	—	—	1	—	3	—	1	2	—	—	—	—	—	—	1	—	—	3	1	5
Coastal Cmd	1	—	—	3	—	—	—	—	—	—	—	—	—	—	—	1	—	—	—	—	1	5	—	1
TOTALS	13	2	11	20	4	20	15	3	15	15	5	19	14	9	20	26	4	21	22	2	33	124	29	137

CHAPTER 12
BATTLE OF BRITAIN DAY, 1940

Aircraft in Fighter Squadrons established (A)/serviceable (B)

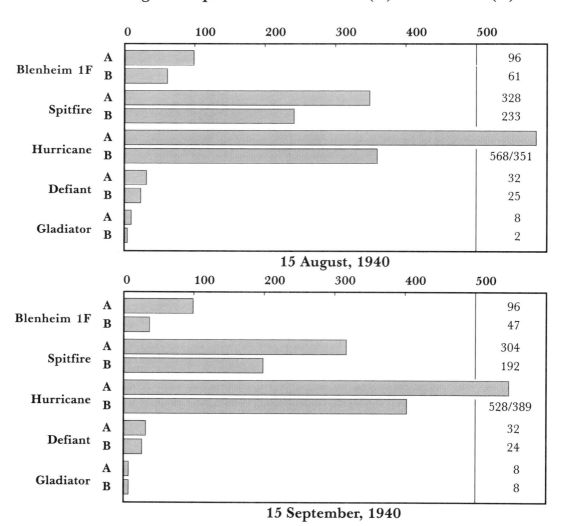

15 August, 1940

15 September, 1940

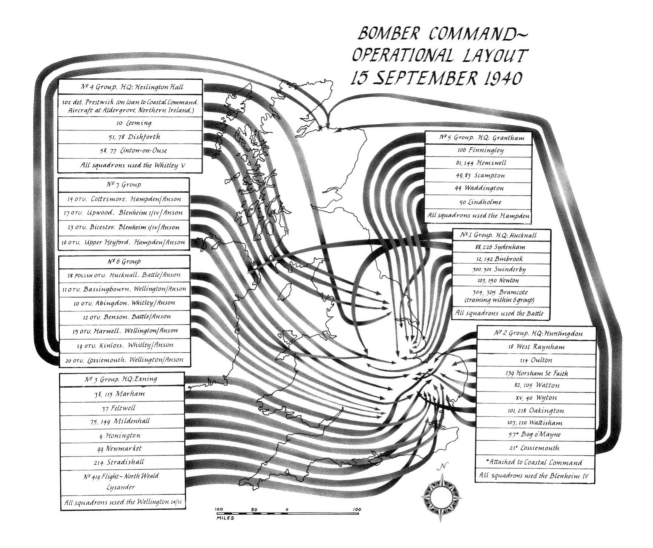

BOMBER COMMAND~
OPERATIONAL LAYOUT
15 SEPTEMBER 1940

N° 4 Group. HQ: Heslington Hall

| 102 det. Prestwick (on loan to Coastal Command. Aircraft at Aldergrove, Northern Ireland.) |
| 10 Leeming |
| 51, 78 Dishforth |
| 58, 77 Linton-on-Ouse |
| All squadrons used the Whitley V |

N° 7 Group

| 14 OTU. Cottesmore. Hampden/Anson |
| 17 OTU. Upwood. Blenheim I/IV/Anson |
| 13 OTU. Bicester. Blenheim I/IV/Anson |
| 16 OTU. Upper Heyford. Hampden/Anson |

N° 6 Group

| 18 POLISH OTU. Hucknall. Battle/Anson |
| 11 OTU. Bassingbourn. Wellington/Anson |
| 10 OTU. Abingdon. Whitley/Anson |
| 12 OTU. Benson. Battle/Anson |
| 15 OTU. Harwell. Wellington/Anson |
| 19 OTU. Kinloss. Whitley/Anson |
| 20 OTU. Lossiemouth. Wellington/Anson |

N° 3 Group. HQ: Exning

| 38, 115 Marham |
| 37 Feltwell |
| 75, 149 Mildenhall |
| 9 Honington |
| 99 Newmarket |
| 214 Stradishall |
| N° 419 Flight - North Weald Lysander |
| All squadrons used the Wellington IA/IC |

N° 5 Group. HQ: Grantham

| 106 Finningley |
| 61, 144 Hemswell |
| 49, 83 Scampton |
| 44 Waddington |
| 50 Lindholme |
| All squadrons used the Hampden |

N° 1 Group. HQ: Hucknall

| 88, 226 Sydenham |
| 12, 142 Binbrook |
| 300, 301 Swinderby |
| 103, 150 Newton |
| 304, 305 Bramcote (training within 6 group) |
| All squadrons used the Battle |

N° 2 Group. HQ: Huntingdon

| 18 West Raynham |
| 114 Oulton |
| 139 Horsham St Faith |
| 82, 105 Watton |
| XV, 40 Wyton |
| 101, 218 Oakington |
| 107, 110 Wattisham |
| 57* Bog o'Mayne |
| 21* Lossiemouth |
| *Attached to Coastal Command |
| All squadrons used the Blenheim IV |

100 50 0 100
MILES

N

September 15, 1940 will always rate as one of the greatest days in our history. Besides marking the zenith of the Luftwaffe onslaught it also proved beyond any doubt that the German Air Force was now certainly incapable of smashing Fighter Command. But with a hoard of splendid Messerschmitt 109s, many soon to become bombers, the enemy would maintain pressure upon Fighter Command, though no longer for very sound reason after Hitler postponed the invasion of Britain. That decision came very much as a result of what has become hallowed as Battle of Britain Day.

Not since 7 September had the Luftwaffe mounted a massive daylight onslaught. Fighter Command seized the opportunity presented by the pause to invigorate 11 Group by bringing back squadrons which had rested and by introducing some like 46 and 229 which in 12 Group had not experienced much fighting but

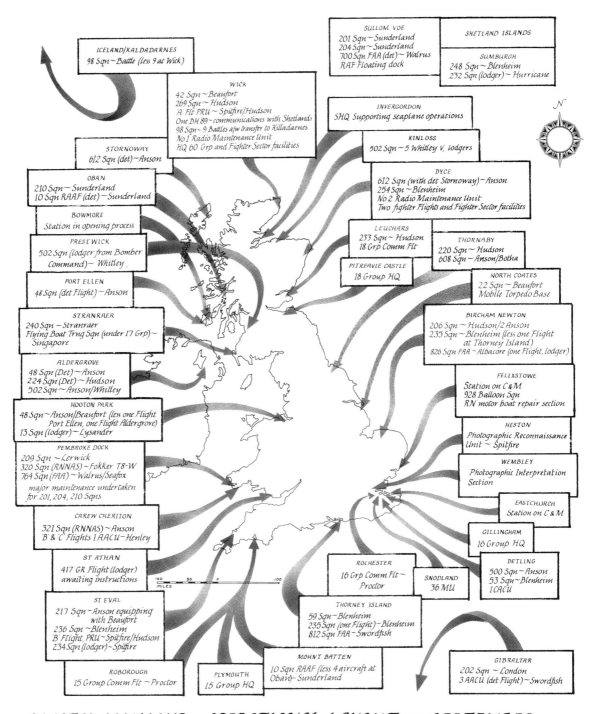

ICELAND/KALDADARNES
98 Sqn ~ Battle (less 9 at Wick)

WICK
42 Sqn ~ Beaufort
269 Sqn ~ Hudson
'A' Flt PRU ~ Spitfire/Hudson
One DH 89 ~ communications with Shetlands
98 Sqn ~ 9 Battles a/w transfer to Killadaenes
No 1 Radio Maintenance Unit
HQ 60 Grp and Fighter Sector facilities

SULLOM VOE
201 Sqn ~ Sunderland
204 Sqn ~ Sunderland
700 Sqn FAA (det) ~ Walrus
RAF Floating dock

SHETLAND ISLANDS

SUMBURGH
248 Sqn ~ Blenheim
232 Sqn (lodger) ~ Hurricane

INVERGORDON
SHQ Supporting seaplane operations

KINLOSS
502 Sqn ~ 5 Whitley V, lodgers

STORNOWAY
612 Sqn (det) ~ Anson

OBAN
210 Sqn ~ Sunderland
10 Sqn RAAF (det) ~ Sunderland

DYCE
612 Sqn (with det Stornoway) ~ Anson
254 Sqn ~ Blenheim
No 2 Radio Maintenance Unit
Two fighter Flights and Fighter Sector facilities

BOWMORE
Station in opening process

LEUCHARS
233 Sqn ~ Hudson
18 Grp Comm Flt

THORNABY
220 Sqn ~ Hudson
608 Sqn ~ Anson/Botha

PRESTWICK
502 Sqn (lodger from Bomber Command) ~ Whitley

PITREAVIE CASTLE
18 Group HQ

PORT ELLEN
48 Sqn (det Flight) ~ Anson

NORTH COATES
22 Sqn ~ Beaufort
Mobile Torpedo Base

STRANRAER
240 Sqn ~ Stranraer
Flying Boat Trng Sqn (under 17 Grp) ~ Singapore

BIRCHAM NEWTON
206 Sqn ~ Hudson/2 Anson
235 Sqn ~ Blenheim (less one Flight at Thorney Island)
826 Sqn FAA ~ Albacore (one Flight, lodger)

ALDERGROVE
48 Sqn (Det) ~ Anson
224 Sqn (Det) ~ Hudson
502 Sqn ~ Anson/Whitley

FELIXSTOWE
Station on C & M
928 Balloon Sqn
RN motor boat repair section

HOOTON PARK
48 Sqn ~ Anson/Beaufort (less one Flight Port Ellen, one Flight Aldergrove)
13 Sqn (lodger) ~ Lysander

HESTON
Photographic Reconnaissance Unit ~ Spitfire

PEMBROKE DOCK
209 Sqn ~ Lerwick
320 Sqn (RNNAS) ~ Fokker T8-W
764 Sqn (FAA) ~ Walrus/Seafox
major maintenance undertaken for 201, 204, 210 Sqns

WEMBLEY
Photographic Interpretation Section

CAREW CHERITON
321 Sqn (RNNAS) ~ Anson
B & C Flights 1 AACU ~ Henley

EASTCHURCH
Station on C & M

GILLINGHAM
16 Group HQ

ST ATHAN
417 GR Flight (lodger) awaiting instructions

ROCHESTER
16 Grp Comm Flt ~ Proctor

SNODLAND
36 MU

DETLING
500 Sqn ~ Anson
53 Sqn ~ Blenheim
1 CACU

ST EVAL
217 Sqn ~ Anson equipping with Beaufort
236 Sqn ~ Blenheim
'B' Flight, PRU ~ Spitfire/Hudson
234 Sqn (lodger) ~ Spitfire

THORNEY ISLAND
59 Sqn ~ Blenheim
235 Sqn (one Flight) ~ Blenheim
812 Sqn FAA ~ Swordfish

ROBOROUGH
15 Group Comm Flt ~ Proctor

PLYMOUTH
15 Group HQ

MOUNT BATTEN
10 Sqn RAAF (less 4 aircraft at Oban) ~ Sunderland

GIBRALTAR
202 Sqn ~ London
3 AACU (det Flight) ~ Swordfish

100   50   0   100
MILES

N

COASTAL COMMAND ~ OPERATIONAL LAYOUT 15 SEPTEMBER 1940

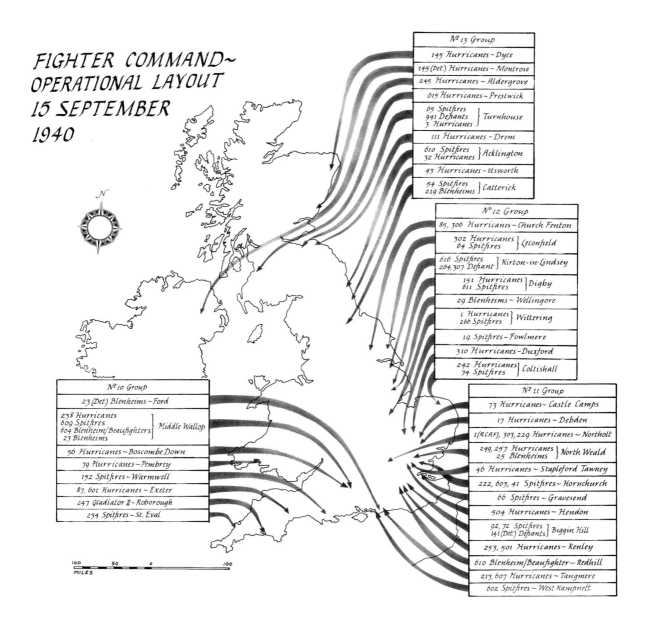

FIGHTER COMMAND~
OPERATIONAL LAYOUT
15 SEPTEMBER
1940

Nº 13 Group
145 Hurricanes ~ Dyce
145 (Det.) Hurricanes ~ Montrose
245 Hurricanes ~ Aldergrove
615 Hurricanes ~ Prestwick
65 Spitfires / 941 Defiants / 3 Hurricanes } Turnhouse
111 Hurricanes ~ Drem
610 Spitfires / 32 Hurricanes } Acklington
43 Hurricanes ~ Usworth
54 Spitfires / 219 Blenheims } Catterick

Nº 12 Group
85, 306 Hurricanes ~ Church Fenton
302 Hurricanes / 64 Spitfires } Leconfield
616 Spitfires / 264,307 Defiant } Kirton-in-Lindsey
151 Hurricanes / 611 Spitfires } Digby
29 Blenheims ~ Wellingore
1 Hurricanes / 266 Spitfires } Wittering
19 Spitfires ~ Fowlmere
310 Hurricanes ~ Duxford
242 Hurricanes / 74 Spitfires } Coltishall

Nº 10 Group
23 (Det.) Blenheims ~ Ford
238 Hurricanes / 609 Spitfires / 604 Blenheim/Beaufighters / 23 Blenheims } Middle Wallop
56 Hurricanes ~ Boscombe Down
79 Hurricanes ~ Pembrey
152 Spitfires ~ Warmwell
87, 601 Hurricanes ~ Exeter
247 Gladiator II ~ Roborough
234 Spitfires ~ St. Eval

Nº 11 Group
73 Hurricanes ~ Castle Camps
17 Hurricanes ~ Debden
1(RCAF), 303, 229 Hurricanes ~ Northolt
249, 257 Hurricanes / 25 Blenheims } North Weald
46 Hurricanes ~ Stapleford Tawney
222, 603, 41 Spitfires ~ Hornchurch
66 Spitfires ~ Gravesend
504 Hurricanes ~ Hendon
92, 72 Spitfires / 141 (Det.) Defiants } Biggin Hill
253, 501 Hurricanes ~ Kenley
610 Blenheim/Beaufighter ~ Redhill
213, 607 Hurricanes ~ Tangmere
602 Spitfires ~ West Hampnett

100   50   0   100
MILES

were well staffed. In the miraculous gift of a pause Fighter Command worked up the newcomers in a manner impossible for many weeks past.

Then came 15 September, one of those lovely, clear, sunny early autumn days when small puffy clouds meander along, enshrining memories of the passing summer. If the enemy was going to return to massed raids then this day was ideal, so the fighters were up early and in waiting, and maybe Dowding had some advanced intelligence to suggest what was afoot across the Channel.

It was shortly before 11:00 that radar stations

in Kent reported enemy forces assembling as so often inland of Boulogne. Command ordered Park to prepare his squadrons for action, warned 10 and 12 Groups and intimated that a large attack was pending. Shortly after 11:00 Nos. 72 and 92 Squadrons were scrambled from Biggin Hill, an act symbolic.

On its way was much of Kampfgeschwader 3 and other bomber formations which, after leaving Belgian bases, had met a huge fighter cover over France and headed for Dungeness, where around 11:30 a score of Biggin's Spitfires presented an unwanted greeting. As the raiders headed for London they were harried by ever more British fighters and shortly before reaching London they received a hammer-blow. Four Hurricane squadrons launched head-on assaults and then Squadron Leader Douglas Bader's 'Big Wing' (two Spitfire and three Hurricane squadrons) broke through the flanking escort and reached the Dorniers. Over 150 fighters were soon running amok among the bombers. No concentrated attack upon London being possible, KG 3 made a curving midday pass across southern districts of the capital, bombing at random as it turned for home as fast as possible. On both sides the losses were considerable, the individual combats many, the pain, the sorrow, the carnage enormous. Bombs exploded over a wide area of southern and southwest London, two unexploded bombs lodging

at Buckingham Palace. Sergeant R.T. Holmes of newcomer 504 Squadron became involved with a Do 17Z of 5/KG 3 which exploded so violently that it put his Hurricane P2725 into a spin. Holmes baled out, landing in a Chelsea back garden; the Hurricane came down in Buckingham Palace Road and the remnants of Dornier Do 17Z-3 1176- 5K+DN fluttered onto Victoria Station and its surrounds.

By that time the 'first up' British fighters were being turned round at their bases while their pilots, aware of considerable success, refuelled, ready for another very likely round not long in coming. This time it was the turn of over 150 Dorniers of KG 2 and KG 76 with KG 26's and KG 53's Heinkels depending for their safety mainly upon the Messerschmitts of JG 26 and JG 54.

By 14:00 they were crossing into Kent on a broad front, and the RAF's response was quite incredible as it felt assured of grand success. Despite the morning losses and battle damage, most squadrons were somehow able to field full strength, for ground crews worn out by the August campaign seemed suddenly to have new

At Cherbourg/Maupertus in September the Bf 109E of JG 2 flown by Helmut Wick when leading the first Gruppe. Note the double Winkel marking, blue pennant of his former Staffel (No. 3) on the cowling and the armoured windscreen. (Michael Payne)

The tail of Wick's aircraft with kill tally. A Ju 34 communications aircraft stands by the trees; behind the tail a visiting Bf 109 of JG 53 wearing a red band around its cowling and unusual Stab marking. (Michael Payne)

life, especially after the German switch largely to night bombing early in September.

As they headed for London the Germans met some 170 eager, refreshed British warriors out to kill and avenge the cruelty inflicted upon Londoners. At first the fight was tough going, for the German fighter pilots were among the best of all. But when the raid reached East London it encountered Duxford's 12 Group 'Big Wing', half a dozen 11 Group squadrons and two reinforcing squadrons from 10 Group. The Hurricanes and Spitfires hurled themselves against the invaders, forcing the bombers to jettison their loads over south-east London and run for home while the Bf 109s were doing their best to save them — and themselves.

What went through the minds of all concerned one can but largely imagine, for the casualties on both sides were high. In the RAF's ranks there was jubilation, for who would have imagined but a few weeks ago that such resounding success was suddenly possible? Among the German bomber crews there must have been ever-increasing fear as more and more RAF fighters weighed in upon them. So much for the 'four day' destruction of Fighter Command! As for the German fighter pilots, they had constantly to bear in mind their small fuel loads quickly used up in the high-speed

manoeuvres. Once home they might well have demanded the truth, for yarns about the RAF being down to its last few aircraft were ridiculous. Add to this the continued activity of Bomber Command, hammering the invasion fleet, penetrating deep into Germany, and even bombing Berlin, and, despite the U-Boats, of vital convoys of fuel and food arriving in Britain, and the situation for the Germans was no longer so encouraging.

As the afternoon continued, more German fighters headed into Kent to provide withdrawal support — by then to a rabble.

At the same time another threat developed, when 27 He 111s of III/KG 55 headed for the Solent before turning for Portland. These were engaged en route by 152 Squadron Spitfires which shot down a bomber and probably forced the inaccurate bombing. Soon after, a far more serious threat developed, and in roughly the same area.

It seems that the KG 55 raid was mounted to divert attention from Bf 110 fighter-bombers of Erpro 210 skirting fast the Isle of Wight and making direct for Supermarine's Woolston works at Southampton where Spitfires were still being built. How long overdue was such a venture! That the Germans confused work at Woolston with activity at the Hamble factory where the Albemarle bomber was under way seems just too incredible to accept. They must have known that Spitfires were built at Woolston long before Castle Bromwich began churning them out fast. Where did they suppose they came from, other than the Southampton region, where 'Supermarine' had been active since the 1920s? If they had made a fundamental error in the entire Battle it must surely have been in failing to destroy the production of Hurricanes and Spitfires. This attempt came too late, and the Solent guns drove the Bf 110s away, to end a glorious day.

By late afternoon, the sky in the south-east was clouded, not in the ordinary way but because the huge number of fighting aircraft had produced enough vapour to entirely cover the previously blue sky.

Late that evening, with the nation's ears tuned to the BBC, an Air Ministry communiqué was quoted announcing that, 'In today's air battle 185 enemy aircraft have been destroyed.' It fostered jubilation throughout the land on this, the best Sunday of the war so far. At last one could sense that, just as 'Winnie' had encouraged us to believe, victory really was possible, incredible as it seemed.

'Come on,' my mother said to me, 'look how late it is', with the clock showing well beyond midnight. As I retired very, very sleepy — like millions — a few, '*the* few', exhausted after combat, and so many more after long hours of war service, ARP duty and factory shifts — it was hard to sleep after all the excitement and

We must take September 15th as the culminating date of the air battle. On this day the Luftwaffe made its greatest concentrated effort in a resumed daylight attack on London. It was one of the decisive battles of the war and, like the Battle of Waterloo, it was on a Sunday. I asked if early results had come to hand. The attack appeared to have been repelled satisfactorily. It was evident that the enemy had everywhere pierced our defences. Many squadrons of German bombers with their fighter escort had been reported over London. Although post-war information has shown that th enemy's losses on this day were only 56, September 15th was the crux of the Battle of Britain. On September 17th, as we now know, the Führer decided to postpone the invasion indefinitely. Thus perished Operation Sealion, and September 15th will stand as the date of its demise.

Winston Churchill,
Post-war recorded recollections

celebration. Dad called to me, 'Reckon your Air Force has done well today, boy!' I was already wondering just which 'Spits' and Hurricanes, and just who, had achieved this miracle. How astonished I would have been had I known that one day I might be in a position to know. . . well, almost!

The fighters in the battles — 15th September 1940

According to the relevant squadron Operations Record Books, the aircraft used were as follows.
Many squadrons were in action twice, i) between 11:00 and 12:30 and ii) between about 13:45 and 16:00.
No. 17 Squadron Hurricanes: ii only) P2794, V6553, V7416, V7408, P2972, P3033, P3027, V7888, P3894, P3536, P3878
No. 19 Squadron Spitfires: i) X4336, R6991, X4179, X4070, X4237, X4352, X4351, X4353; ii) X4170, N3199, X4070, X4336, X4179, P9431, R6991, X4237, X4353, X4352, X4351, X4173, X4331
No. 41 Squadron Spitfires: i) X4343, P9324, X4068, X4338, X4344, R6687, R6619, X4409, P9427, R6605 — operated again, X4345 replacing X4068
No. 46 Squadron Hurricanes: i) V7438, V6852, P3066, R4182, V7442, V7443, P3816, N2497, N2599, V6550; ii) all operated again except N2497 and N2599 replaced by P2968 and V6582
No. 66 Squadron Spitfires: i) X4322, X4020, R6800, R6927, X4253, X4326; ii) X4302, N3029, X4176, R6925, R6603, R6771

No. 72 Squadron Spitfires: X4337, R6881, X4416, N3068, K9940, X4340, X4063, P9460, X4252, K9989; ii) all operated again except K9940 and X4063

No. 73 Squadron Hurricanes: i) Aircraft 'J', 'B', 'K', P2975, L2036, P3868, P3785, P8812, P3226; ii) 'B', 'N', P2975, P3785, L2035, P3226

No. 74 Squadron Spitfires: Mk IIs i) P7363, P7364, P7312; ii) P7368, P7367, P7329

No. 92 Squadron Spitfires: P9371, X4038, R6767, R6606, R6616, N3248, P9544, R6760, R6622, X4051; ii) all flew second sorties except R6767, P9544 and R6622; also K9998 and P9513

No. 152 Squadron Spitfires — 6 of 'B' Flight operated off Portland

No. 222 Squadron Spitfires: afternoons only, K9939, L1089, X4341, P9878, P9469, N3202, K9993, P9397

No. 238 Squadron Hurricanes: P2836, P3920, P3426, P2983, P3219, P3920, P3618, P3836, P3230, P3611, P3833, P2681, P3178

No. 242 Squadron (led Nos. 19, 302, 310 and 611 Squadrons of 12 Group): i) V6576, 2982?, V7467, V6576, P3151, R4385, V6578, V7203, P3054, 2884, R4115; ii) all flew second sorties except V6576, R4385, V6578, R4115 — replaced by P3048, P3458

No. 249 Squadron Hurricanes: i) V6559, V6683, P3834, V6556, V6622, V6685, P3579, V6594, V6635, V6680 and one unknown; ii) V6559, V6683, P3834, V6566, V6622, P3615, V6693, V6617, V6635, V6680 and two unknown

No. 253 Squadron Hurricanes: P2958, R2686, V7466, P5179, V6637, N2588, P3609, P3537; ii) P5172, P2865, P2958, N2455, P5179, N2588, R2686, V6637, V6698

No. 257 Squadron Hurricanes: i) V6557, V7357, P3705, P3776, V7254, P3642, R4190, P3893; ii) R4190, P3898, P3705, P2835, V6557, V7351, P2960, P3775, V6555 (Stanford Tuck)

No. 302 (Polish) Squadron Hurricanes: i) R2684:B, P3935:D, P2954:E, P3867:F, V6569:K, R4095:M, P3812:L; ii) 'B', 'F', 'L' with V6571:Q, P2752:R and P3812:Z

No. 303 (Polish) Squadron Hurricanes: P3089, V6665, P3939, R2685, P3120, P3577, V7244, V7235, V7289, P2903, V6673, V7465; ii) P3089, V7465, V7235, V6673, L2099, V6684, P3577, R2685, P3120, P3939

No. 310 (Czech) Squadron Hurricanes: i) R4089, V7304, L2713, R4087, V6619, P3612, R4085, V6608, P3143, P3056, V6542, V6556; ii) R4085, V6608, P3143, P3056, V6556, V6579, P3887, L2713, R4089, R4087, V6619, P3612

No. 1 Squadron RCAF Hurricanes: P3859, L1973, P3080, '323', V6669, P3672, V7288, P3647, V6605, V6609, P3876, V6603; ii) V6603, V6609, P3647, L1973, P3859, V6671, P3672, V6669, V6605

No. 501 Squadron Hurricanes: i) P3397, V7403, V6545, P3820, L1572, P5193, V6600, V6672, V6570, P2760, V7357, V6645, P5194, V7433, '2760'; ii) V6672, P5193, V6545, P3820, V7357, V6645, '5494?', L1657, V6600

No. 504 Squadron Hurricanes: P3415, P3774, P2987, P3388, P3614, N2705, N2481, L1913, P3414, L1583, N2725, P2908; ii) P3429, P3774, P2987, P3388, P3614, N2705, P2908, P3414

No. 602 Squadron Spitfires — afternoon only: X4411, X4414, N3242, X4382, X4389, R6780, X4269, R6601, X4412, R6839, X4390, X4160

No. 603 Squadron Spitfires: i) R7019, X4359, N3267, X4324, X4323, X4348, P9440, P9499, X4274, R6836, X4394, X4250; ii) R7019, X4359, N3267, X4323, X4324, R6836, P9499, K9803, X4274, X4378, P9440, X4250

No. 605 Squadron Hurricanes: i) P3580, V6699, P3583, P3677, P3832, L2018, P3308, N2352, P2589, P3737, P3828, L2122; ii) P3677, L2012, P3583, P3832, P3965, P2589, P3737, P3828, L2122; iii) P3677, L2012, P3583, P3832, P3965, P2589, P3107, P3737, P3828

No. 607 Squadron Hurricanes: aircraft used in the two operations uncertain, combats in second scramble only, serial numbers uncertain

No. 609 Squadron Spitfires: i) R6691, N3133, L1096, X4107, K9997, R6922, R6979, N3223, R6961, R6631, R6699, R6690, X4165, R6922; ii) N3280, X4107, L1096, R6691, N3113, R6979, R6922, X4165, N3223, R6961, R6631, R6699, X4234

No. 611 Squadron Spitfires: i) P7291, P7305, P7283, P7383, P7354, P7302, P7303, P7314, P7322, P7322, P7323, P7299, P7284, P7282; ii) P7284, P7323, P7282, P7291, P7283, P7302, P7303, P7305

No. 615 Squadron Hurricanes: operated in afternoon only, Brooklands area, aircraft used uncertain

Sorties flown by Fighter Command and Luftwaffe during and related to operations against the United Kingdom 13 August-15 September 1940

Fighter Command listing includes all types of operational sorties flown. Luftwaffe sorties marked * are British Official approximations — and often quite inaccurate

Date (to period ending 06:00)	Fighter Command			Luftwaffe	
	Patrols	Sorties		Sorties	
		Day	Night	Day	Night
August					
13	192	889	27	1,485	?
14	132	494	26	489	?
15	227	974	?	1,786	?
16	163	895	?	1,715	?
17	100	288	15	560*	?
18	155	766	?	650*	72*
19	130	403	?	600*	150*
20	166	477	1	120*	50*
21	181	620	10	120*	50*
22	?	?	44	190*	250*
23	200	507	?	?	120*
24	187	936	45	1,030	170
25	150	481	43	730	150
26	197	787	42	1,088(total)	
27	?	288	47	225(total)	
28	187	739	22	636	340
29	125	498	28	720	220
30	208	1,054	—	1,345	260
31	192	978	29	1,450	170
September					
1	?	661	29	640	180
2	100	751	29	972	75
3	123	711	34	586	90
4	123	677	20	750	197
5	121	672	50	685	218
6	144	987	44	722	75
7	143	817	44	400*	260
8	65	215	23	170*	200*
9	68	441	25	400*	?
10	?	?	41	?	?
11	114	637	58	?	125*
12	81	190	5	50*	120*
13	98	209	?	90*	?
14	?	?	28	400*	140*
15	115	705	68	930 + *	175*

Luftwaffe losses during operations 8-15 September 1940

a indicates shot down *b* crashed during sortie *c* seriously damaged

September	8			9			10			11			12			13			14			15		
Type	a	b	c	a	b	c	a	b	c	a	b	c	a	b	c	a	b	c	a	b	c	a	b	c
Do 17P	—	—	—	—	—	—	—	—	—	—	—	—	—	—	—	—	—	—	1	—	—	—	—	—
Do 17Z	3	2	—	—	—	—	1	—	—	—	—	—	—	—	—	—	—	—	—	—	2	16	—	4
Do 18	—	—	—	—	—	—	—	—	—	—	—	—	—	—	—	—	—	—	1	—	—	—	—	—
He 59	—	—	—	—	—	—	—	—	—	—	—	—	—	—	—	1	—	1	—	1	—	—	—	—
He 111H	—	—	—	2	—	1	—	—	—	9	1	3	—	—	—	—	1	—	3	—	—	9	1	2
He 111P	—	1	1	—	—	—	—	1	—	—	1	—	—	1	—	—	1	—	—	—	—	3	—	—
He 115	1	—	—	—	—	—	—	—	—	—	—	—	—	—	—	—	—	—	—	—	—	—	—	—
Hs 126	—	—	—	—	—	—	—	—	—	—	—	—	—	—	—	—	—	—	1	—	—	—	—	—
Ju 88	1	3	2	5	2	—	1	1	—	—	—	—	1	2	1	—	1	1	—	—	1	2	—	2
Bf 109	—	2	—	12	1	1	—	—	—	6	1	1	—	—	—	—	1	—	3	—	2	18	1	1
Bf 110	—	—	—	3	—	1	—	—	—	6	1	1	—	—	—	—	—	—	—	—	—	—	—	—
TOTALS	5	8	3	22	3	3	2	2	—	21	4	5	1	3	1	1	4	2	6	1	7	48	2	9

RAF losses during operations 8-15 September 1940

a indicates failed to return/shot down, *b* battle casualty, *c* seriously damaged

September	8			9			10			11			12			13			14		
Type	a	b	c	a	b	c	a	b	c	a	b	c	a	b	c	a	b	c	a	b	c
Blenheim F	—	—	—	—	—	—	1	—	—	—	—	—	—	—	—	—	—	—	1	—	—
Beaufighter	1	—	—	—	—	—	—	—	—	—	—	—	—	—	—	—	—	—	—	—	—
Defiant	—	—	—	—	—	—	—	—	—	—	—	—	—	—	—	—	—	—	—	—	—
Hurricane	3	—	—	14	2	2	—	—	—	18	—	3	—	2	—	1	—	—	7	—	1
Spitfire	—	—	—	5	1	1	—	—	—	13	—	3	—	—	—	—	—	—	6	1	2
Battle	—	—	—	—	—	—	1	—	—	—	—	—	—	—	—	—	—	—	—	—	—
Blenheim B	—	—	—	—	—	—	—	—	—	—	—	—	—	—	—	1	—	—	—	—	—
Hampden	—	—	—	—	—	—	—	—	—	2	—	—	2	1	—	1	—	—	—	—	—
Wellington	—	—	—	—	—	—	—	—	—	—	1	—	1	1	—	—	—	—	—	—	—
Whitley	—	—	—	—	—	—	1	—	—	3	—	—	—	—	—	—	—	—	—	—	—
Coastal Cmd	3	—	—	—	—	—	1	—	—	5	—	—	—	—	—	2	—	—	1	—	—
TOTALS	7	—	—	19	3	3	3	—	—	41	1	6	3	4	—	3	—	—	16	1	3

September	15			TOTAL			September	15			TOTAL		
Type	a	b	c	a	b	c	Type	a	b	c	a	b	c
Blenheim F	—	—	—	1	1	0	Blenheim B	—	—	—	1	0	0
Beaufighter	1	—	—	2	0	0	Hampden	—	—	—	5	1	0
Defiant	—	—	—	0	0	0	Wellington	—	1	—	1	3	0
Hurricane	19	1	4	62	5	10	Whitley	2	—	—	6	0	0
Spitfire	6	—	3	31	2	8	Coastal Cmd	—	—	—	12	0	0
Battle	—	—	—	1	0	0	TOTALS	28	2	7	122	12	18

CHAPTER 13

ARE THEY COMING?

The intensity of the German air assault over the past week was generally assumed to mean that the invasion was about to be mounted. The question was, 'When?'

At the start of September, 27 infantry divisions formed the protecting Home Force. About a dozen were fairly well equipped, the rest half trained — and none of the Mobile Brigades had experienced 'blitzkrieg' warfare. The main reserves in the Midlands would be drawn upon while forward troops fought any landing and the RAF attacked its supply forces. About 500

light tanks, 500 anti-tank/light guns and 350 heavier type tanks were operational, so the army was far from well supplied. The LDV — which became the Home Guard on 31 July — was half a million men strong and was prepared to hamper enemy movement. Its younger members had been formed into mobile brigades — of a sort, for they relied upon motor cycles, commandeered vans and bicycles. Shades, indeed, of a familiar family entertainment — *Dad's Army* — although it was a far better force than often portrayed! Off the East Coast a mine barrage

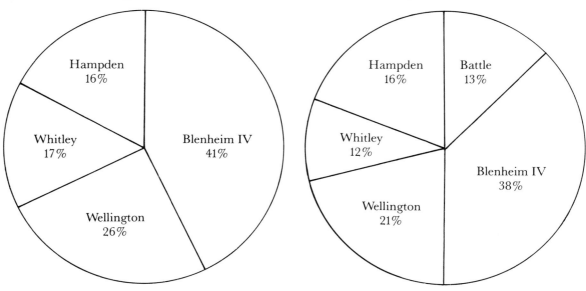

Composition of RAF Bomber Command by aircraft types — 15 August, 1940

Hampden 16%
Whitley 17%
Blenheim IV 41%
Wellington 26%

Composition of RAF Bomber Command by aircraft types — 15 September, 1940

Hampden 16%
Battle 13%
Whitley 12%
Blenheim IV 38%
Wellington 21%

Aircraft available in RAF bomber squadrons, 15 September, 1940 established/serviceable
(A)   (B)

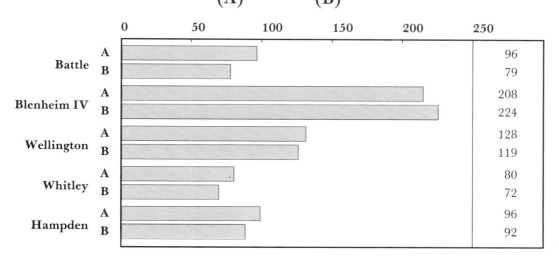

		A	value
Battle	A		96
	B		79
Blenheim IV	A		208
	B		224
Wellington	A		128
	B		119
Whitley	A		80
	B		72
Hampden	A		96
	B		92

had been sown, small minefields barring approaches to many southern ports. Taken all round, the defences were not insignificant.

Across the Channel the first assault wave was still moving into place. In ports between Flush-

A German photograph of preparations aboard barges — possibly at Antwerp — and including the Ascenseur *of Antwerp,* Ben-Hur *and* Lea. *Square bows allowed several to be pushed, straight sides permitting grouping.* (Bundesarchiv)

Not the image one had at the time of German troops training to overcome us. Still, they are showing great spirit — and enjoying themselves. The tug would have been used to push some barges to England — hopefully! (Bundesarchiv)

ing and Le Havre suitable ships, motor boats, inland waterway barges and their tugs had been assembled, a German manifest of 4 September listing 168 transports, 1,600 motor boats, 419 tugs and 1,910 large 'Rhine-type' barges, many stolen from their rightful owners. There were, according to the German Navy, more than enough ships for the task. Everything was to be in place by 19 September, the Navy adding that it would take ten days to lay minefields to prevent flank attacks and generally to prepare for sea. Hitler would therefore need to have given the executive command on 11 September for the assault intended to be launched on the 21st.

There was, for him, just one little snag... the Luftwaffe had failed to destroy Fighter Command and did not control the sky over the English Channel. Hitler therefore advanced the decision date to 14 September, giving the Luftwaffe three more days to act decisively. Instead both 11 and 12 September brought indecisive

action, so on the 13th the Navy told Hitler that the invasion was not yet feasible. On 14 September Hitler on staff advice further postponed action to the 17th. On the 15th senior naval officers rated the event a 'dangerous gamble' after the Luftwaffe was given a hiding on what became known as Battle of Britain Day.

Bad weather then rolled in, interfering with minelaying. Even had the go-ahead been given on the 17th — when the RAF was proving itself very much intact and effective — no invasion launch would have been possible before 8 October, due to the need for suitable tidal considerations. There was also the assumption that on the selected day the sea state would allow towed inland watercraft to complete a Channel crossing. Bearing in mind the enormous amount of training and preparation needed to mount the 1944 Allied Normandy landings one cannot but question the readiness of the Germans to mount a successful sea crossing, land, advance and then be capable of supporting such a huge and difficult venture.

They had made some preparations for air support, by bringing the Stuka force close to the Dover Straits, and also gathered more Bf 109s. Luftflotte 5 was deprived of He 111s of KG 26 and Ju 88s of KG 30 now based in Belgium

Big Wing

By the Official closing date of the Battle of Britain (31 October) 2,698 German aircraft were claimed as destroyed. Post-war examination of Luftwaffe records suggested 1,733. Comparative German claims amounted to 3,058 British aircraft; 915 fighters is the British official figure. Would the British have scored higher using different tactics?

Dowding sited half his effective fighter force in 11 Group and the south-east, relieving squadrons when they tired. There had, however, been smouldering criticism that he should have held more squadrons in 11 Group and adjacent 12 Group Sectors, for the short range of the Bf 109 limited it to day fighting thereabouts, and the criticism was to flare up after the Battle was won.

Dowding's aerodromes had insufficient room for more squadrons and would have easily become congested, ideal targets, and left other parts of Britain wide open to attack. Supporting, maintaining, operating more squadrons would not have been easy. Coastal convoys, highly vulnerable to attack, had to be covered, even escorted. Fighter conservation was essential too, for there was no early indication of the length of the campaign. In consequence Park had to field small responses during much of the Battle.

Both Dowding and Park were criticized for their work, particularly by the rather forceful Air Vice-Marshal Trafford Leigh-Mallory, No. 12 Group commander. When called upon to aid 11 Group by guarding its territory north of the Thames 12 Group fielded from Duxford a formation of three, four, even seven squadrons. Usually leading the 12 Group contribution was Squadron Leader Douglas Bader, who had lost both legs as a result of a flying accident in 1931. By 'stealth', along with courage, tenacity and skilful use of his two metal legs, he had managed to resume flying duties on the outbreak of war and spent a while at Duxford in 1939 before in the summer of 1940 taking command of Coltishall's 242 Squadron, which generally led Leigh-Mallory's formation.

There was considerable support in Air Ministry for the 'large formation' and when the differences of opinion began to be strongly aired the Air Staff ordered an enquiry. The heart of the matter was that the two Group commanders faced very different threats. Park, often receiving only a few minutes warning of attack, had to respond fast, his squadrons sometimes taking off as bombs fell on their airfields. They rarely had time to unite prior to combat, whereas 12 Group had ample warning time, allowing its squadrons to formate prior to engaging. It was paramount for 11 Group squadrons to guard their bases as well as engage incoming raids and difficult even for squadrons to pair off in time for action. Initial interception by 11 Group squadrons undoubtedly raised 12 Group success rate. The 12 Group squadrons could not resist the temptation to score more by chasing raiders well into the 11 Group area, thus leaving northern 11 Group stations unprotected. The size of 12 Group formations confused the raid reporting and controlling system into mistaking them for enemy forces, resulting in wasted and dangerous effort. So went the arguments.

The outcome was undoubtedly harsh, for in November 1940 both Dowding and Park were 'rested', the former joining the British Mission in the USA and Park being given a post, albeit important, in Training Command, before he distinguished himself yet again in Malta. Doubtless they had earned a period of respite after their outstanding, unequalled efforts. Perhaps Leigh-Mallory was a very suitable choice to head 11 Group when it gradually switched to an offensive role requiring large formations. Maybe Air Chief Marshal W. Sholto Douglas, Deputy Chief of the Air Staff, was a sound choice as Dowding's successor. Nevertheless, the changes shocked many at the time and were made in a most ungenerous manner. The British have a poor record in rewarding successful leadership, tantamount to almost punishing it, as in the removal of Dowding and Park after proving such brilliant leaders.

Above *Sergeant John Hannah was 18 years old when during a raid on Antwerp on 15 September he extinguished a fire in a Hampden in which he was wireless operator/air gunner. Two other crew members had baled out. Hannah's courage earned him a Victoria Cross.* (IWM)

Below *Well, well! As life jacketed troops in 'bathing costumes' try to get a gun ashore a trooper on the left is taking some nice holiday snap shots with his fine Leica. Somebody else snapped him evidently!* (Bundesarchiv)

and the Netherlands. That freed Scotland and its naval anchorages from repeated attention. On the morning of 7 September, the day of the first huge London raid, there were serviceable about 600 bombers and 700 fighters in Luftflotte 2 available for independent operations or supporting the 16th Army in its invasion attempt. To its west Luftflotte 3 could field 350 bombers and 100 fighters. All that they needed was control of the air and the Channel, and they had neither.

As they gazed greedily northwards the Germans must surely have wondered just how it was that a few fighter pilots had managed to thwart the vaunted Luftwaffe. Their main problem was that they never came to terms with the skilfully prepared and brilliantly conceived defence of the United Kingdom, undoubtedly imagining that they could generate enough force and terror to destroy the most stout hearted. Their intelligence deductions misled them into much wasted time and effort. They had not thought out the air campaign, whereas the British had and were still devising the means for victory.

The withdrawal of German units from Norway was soon discovered, which meant that an invasion of Scotland was no longer to be feared. The strength of invasion forces in France and the Low Countries was not clearly known and

the task of discovering it was placed in the hands of RAF Bomber Command, Coastal Command and in particular the Photographic Reconnaissance Unit, an organisation worthy of special consideration.

The decision of 22 March 1939 to form at Heston a Photographic Development Unit to operate camera-equipped 'high speed' aircraft

Above *Did they really mean to invade us aided by mules? In the highly mechanized, mighty Wehrmacht horses and mules were used extensively.* (Bundesarchiv)

Below *More businesslike, these two, obviously feeling the Channel air bracing while their men wrestle with the business of disembarking from a very large and quite unsuitable barge.* (IWM)

with 'invisibility' qualities was implemented when hand-picked staff for the unit began arriving on 3 October 1939. On 18 January 1940 the unit's first PR operation from Britain took place when a Spitfire left Stradishall to photograph Terschelling. On 1 April the Development Unit became the operational Photographic Reconnaissance Unit.

On 1 July 1940 'A' Flight was formed and at once ordered to Wick to watch from there for movements in Norwegian ports. Then 'B' Flight shifted to St Eval to observe Brest and the west and north-west coasts of France.

Both Flights dispatched their first operational sorties on 3 July. By then fine photographs of the Channel ports and French coastal areas taken from pale pink, cream and light blue coloured Spitfires flying high were being secured. Two more Flights, 'C' and 'D', formed on 24 July with Spitfires at Heston, concentrating upon photography of the Channel ports.

By the end of July 78 sorties had been flown from Heston, 57 bringing back photographs. Another 93 were flown in August, and although

Invasion build-up details were secured largely from photographs secured by specialized blue, cream or pink painted Spitfires of the PRU. 'One-off' aircraft, each had a personalized camera fit.

there were signs of invasion preparations none appeared far advanced. No barges were evident on photographs produced after a sortie to Ostend by Spitfire R6879 on the 28th but three days later 18 had arrived and within hours a fast build-up of ships and barges was being recorded. Between 1 and 4 September about 100 barges arrived at Flushing and on the 6th and 7th many reached Calais and Dunkirk. On 4 September cameras in the first production Spitfire, K9787, secured pictures of Boulogne, and those in N3117 recorded 270 in Ostend alone on 7 September. It was believed that the invasion was about to be mounted.

Early that evening, while fires raged in Woolwich and London's dockland, the Combined Intelligence Committee met and soon informed the Chiefs of Staff that tidal conditions favoured an invasion between 8 and 10 September. Invasion believed near, Alert No. 1 was signalled widely and at 19:07 the codeword 'Cromwell' was flashed to Eastern and Southern Army Commands and GHQ Reserve, but not to the Home Guard. The codeword implied 'imminent action' and when some Home Guard units discovered the alert they rang the church bells to warn their areas. A stop had to be quickly put to that, and next day Home Guard members were told not to ring the bells unless they

Blenheims and Hudsons also undertook PR sorties, among them this 'LY' marked Blenheim IV shot down in Holland. (via G.J. Zwanenburg)

had actually set eyes upon at least 25 German paratroops. Among the PR fliers taking a look along the French coast on 8 September was, again, Spitfire K9787 (virtually 'the first of the few') which between 10:00 and 11:30 operated between Zeebrugge and Calais. That month 100 out of 126 sorties from Heston were effective as well as eight from Wick and 30 from St Eval.

Alert No. 1 meant that the Navy, its capital ships sailing south, would need to be ready to react rapidly. The RAF, expecting the landing within three days, placed 24 bombers at 'readiness' and ordered half of the remainder to be prepared to attack German forces at sea. All troops were ready between dusk and dawn and at eight hours readiness in daylight. The situation was then far from eased when four spies, caught after rowing across the Channel and landing on the south coast, admitted they had come to report upon movements of the reserve forces.

Whilst no details of all these matters were revealed, there was public awareness of impending invasion. Matters were not helped when

alarming rumours quickly spread that an invasion attempt had been made, and that many bodies were being washed ashore, some horribly burned, from sunken ships. There was little truth in these tales, but the bodies were from invasion training incidents or from the air battle.

Late in June 1940 Bomber Command's invasion task was decreed — the sinking of ships in their ports and during their invasion voyages. In this the Fleet Air Arm would assist. On 4 July invasion ports and barges were added to Bomber Command's target listing, but in August 1940 the targets were deemed still not ready for massive attention, although 2 Group Blenheims frequently attacked barges on Dutch and Belgian waterways. The Hampden raid of 12 August on the Dortmund Ems Canal undoubtedly delayed barge assembly.

During the first week of September Bomber Command continued attacking industrial targets, utilities and communications, which included small-scale penetrations to Berlin, Magdeburg, Stettin, Munich and sending handfuls of Whitleys to Italy. On 2/3 September 29 Wellingtons carrying, among many other incendiaries, 15 examples of 250-lb light case fire bomb, set out with the intention of setting light to

An oblique shot from a PR sortie showing 'Rhine barges' assembled for the invasion attempt. (IWM)

forests in Germany's Schwarzwald and Thuringerwald. Bosch works at Stuttgart, oil plants at Ossage and Rheinmettal Borsig's Berlin factory, all were attacked by Hampdens, Wellingtons and Whitleys while Blenheims intruded on airfields and the German's big guns at Cap Gris Nez. That was until 7 September when, invasion alert effective, the bombers began destroying the assembled vessels in the Channel ports.

That first night 26 Hampdens called on Ostend, dropping 194 x 250-lb HEs and 360 x 4-lb incendiaries onto loading vessels, while 13 Blenheims dealt with Dunkirk's assembly and 11 Battles of 1 Group delivered 17 x 250-lb and 153 x 40-lb HEs and 10 x 25-lb incendiaries. In daylight next day Blenheims attacked destroyers off the Dutch coast; at night 18 Blenheims raided Ostend, repeating that attack 21-strong the next night, while Battles called on Calais. On 10/11 September 14 Hampdens and

six Blenheims bombed Calais and 15 Hampdens and nine Blenheims Ostend, while more Blenheims tackled invasion shipping in Boulogne and Flushing. There was even more bombing of the invasion fleet on 11/12 including 20 Wellingtons which joined 11 Blenheims raiding Ostend.

Throughout each day PRU's Spitfires repeatedly photographed the invasion ports, bringing back vital evidence of the build-up — and destruction. Nine such flights were made on the 9th and again on the 11th, and five on the 13th before that night 91 bomber sorties were directed against the invasion fleet. Thereafter, until a return to industrial targets on 23/24 September, most of the night effort was directed at the Channel ports. Details of those raids are given on page 186. By 17 September, in Dunkirk alone, 84 barges had been sunk or damaged, 200 by two nights later. Photo reconnaissance on 20 September then surprisingly showed ships leaving the ports and leaving for Germany. On 18 September, 1,004 barges were visible between Flushing and Boulogne — only 691 by the end of the month. Initially it was thought that they had been dispersed in an effort to protect them from air attack. On 31 October PR flights revealed only 448 barges still in their ports, a mere 45 of them in Flushing.

Hitler, with the air war not won, his landing force nightly bombarded and his Navy warning of the hazardous nature of the venture, had on 17 September decided to postpone Operation Sealion till October. By 21 September a tenth of the fleet had been dispersed. Constant movement makes the number of vessels committed variable, but German figures for 21 September list:

	Assembled	Lost/damaged
Transport vessels	170 + 4 in transit	21
Barges	1,918 + 424 in transit	214
Tugs	386	5

British reliance for up-to-the-minute news on the composition of the invasion force depended very much upon Heston's PRU and its London photo interpretation unit. The enemy, certainly aware of this activity, on 17 September laid a stick of HE bombs across Heston, one of which fell on the tarmac by the main hangar. Then on 18 September HEs and fire bombs fell on Heston's eastern end. Next night brought real trouble when at 22:48 a raider circled the aerodrome before carefully placing a parachute mine on the tarmac by the main hangar, which was blown apart, along with its contents. Blast, the weapon's main donation, tore through the Operations Block, badly damaging a smaller hangar's roof. Five Spitfires and ten other aircraft were variously damaged. Next day Air Marshal Sir Arthur Bowhill, AOC-in-C Coastal Command, hurried along to view the serious damage.

For the Luftwaffe, while an intended invasion remained, the wearing down of Fighter Command continued, although the loss of so many bombers and skilled crews with vital invasion tasks could not be brushed aside. On 12 October Hitler decided to postpone the invasion; not until January 1941, however, was Operation Sealion abandoned. On that basis it could well be argued that the Battle of Britain continued long after October, although the postponement of the invasion on 12 October until 1941 might well be a chosen date upon which to consider the Battle completed.

Assessment of invasion barge build-up from Spitfire PR photographs

September	1	3	5	6	7	8	9	11	14	16	18	23	27	Oct. 21
Beveland canal	71	240	40											
Hanasweert	80		80					38	38					
Ghent/ Terneuzen	200		200		120									
Terneuzen														
Ostend		+50	+110	273	302	300		250	250	250	250	227	170	65
Boulogne			+50	61	11	65	70	90	90	102	150	230	230	125
Flushing			+100		130	200		200	150	145	145	140	75+	15
Middleburg			70										50	18
Le Havre				15					34		205	200	220+	54
Calais				53	85	86		140	120	120	266		140	160
Gravelines								40	40	40	15	36	51	40
Dunkirk				65	97			110	110	100	140	220	220	130
Dunkirk Canal				100							80			
Ghent					120									
Delfzyl								150	150	150	150	150	150	240
Ijmuiden									20				62	62
Antwerp									625	625	625	600		500
Emden												65	75	133
Amsterdam												300	300	180
Rotterdam												650	400	446

Bomber Command raids on invasion ports 13/14-22/24 September 1940

Date	Antwerp	Boulogne	Calais	Dunkirk	Flushing	Le Havre	Ostend
13/14	15 Wellingtons	9 Hampdens —	9 Whitleys 11 Blenheims	9 Whitleys 8 Blenheims	— —	— —	10 Hampdens 10 Blenheims
14/15	10 Whitleys	10 Battles	—	3 Blenheims	—	—	4 Blenheims 17 Wellingtons
15/16	—	11 Blenheims	27 Wellingtons	23 Blenheims	—	—	—
16/17	24 Hampdens	—	—	—	4 Hampdens	—	8 Wellingtons
17/18	20 Hampdens	20 Battles 13 Blenheims	22 Wellingtons	27 Blenheims	8 Hampdens	—	15 Wellingtons 10 Whitleys
18/19	5 Whitleys	7 Battles	11 Blenheims	9 Blenheims	6 Wellingtons	22 Wellingtons 25 Hampdens	16 Blenheims
19/20	—	—	—	—	4 Hampdens	—	5 Hampdens
20/21	10 Hampdens	10 Battles 7 Hampdens	19 Wellingtons	25 Blenheims	10 Wellingtons	—	14 Wellingtons
21/22	—	21 Whitleys	16 Wellingtons 6 Battles	21 Blenheims 14 Wellingtons	—	—	8 Hampdens 5 Blenheims
22/23	3 Hampdens	8 Hampdens 4 Wellingtons	8 Wellingtons 12 Blenheims	5 Blenheims —	5 Hampdens	10 Hampdens 11 Wellingtons	10 Blenheims 3 Hampdens
23/24	—	9 Battles	26 Blenheims 2 Battles	—	—	—	13 Blenheims

Additional attacks:
17/18 Terneuzen— 7 Hampdens
18/19 Terneuzen— 7 Whitleys
22/23 Terneuzen— 6 Whitleys
25/26 Ostend and Dunkirk— 16 Battles
25/26 Boulogne and Calais— 18 Blenheims and 27 Wellingtons
26/27 Le Havre— 13 Wellingtons and 15 Whitleys

CHAPTER 14

FORGOTTEN ONES

'Last night, Anson bombers of Coastal Command attacked the docks at Brest, and yesterday Hudsons bombed shipping off Norway. Blenheims of Coastal Command bombed the docks at Le Havre and engaged enemy aircraft over the Channel. Three oil tankers bringing petrol vital for our fighters were escorted into Milford Haven by Sunderlands and Ansons, while high-flying PR Spitfires photographed the enemy coastline from Bergen to Bordeaux. Blenheim fighters escorted an Empire Flying-Boat safely during the last stage of its flight to Britain. Over the Channel an Anson escorting a convoy fought off attacks by four Messerschmitts. A Beaufort torpedoed a 6,000-ton vessel in Calais roads. Whitleys manned by Bomber Command crews, Stranraers, Blenheim fighters, Hudsons and Ansons again escorted convoys approaching our north-west ports. From these operations three of our aircraft are missing.'

On no account would such an Air Ministry communiqué have been released, for 'security reasons', yet its like could have appeared on many Battle of Britain days. Sad that the heroism of those who served with Coastal Command throughout the 1939-45 war has received scant attention, that their contribution to the winning of the Battle of Britain has gone almost unnoticed, maybe due to its complex and extensive nature. (A detailed survey of the work of the Command, its squadrons and aircraft can, incidentally, be found in *Aircraft for the Few*, companion volume to this.)

'Ansons bombing Brest?' you may question. Certainly seems unlikely, yet three times in September 1940 217 Squadron's 'faithful Annies' did just that. We are apt to think of Ansons as trainers and light transports, but they performed well, operationally, in Coastal Command.

Even prior to hostilities, and indeed beyond their European conclusion, Coastal Command's squadrons were fully operational. It was Coastal Command Anson crew of 608 Squadron that, early on 1 July 1940, spotted a half-

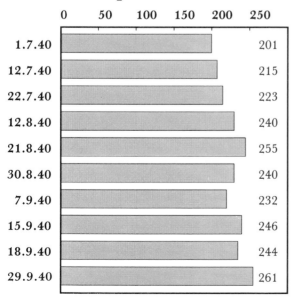

Numbers of serviceable aircraft in RAF Coastal Command Squadrons.

Date	Number
1.7.40	201
12.7.40	215
22.7.40	223
12.8.40	240
21.8.40	255
30.8.40	240
7.9.40	232
15.9.40	246
18.9.40	244
29.9.40	261

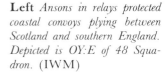

Above *Ansons of 217 Squadron really did bomb Brest! Two of the squadron's aircraft, N9742 and K6285, are seen here earlier in September 1940 and in the hands of 321 Dutch Squadron.* (IWM)

Left *Ansons in relays protected coastal convoys plying between Scotland and southern England. Depicted is OY:E of 48 Squadron.* (IWM)

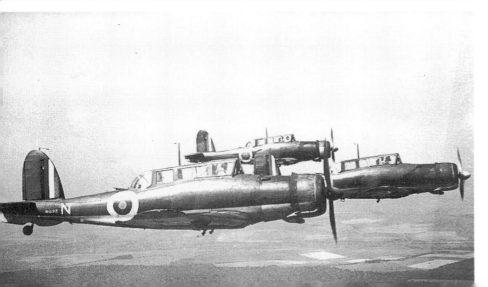

As well as with its Swordfishes the Fleet Air Arm was ready to tackle an invasion with a few Blackburn Skuas. One was N:L2934.

The Roc was the turreted version of the Skua. Its turret added firepower but too much weight. What part if any the Roc played in the Battle is uncertain, but an operational Flight was based for a short time at Cambridge possibly there to strafe any east coast landing? Illustrated — L3114-E, L3119-O.

submerged He 59 floatplane off West Hartlepool, an item some rate as the first fighter success of the Battle. In direct contrast, Hudsons of 220, 224 and 233 Squadrons next day carried out typically hazardous daylight attacks on MVs and destroyers sailing in convoy off Lotbrerg, in the face of flak and fighters and at a time when invasion from Norway was thought feasible. Then, after dark, a dozen Swordfish of 825 Squadron Fleet Air Arm (among those seconded to work with the Command) set off to bomb barges in the River Maas. Only three were successful, 'B' and 'H' failing to return and three others crashing — 'R' near Harwich, 'L' at Birchington and 'M' on Harrocks Island, Suffolk — in a venture typical of many worthy of long stories. That same night another six, of 812 Squadron, set off from North Coates to the same target area, which only one crew located and in the face of intense flak. Their companions in five Albacores of 826 Squadron, Bircham Newton, attacked a ship off the Hook. Such operations by the FAA were many times repeated, along with mining, often from dangerously low levels in heavily defended areas of the Maas, the Scheldt, Ems Estuary and Hubert Gat. The Fleet Air Arm's part in the Battle is scarcely remembered.

Bircham Newton's Blenheims, and Hudsons of 206 Squadron, long active against shipping, were allocated search and strike areas off the Dutch and Belgian coasts. As early as 6 July their low- and medium-level reconnaissance flights — supporting the Command's high-flying spies — were watching barge movements. Leuchars-based Hudsons of 220 and 224 Squadrons conducted their anti-invasion and merchant shipping strike operations off Norway, frequently bombing harbours and fringe targets and, aided by Wick's 269 Squadron, typically attacked an ammunition dump at Faltoens, near Bergen, on 9/10 July

An ever increasing part in the fighting was soon taken by Blenheims after two squadrons, Nos. 53 and 59, which had specialized in reconnaissance for the BEF, joined Coastal Command on 3 July. No. 53 moved to Detling, No. 59 to Thorney Island, and both began attacking shipping in the Channel and its ports, along with coastal aerodromes and other fringe targets. On 11 July three crews of 59 Squadron searching for E-Boats south-west of Selsey Bill engaged instead a Do 17 which retired behind a smoking engine. Such confrontations became commonplace. Next day a 59 Squadron crew discovered two ships in Cherbourg harbour and, in the face of heavy AA fire, tried to sink them. A dozen Me 109s soon were engaging the Blenheim, whose crew amazingly fought them off, although the gunner was wounded.

The Ministry Says...

The Anson machine is not itself for fighting, but the fact has not deterred Anson crews from entering a scrap with enemy fighters. Last month three Anson machines engaged on reconnaissance engaged no less than nine Messerschmitts over the Channel. They destroyed two and crippled another without loss.

Air Ministry Communiqué, 17 July

Strike operations formed one part, the more spectacular, of Coastal Command's war.

Most of the Command's flying at this period of the war involved the protection of coastal convoys, for only the score or so of Sunderlands in hand had sufficient endurance necessary for prolonged ocean patrols. Most escort duty was carried out by the Command's Anson squadrons, and for Detling's No. 500 (County of Kent) Squadron that meant having its 'Annies' in the thick of the summer fighting — and bombing — along a lengthy front from Sussex to Essex. 'L' Love was on 12 July escorting east coast convoy FS19 (21 MVs and 2 destroyers) when at 07:40 nine He 111s attacked. Pilot Officer Pain and crew tackled them, claiming a Heinkel just before fighters arrived. Three survivors were rescued, although the MV *Hornchurch* was sunk. Another incident involved Sergeant Barr and crew in G/500 Squadron escorting 34 ships forming convoy FS24 on 18 July when, at 11:03, four Bf 110s dashed in and began strafing the vessels. Again an Anson crew decided to engage raiders, one of which soon plunged into the sea with a burning engine. By that time RAF fighters had arrived, but 500 Squadron maintained the victory was theirs.

Attacks on U-Boats brought usually brief,

exciting but often unrewarding moments during many, many hours of monotonous patrolling. Even when submarine attacks were accurate the results were usually indecisive, for the bombs simply did not have the charge needed to sink a U-Boat. One such attack was made on 12 July by a Fokker T8-W floatplane 'P' Peter. Before the Netherlands fell a handful of these seaplanes escaped to Britain and, manned by Dutch Navy personnel, operated out of Pembroke Dock along the Welsh Coast, where on this occasion the crew attacked a U-Boat 40 miles north of Holyhead without success. The weapon needed was the depth charge, which Sunderlands of No. 10 (RAAF) Squadron began using in July.

Throughout the campaign Sunderlands performed with distinction, and far from home, for the aircraft's operational radius was over 500 miles. On 2 July Sunderland H/210 Squadron managed to sink U-Boat U-246 with a direct hit using a 250-lb AS bomb — luck indeed — after which the Navy picked up 41 survivors. The tables were soon turned when that morning K/204 Squadron reported the sinking of the *Andora Star*. Several lengthy flights by Sunderlands included a reconnaissance flown by Pilot Officer Lindsey in L5802 'U' of 201 Squadron. Operating from Sullom Voe he flew to Narvik then to Harstaad, where, although most of his bombs hit an oil storage area, none exploded. Chagrin all round! By touch down the sortie had lasted some 15 hours. Another long flight had been undertaken much earlier, 12 July, when Squadron Leader Pearce took N9049 of No. 10 (RAAF) Squadron for a midday reconnaissance of Bordeaux and St Nazaire, a journey of 12 hours in very dangerous air space.

The Sunderland's manoeuvrability came in very useful when on 15 July Flight Lieutenant Birch in H/10 (RAAF) Squadron battled with He 111s attacking the convoy over which he was patrolling and on 2 August when V/201 Squadron fought a Do 17 north of the Shetlands. Close to the *Britannic* on 14 August J/210 Squadron battled with a Fw Condor, was damaged and forced to make for home. Shots in the hull of a flying-boat could indeed bring a particularly alarming homecoming... The common idea that a flying-boat might readily land on the open sea was often proved wrong and when Sunderland B/10 (RAAF) Squadron off Slyne Head came across a lifeboat from the *City of Benares*, the sea state prohibited putting down. A total of 39 Sunderlands and crews served in four squadrons during the Battle, acquitting themselves with great distinction. Three were posted missing on operations and another three crashed.

The Ministry Says...

The performance of the Sunderland flying-boat which went to Tromso during Sunday is one of the most spectacular flights of the war. It represents a direct flight of longer than from London to Rome and back. It came down to 50 feet above the water and the crew saw eight He 115s at their moorings. The front gunner got two bursts into at least two of the enemy aircraft, then the Sunderland climbed to 600 feet for a bombing attack. Three heavy bombs were released from this height scoring one direct hit and two misses.

Air Ministry Bulletin, 27 August

One of Coastal Command's main tasks was to watch for indications of invasion activity by flying a variety of patrols over a host of specified sea areas. It was also responsible for the observation of the movement of barges to be used in the expected invasion. Prominent in this and many other activities were Blenheims of 53 and 59 Squadron, particularly active against airfields when fighting was at its most intensive. On 21 August 53 Squadron raided Abbeville airfield and 59 Squadron bombed Caen/Carpiquet. The same day Blenheim

fighters of 236 Squadron, St Eval, had earlier protected a civilian Empire Flying Boat heading westward from the Scillies, and six Hudsons of 206 Squadron tackled two large merchant ships. No. 236 Squadron, which received Blenheim IVs on 13 July 1940 when it joined the Command, operated them in both low attack and escort duties, engaging enemy raiders when opportunity presented itself. No. 236 was dealt a harsh blow on 21 August when at 13:52 three Ju 88s attacked St Eval, badly damaging the squadron's hangar and five Blenheims therein as well as wounding three men in the orderly room. By chance another six Blenheims had just left to escort a Sunderland along the Channel when their crews spotted the Ju 88s, one of which some chased to Land's End without scoring a kill.

Also very active at this period was 235 Squadron at Thorney Island, from where it mounted defensive patrols over the aerodrome on most days between 13 and 30 August as well as escorting British minelayers. On 22/23 August six Blenheims of 53 Squadron carried out one of the earliest intruder raids, engaging a German bomber landing at St Omer while other Blenheims of 59 Squadron attended to Dinard. On 24/25 August 13 Blenheims delivered raids on Flushing and oil tanks at Cherbourg. At the same time four Albacores of 826 Squadron set off from Bircham Newton for Vlaardingen. Flak was intense, target location in a friendly nation's territory difficult, and only 'C' Charlie attacked, gliding quietly down from 13,000 to 5,000 feet to drop six 250-lb GPs and eight 25-lb incendiaries, a fair load from a biplane.

Early September found all the strike and escort squadrons very busy. On the 1st Blenheims from Bircham Newton were covering a naval force, while three Ansons and also three Beauforts of 22 Squadron searched for any U-Boats nearby. During the evening Blenheims bombed Lorient, then on 3 September the Thorney squadron raided Ostend. Next afternoon three crews of 235 Squadron discovered a Do 18 seaplane some 18 miles off the North Foreland, but it escaped before they were in a

For medium-range patrol and strike Coastal Command used the Hudson, adapted from the Lockheed 14 airliner. VX:M P5143 is shown on patrol from Bircham Newton. (IWM)

position to engage. On 11 September five Beauforts of 22 Squadron mounted a late afternoon strike against four large MVs in Ostend Roads, getting hits on one in the face of murderous fire from five escorting flak ships. Equally eventful was the activity produced when, after reconnoitring Texel, 235 Squadron-escorted Albacores bombed shipping off Calais. Pilot Officer Coggins claimed two intercepting Bf 109s but a Blenheim was also shot down and another lost to intercepting Bf 109s when others of the squadron escorted 59 Squadron raiding Boulogne. 'Battle of Britain Day, 1940', also saw the Blenheims in action, five of 53 Squadron attacking shipping off Sangatte during the late afternoon. After dark 13 crews of 53 and 59 Squadrons visited Le Havre and six naval Swordfish from Thorney Island mined off Flushing. The air maritime forces were very active indeed throughout the fight. It was, however, far from plain sailing for Coastal Command as August was also the month when difficulties with its equipment and manning levels began producing serious problems.

High hopes, soon brutally dashed, were directed towards long-awaited new types of aircraft. One was the mixed-role Blackburn Botha, the intended Anson replacement which, in the hands of Thornaby's 608 Squadron, began coastal escort duties on 10 August. Even before its operational debut it had been roundly condemned due to its inability to maintain height on one of its unreliable engines and also because of the very poor view, rendering it useless as an observation platform. Coastal Command persevered with it, but the Botha's career was brief and the squadron was relieved to re-equip fully with Ansons.

Another new type was the Bristol Beaufort torpedo bomber initially viewed as a standby aircraft in case the Botha failed, and originally intended for use only in the Far East. Problems with its Taurus engines caused it to be switched to Home Service. About 100 had been built by mid-1940, many of which had to be returned to the manufacturers for major modifications. That meant the Command had no reliable torpedo bomber to fight any invasion shipping, although a few Beaufort and Swordfish sorties operated with their prime weapons just before the Battle ended. Usually those types bombed and mined, roles they were also intended for. Against large ships the torpedo was a necessary prime, but costly, weapon.

A third disappointment was the small Saro

Torpedoes were the prime and very expensive anti-shipping wartime weapons. Delivery was never easy, as 22 Squadron's Beaufort crews found. L4516 OA-W operated with the squadron between April and December 1940. In the distance a Swordfish which the Fleet Air Arm courageously operated from North Coates. (IWM)

Lerwick flying boat, whose troubled history rivalled that of the Botha. In this case the failings were mainly aerodynamic. Until 26 July No. 209 Squadron persevered with the aircraft, flying anti-submarine patrols off the west coast. Operations ceased, then on 3 August all flying was stopped until modified engines, floats and controls were fitted. Meanwhile, the Supermarine Stranraer biplane flying-boats which the Lerwick was intended to replace soldiered on with 240 Squadron and into 1941 performing very reliably.

Aircraft problems were paralleled by another of a very different nature — lack of sufficient crews to man the Command. The problem did not escape the notice of the Prime Minister, who seemed convinced that poor serviceability and not bad management and crew shortage were responsible for reduced levels of aircraft available for operations. He pressed Air Chief Marshal Sir Frederick W. Bowhill, AOC-in-C Coastal Command, for explanations. Nothing could be done to improve the situation until

Coastal OTUs provided the necessary output.

Mid-August saw a boost given to the Command's strength when two squadrons of Fairey Battles were seconded to it and initially placed at Thorney Island before settling at Eastchurch for operations. The inadequate range of the Battle rendered it useless to Bomber Command except in an anti-invasion role for which Battle squadrons trained. Nos. 12 and 142 Squadrons were, however, lent to Coastal Command specifically for attacks on Boulogne's E-Boats to stop them from interfering with Channel shipping. Those operations commenced on 13 August, and four days later, escorted by Coastal Command's Blenheim fighters, both squadrons bravely carried out an evening raid on Boulogne. When the possibility of invasion much increased, both squadrons returned to Bomber Command and joined No. 1 Group's night attacks, mainly on Calais and Boulogne, as the invasion force prepared itself.

By the end of the Battle of Britain Coastal Command's future campaign was very evident. The U-Boat menace was clearly set to become a major and alarming threat to all supplies, not least oil. The Battle of Britain, with ample justification, may be viewed as an early part of the Battle of the Atlantic. That became evident when long-range Blenheim escort fighters were switched to operate off Northern Ireland to scare away KG 40s Fw 200 Condors increasingly harassing shipping entering the north-west approaches to Liverpool and Glasgow, ports already being bombed. Hudsons were brought from Leuchars to assist and patrolled from Aldergrove, where detached Whitleys of 102 Squadron, Prestwick-based in October, also employed their considerable duration to protect convoys. Coastal Command was indeed the most ubiquitous of all RAF Commands.

Coastal Command operational strength — 18:00 hrs

	1 July				31 August				29 September				31 October			
	a	*b*	*c*	*d*	*a*	*b*	*c*	*d*	*a*	*b*	*c*	*d*	*a*	*b*	*c*	*d*
Anson	2	18 ⎫			6	21	126	68	6	21	126	58	6	21	126	43
Anson	4	14 ⎭ 92	73													
Botha	—	—	—	—	—	—	—	—	—	—	—	10	—	—	—	6
Blenheim	3	16	48	15												
Blenheim F	—	—	—	—	2	24	48 ⎫		2	24	48 ⎫		2	24	48 ⎫	
Blenheim F	—	—	—	—	2	16	32 ⎭ 40		2	16	32 ⎭ 47		2	16	32 ⎭ 46	
Blenheim GR	—	—	—	—	2	18	33	24	2	18	36	28	2	18	36	19
Fokker T8W	—	—	—	3	—	—	—	3	—	—	—	—	—	—	—	—
Hudson	5	21	105	56	5	21	105	44	5	21	105	46	5	21	105	50
Beaufort	1	21	21	—	1	21	21	—	1	21	21	14	1	21	21	4
Battle	—	—	—	—	2	16	32	22	—	—	—	—	—	—	—	—
Sunderland	1	6 ⎫			4	6	24	15	4	6	24	16	4	6	24	10
Sunderland	3	4 ⎭ 22	12													
Lerwick	1	6	6	0	1	6	6	0	1	6	6	0	1	6	6	0
London/-Stranraer	1	6	6	4 Str	—	—	—	—	—	—	—	—	—	—	—	—
Stranraer	—	—	—	—	1	6	6	3	1	6	6	4	1	6	6	5
Wellington	1*	3	3	3	1*	3	3	0	1*	3	3	0	1	3	3	0
Whitley	—	—	—	—	—	—	—	—	—	—	—	12	—	—	—	6
FAA attached:																
Albacore	1	—	—	7	1	—	—	5	1	—	—	8	1	—	—	0
Swordfish	3	—	—	24	1	—	—	8	1	—	—	8	1	—	—	2
Walrus	—	—	—	1	—	—	—	3	—	—	—	5	—	—	—	2
PRU Spit**	1	?	?	?	1	?	?	?	1	?	?	?	1	?	?	?
TOTALS	26	115	303	198	29	158	436	235	27	142	407	256	27	142	407	193

Legend: *a* = number of squadrons
    b = squadron establishment
    c = total aircraft establishment
    d = number of aircraft serviceable
    * = One Flight, only
    ** = full details unknown

CHAPTER 15

NIGHT AND DAY

As the nation celebrated the glorious victory of the 15th, Hermann Göring was still voicing crazy notions about destroying Fighter Command in four days. Long four days! At night, however, his bombers were inflicting fearsome damage, as on 15/16 September.

Typifying many to come, it saw the vanguard of bombers arrive from Le Havre, causing London's sirens to warn at 20:09 and its guns to start firing the first of the night's 8,937 rounds at 20:14. Two hours later raiders began heading in from Dieppe, and between 01:00 and 03:00 a contingent came from Dutch and Belgian bases via Essex or the Thames Estuary. In their eagerness to destroy London, they managed to wreck the central tower of the prominent Strand Shell Mex building and damage the Gaiety Theatre along with St Thomas's, Guys and Lambeth Hospitals. Bursting shells wrenched the sky apart until 04:30, and searchlights prodded it almost continuously from 23:15 until All Clear sounded at 05:36. By that time Liverpool, the Midlands and South Wales had also been damaged. Although London was bombed on 42 consecutive nights, other areas frequently came under night attack.

Throughout 16 September Fighter Command reviewed its claims of the 15th. *If* 185 German aircraft had been brought down, where were the wrecks? Proven reports quickly suggested the score to be about one third of the original claim. Although there had been confused fighting, it appeared that pilots had often concentrated upon ensuring one kill. Even if

the score was lower than originally believed, the 15th had seen the Luftwaffe well and truly thrashed, Monday's poor weather providing a good excuse for it to avoid more harsh treatment. Nevertheless, during a morning when six shells were hurled towards Dover, over 300 German aircraft ventured high over Kent without flaunting their presence in the face of 21 RAF

London's underground station at Piccadilly Circus provided excellent night shelter.

squadrons. Then the clouds rolled in low, cloaking lone callers at many RAF stations. Besides the five German aircraft destroyed during the day, a captured He 115 floatplane was towed upside down into Eyemouth by fascinated fisherfolk.

Nightfall again protected London bombers, which brightly lit much of the East End with seven huge fires, 80 fire pumps being needed just at West Smithfield. Parts of Birmingham were hit, and at Wakefield Prison incendiaries caused a fire. Come 17 September and the Luftwaffe fielded first more lone operators, bring-

Left *After leaving any shelter one always wondered what familiar old friend might be no more. In this incident on 22 August it was a cinema in Edmonton, North London.* (IWM)

Below *The King and Queen surveying the damage on one of the occasions that Buckingham Palace was hit, while Mr Churchill, ever the politician, contemplates the photographer!* (IWM)

ing trouble to Caterham, Portsmouth and Speke. Mid-afternoon saw a large formation mainly of Bf 109s over Kent, their strong top cover hoping to pounce upon any of the 28 squadrons of British fighters responding. JG 53 managed to cripple 501 Squadron with a lightning strike before the day's losses became about equal, although every German coming down over land was a loss to his side, whereas an RAF pilot baled out possibly to fight again soon. High aircraft production and ample stored reserve increasingly ensured that.

After dark a new, vicious obscenity developed, the first large-scale use of 1,000-kg blast weapons. Adapted from sea mines and originally thought erroneously to be magnetic mines, these cylindrical objects were about eight feet long and two feet in diameter. Each descended suspended from a 27-foot diameter green silk parachute, drifting down at about 40 mph to ensure a soft landing. Thin case and large charge combined to produce a colossal hollow bang, tremendous shock waves and extensive blast damage over a quarter-mile radius — assuming the weapon's fusing worked, which it often did not. Mine incidents believed to have been brought about by Heinkels of KG 4 and Kgr 126 totalled 21 by dawn on the 18th. Serious effects and giant craters had resulted from the nine which had exploded, including two at Petts Wood and Rochester. Another dangled alarmingly in Shoreditch High Street. The Government's verdict was that this was a weapon aimed 'against the morale of the people'. While no official announcement was made concerning the mines, their arrival was soon general knowledge, with secrecy adding to fear and rumour. Anger was added when news widely spread that among the dozen huge fires that night were those burning in famous London stores in Oxford Street, among them D.H. Evans and John Lewis which demanded attention from hundreds of firemen whose hoses seemed to snake everywhere. Ten huge fires also blazed in the East End.

Three multi-wave operations mounted on 18 September against the south-east had a ratio

Whatever the study of paper returns may have shown, the fact is that the situation was critical in the extreme. The majority of squadrons had been reduced to the status of training units, and were fit only for operations against unescorted bombers. The remainder were battling daily against heavy odds. The indomitable courage of the fighter pilots and the skill of their leaders brought us through the crises, and the morale of the Germans eventually cracked because of the stupendous losses which they sustained.

Air Chief Marshal Sir Hugh Dowding, Commander-in-Chief Fighter Command

of about four fighters to one bomber and either crossed Kent or rounded the Foreland into the Thames Estuary to attack riverside targets. The first operation included a raid on Tilbury; the second resulted in Gillingham being attacked at 12:55 and caused 28 casualties; the third involved a high speed dash by KG 77s Ju 88s to the Medway Oil Company's Port Victoria store on the Isle of Grain. Also bombed in another phase of this last operation were Chatham, Tilbury/Gravesend and Maidstone, while half this force, fighters, flew high over Kent hoping to surprise RAF interceptors. Inexperienced crews flying Ju 88s of III/KG 77 hurrying along the south side of the Thames heading for Gravesend had been pounced upon by 14 squadrons, including the 12 Group Wing which disposed of nine bombers. During this operation there were far too many reports to simply dismiss the inclusion of two four-engined bombers within a diamond formation of 15 He 111s.

Despite a staggering 13,000 rounds of discouraging AA shells hurled aloft the following night from 61 IAZ sites, firing almost continuously for three hours, fire consumed Plessey's main works, the cordite section of ICI's Waltham Cross factory and a 30-inch gas main at Southall. At 23:30 a parachute mine exploded near Westminster's County Hall and 30 fire pumps rushed to the scene. Among five other huge blazes one overtook Taylor's Depository in Pimlico.

Events of the last few days must have increased Hitler's belief that an invasion could be a risky venture, indeed might even end in disaster for his forces, which view the British Government would have disputed. On 19 September he ordered the invasion, planned to start on 21 September, to be postponed. Although there were no large raids that day single aircraft raided London, killing four occupants in Croydon with an oil bomb and machine-gunning Hackney from low level. A mine exploded at Barnes while attempts were being made to make it safe, and Clifford Bridge was destroyed.

The small-scale activity on the 19th preluded central London's worst night raid so far, during which the first bombs in Whitehall fell near the Scottish Office and the War Office. Gunners naturally hastened to its defence and some

of the 2,418 rounds fired from 49 sites clouted the foe. The first success came to ZE6 or ZE11 when the tail was shot away from a He 111P of 3/KG 55 which at 23:05 crashed at Spellbrook, north of Harlow. The second came at 00:17 to ZS18 Raynes Park, whose victim, a Ju 88 of KG 51, smashed into nearby houses and the garden of Blinchley House, Merton. Potentially horrific incidents that night came when UX mines landed at St Stephens Church in East Ham and on the LMS line near Leyton. An horrific incident involving a mine at Tilbury's Ladywell Institution was averted by evacuating the inmates. Tragically less fortunate were 60 who suffered when a direct hit wrecked a trench shelter in Lordship Lane, Tottenham. Among well-known places hit were the Inner Temple hall and library, Senate House and London University in Holborn, Westminster's County Hall and Peter Robinson's in Oxford Street. By dawn London's casualties totalled 390. It was not only London that was being bombed, one

The crew of a 29 Squadron Blenheim day fighter set off on a night patrol. (IWM)

bomb exploding on the 20th in a Lyneham hangar.

Next day a two-raid fighter sweep over Kent cost the RAF seven Spitfires and four pilots killed when their formation was bounced by top cover. Meanwhile the German invasion fleet started to disperse.

While very high over the south-east on the 21st Bf 109s roamed, small numbers of Ju 88s also made a nuisance of themselves, one of Lehr 1 flying low level to Brooklands to place four bombs, three on the landing ground and one in the Hurricane assembly shop. Luckily the latter did not explode before it had been courageously removed from the building. It was fortunate too that when the 93rd parachute mine delivered itself into central Ipswich it only partially exploded. Impossible to defuse, it had instead to be blown in situ. Even the controlled explosion produced a crater 50 feet wide and 25 feet deep, demolished 70 houses, damaged 750 and broke windows as far as 650 yards away.

Night raiders penetrating a hail of 4,124 AA shells over London on the 21/22nd dropped an unexploded mine on Hornchurch's landing ground, seriously damaged Allen and Hanbury's Bethnal Green medical works and started a fire in Howard's Timber Yard, Poplar, attended by 80 pumps. On 22/23 September a parachute mine exploding at Ilford demolished a hundred houses and damaged many more, while in Poplar and Lambeth direct hits killed over 50 in shelters. The British Museum's King Edward buildings were damaged and Mile End 'tube' station was closed by a direct hit.

On the 23/24th London was under Red Alert from 19:56 to 05:27 and fire engulfed Clarnico's, trapping over 100 in the factory's basement shelter. By midnight 24 serious fires were burning in West Ham. Searchlights were exposed 220 times, 7 times illuminating raiders for 42 AA sites which loosed off 5,565 rounds. A Vickers Twin Mk 8 firing from Waltham Cross exploded a descending mine, and SM11 guns brought down He 111H-3 1H+GP of 6/KG 26 at Q3981, Chobham, from which three men became PoWs. Heavy night raids employing from around 150 to 230 bombers against London, daylight forays by fighters intended to wear out RAF pilots, few bombers and cloud-covered attackers formed the backbone of activity while the Germans formulated new means of reducing British resistance. Attacks were then switched — too late to influence the Battle — to concentrating upon flattening fighter production sources.

Numbers of Guns and Searchlights Deployed

Date	Heavy guns	Bofors guns	Searchlights
31 July	1,267	390	4,193
28 August	1,327	447	4,242
28 September	1,378	479	4,278
26 October	1,405	542	4,524

The Gunners' Success — 30 September

About 250 rounds of AA fire were needed to bring down an enemy aircraft by day. At night 20,000 rounds were expended to bring down one raider, 11,000 rounds by 31 October.

Gunners' Claims — much inflated

Total	In daylight	At night
To 31 August	178	28
For September	122	23
For October	21	18

Above *Too late, the Luftwaffe attacked Southampton's Supermarine works, seen by the river at the top of the photograph (the topmost 'C'). As here, concentration was mainly on the dock area.* (IWM)

Below *Ju 88s of KG 77 participated in several of the later bomber operations during the Battle. One of their aircraft, 3Z:HS, is seen here in night camouflage.* (Bundesarchiv)

Two groups of bombers operating on 24 September over the Medway area — one entering over Dover and the other by way of the River Crouch — were challenged by 18 fighter squadrons. Soon after 13:00 from the Cherbourg direction came 18 Bf 110s of Erpro 210 with ZG 76 providing top cover and making direct for Supermarine's Woolston works, upon which each dived, delivering a 250-kg bomb. Five scored hits on the factory area without causing serious damage. One bomb, however, killed and wounded skilled and senior staff in a shelter, and for the loss south of the Isle of Wight of only one bomber. Higher level raiders also tried unsuccessfully for Woolston. After dark London suffered again, while Berlin was bombed and a Wellington delivered 91,500 propaganda leaflets to residents there and at Hanover and Hamburg.

London was under Red Alert from 20:10 to 05:30 on 24/25 September, some raiders over the IAZ trying to fire the colours of the day. That did not discourage its gunners from firing another 5,480 rounds. Very heavy bombing commencing at midnight caused incidents at Camberwell, Chelsea, Islington, Kensington, St Mary's Hospital, Chancery Lane, Queen's Hall, University College, Lambeth, Marylebone Road, St Pancras, Waterloo Station, Wormwood Scrubbs, Earl's Court Station, Kew

Bridge and *The Times* building in Queen Victoria Street. Over North Woolwich a parachute mine burst in the air, more mines falling at Mitcham and Luton. In dealing with the London fires, 58 pumps were needed in Hampstead, 48 at the Southampton Buildings in Bloomsbury and 20 at Maples Tottenham Court Road store.

Dispersal of the invasion assembly released sufficient aircraft to reinforce Luftflotte 3 to allow it to resume large-scale daylight operations on 25 September with a morning attack by He 111s of KG 55 on the Bristol Aeroplane works at Filton. No. 10 Group, after incorrect intelligence indications had pointed to Raid 22H attacking Yeovil, positioned squadrons of fighters accordingly. As a result 90 tons of HEs and 24 oil bombs caused serious damage to Filton's aero engine and airframe works as well as nearby villages and communications. Casualties amounted to 60 dead and 150 injured before Nos. 152 and 238 Squadrons struck down at least three of the withdrawing Heinkels and AA gunners another. Two escorting Bf 110s were also destroyed. Several Ju 88s of LG 1 later dive-bombed oil installations at Portland and Plymouth, where a crane was destroyed. Next day No. 504 Squadron moved to Filton, providing local defence.

Encouraged by its achievements KG 55 repeated its success on 26 September. Shortly before 16:00 Raid 20H, a group of about 60 enemy aircraft, was discovered by radar. Proceeding along the west side of Southampton water it then turned north-easterly hiding behind large elongated clouds and clearly heading for Southampton where, at 16:28, 27 Bf 110s attacked the Itchen and Woolston Vickers-Supermarine works, six dive-bombing, the remainder attacking from 14,000 feet. A quarter of an hour later, after tracking in over the New Forest, came 35 Heinkels escorted by 50 fighters to destroy the factory. Some of the 70 tons of bombs used strayed onto Dawks gas works killing 11 and injuring 16, and another 11 were killed at the docks. Twelve squadrons of fighters ordered to intercept mostly flew too high. It was

left to Solent guns to challenge the raiders before four squadrons went into action — after the bombing — shooting down a He 111 and two ZG 26 Bf 110s on the Isle of Wight for the loss of six aircraft and two pilots killed. Casualties at Supermarine's were serious, nearly 100 more dying in and around the works factory, where Spitfire production and Supermarine's heavy bomber prototype were devastated. As a result Spitfires were soon being constructed widely in the area to prevent a repeat attack.

Air-bursting mines prompted immediate interest in the possibility of gun laying radar detecting a slowly descending mine to allow gunners to destroy the obscenity. Forlorn hope, for when a Lysander flew over Richmond Park and released four canisters simulating mines, only gun site ZS20 located them. On the 25/26th, after the London sirens wailed at 20:44, gunners fired another 7,714 rounds; and next night, settling for 4,418 shots, failed to prevent mines landing in Uxbridge and Hornsey, and the west frontage of the House of Commons building from being battered.

On 26/27 September German bombers operated widely south of a line Liverpool to Hull and caused very many incidents. Standard Motors at Coventry was considerably damaged and one of eight HEs which hit RAF Northolt struck a barrack block so steeply that it passed through two reinforced floors. Serious damage was also caused in Birkenhead and Liverpool.

By day the Luftwaffe was still trying to exhaust Fighter Command. Bf 109s and '110s repeatedly rode over Kent attempting to lure RAF fighter pilots into tiresome high-altitude and wasteful combat. In Phase One on the 27th the Observer Corps reported six large bombers circling Kenley. The only bombs were reported in the Dover area. Ju 88s of KG 77 attempted two raids on London and lost 13 of their number to British fighters, which forced back the rest. Bf 110s of LG 1 fared little better, losing seven of their number over Kent and Surrey. Mid-morning saw other Bf 110s of ZG 26 heading inland towards Bristol. Fighter interception, particularly by 504 Squadron, forced them to

jettison their loads outside the city. Five were shot down. It turned out to be a day of mutual heavy losses.

On 28 September the Luftwaffe mounted two main attacks employing Bf 110 and Ju 88 fast bombers protected by masses of Bf 109s over the south-east. From four large morning raids only six enemy aircraft managed to penetrate to central London after 24 RAF squadrons reacted. Afternoon activity aroused a 25-squadron response to deal with about 40 bombers and 120 fighters, all flying high. Other fighters engaged about 50 Bf 110s off Portsmouth. After dark 121 raids approached London, 65 crossing its heart between 18:46 and 07:12 and causing the guns to fire for nine hours. Major incidents occurred at Lambeth and Nine Elms goods yards, the Albert Embankment, and Southwark, where three HEs destroyed St Peter's Crypt Shelter, killing 18 outright and trapping many. Difficult, isn't it, to believe such things really happened in familiar London places?

On 30 September four operations were mounted over the south-east, the third involving Ju 88s of KG 30 and KG 51. Aiming at Kingston and apparently RAF Uxbridge, six Ju 88s dive-bombed Greenford in error, drop-

Contrast in camouflage is shown between two Bf 110Cs of ZG 26 (Horst Wessel). (Bundesarchiv)

ping about a hundred bombs in that area and severely damaging over 400 houses and causing widespread disruption of electricity supplies. Weybridge and Slough were listed targets in the fourth assault. Two operations were also mounted against Portland and considerable damage was caused by two raids on Bexhill. Bombing operations were attempted widely over the south-east and London, and a Bf 109/110 feint off Dorset before 40 escorted He 111s of KG 55 headed towards Yeovil. This time 10 Group's intelligence indications were proved right. Four squadrons engaged the intruders, Nos. 56, 152 and 504 Squadrons ferociously. They shot down four but the rest, on being turned back, jettisoned their loads around Sherborne. In a hectic day's fighting the Luftwaffe lost in combat 24 Bf 109s along with five very seriously damaged and five more put out of action. Four Ju 88s, and a Do 17Z were destroyed and eight more bombers very seriously battered. RAF fighter losses amounted to 26 aircraft destroyed, five badly damaged and 15 pilots killed as a result of action.

Luftwaffe losses during operations 16-30 September 1940

a indicates shot down *b* crashed during sortie *c* seriously damaged

	16			17			18			19			20			21			22			23		
	a	b	c	a	b	c	a	b	c	a	b	c	a	b	c	a	b	c	a	b	c	a	b	c
Do 17P	—	—	—	—	—	—	—	—	—	—	—	—	—	—	—	—	1	—	—	—	—	—	—	—
Do 17Z	—	—	—	—	—	—	—	—	—	—	1	2	—	—	1	—	2	—	—	—	1	—	—	—
Do 215	—	—	—	—	—	—	1	—	—	—	—	—	—	—	—	1	—	—	—	—	—	—	—	—
He 111H	—	—	—	—	—	—	—	—	—	—	—	—	—	—	—	—	—	—	—	1	—	2	—	—
He 111P	—	—	—	—	—	—	—	—	—	—	—	1	—	—	—	1	—	—	—	—	—	—	—	—
He 115	1	—	—	1	—	—	—	—	—	1	—	—	—	—	—	—	—	—	—	—	—	—	—	—
Ju 88	2	2	—	3	1	1	10	1	—	6	—	2	—	1	2	2	2	—	1	1	—	1	1	—
Ju 88C	1	—	—	—	—	—	—	—	—	—	—	—	—	—	—	—	—	—	—	—	—	—	—	—
Bf 109	2	—	1	3	—	—	6	1	1	—	—	—	—	2	1	—	—	—	—	—	—	8	1	3
Bf 110	—	—	—	—	—	—	—	—	—	—	—	—	—	—	—	—	—	—	—	—	—	—	—	—
TOTALS	6	2	1	7	1	1	17	2	1	7	2	4	1	3	5	3	5	—	1	2	1	11	2	3

	24			25			26			27			28			29			30			GRAND TOTAL FOR SEPT.		
	a	b	c	a	b	c	a	b	c	a	b	c	a	b	c	a	b	c	a	b	c	a	b	c
Do 17P	—	—	—	—	—	—	—	—	—	—	—	—	—	—	—	1	—	—	—	—	—	0	1	2
Do 17Z	1	—	1	—	—	—	—	1	—	—	—	—	—	1	—	—	—	—	1	1	2	29	9	17
Do 18	—	—	—	1	—	—	—	1	—	—	—	—	—	1	—	—	—	—	—	—	—	4	1	3
Do 215	—	—	—	—	—	—	—	—	—	—	—	—	—	—	—	—	—	—	—	—	—	2	0	0
He 59	—	—	—	—	—	—	—	—	—	—	—	—	—	—	—	—	—	—	—	—	—	1	2	1
He 111H	1	—	—	4	1	1	1	—	—	—	—	—	1	—	3	—	—	3	2	—	—	33	20	33
He 111P	—	—	—	1	—	1	—	—	1	—	—	—	—	—	—	3	2	—	—	1	—	7	10	6
He 115	—	—	—	1	—	—	—	—	—	—	—	—	—	—	—	—	—	—	—	—	—	4	3	0
Hs 126	—	—	—	—	—	—	—	—	—	—	—	—	—	—	—	—	—	—	—	—	—	0	0	1
Ju 87	—	—	—	—	—	—	—	—	—	—	—	—	—	—	—	—	—	—	—	—	—	0	1	0
Ju 88	1	1	1	—	—	—	—	2	—	15	—	—	1	—	1	—	3	—	5	2	2	81	29	21
Ju 88C	—	—	—	—	—	—	—	—	—	—	—	—	—	—	—	—	—	—	—	—	—	1	0	0
Bf 109	—	—	2	1	1	—	1	—	—	14	2	3	2	—	1	1	—	2	26	3	5	182	37	47
Bf 110	3	—	—	2	—	1	3	—	—	18	—	2	—	—	—	—	—	—	—	—	1	75	5	9
TOTALS	6	1	4	9	3	3	5	3	1	47	2	6	4	7	2	1	10	6	32	6	12	419	118	130

Every night until 3 November — and of course many beyond — the Luftwaffe attacked Greater London, using an average of 160 bombers. In the course of September's night raids, 5,300 tons of bombs had been aimed at the capital, whose proximity to many new German bases, and its size, made it an easy night target, whose defence still mainly rested with blind-fired gun barrages. Dowding, despite his protestations, was instructed to switch some Hurricanes to night fighting, and forecast that only radar equipped night fighters were likely to make night kills. By 30 September in the IAZ alone there were 196 guns — 145 3.7-inch, 48 4.5-inch and 6 3-inch — and the numbers were increasing. By 31 October the IAZ was to hold 233. Fighters patrolled, whenever possible, with interceptions almost impossible. Little wonder that the Luftwaffe was putting so much effort into the night sky and scoring worthwhile success largely by chance.

RAF losses during operations 16-30 September 1940

	16 a	16 b	16 c	17 a	17 b	17 c	18 a	18 b	18 c̄	19 a	19 b	19 c	20 a	20 b	20 c	21 a	21 b	21 c	22 a	22 b	22 c
Blenheim F	—	—	—	—	—	—	—	—	1	—	—	—	—	—	—	—	—	—	—	—	—
Beaufighter	—	—	—	—	—	—	—	—	—	—	—	—	—	—	—	—	—	—	—	—	—
Defiant	—	—	—	—	—	—	—	—	—	—	—	—	—	—	—	—	—	—	—	—	—
Hurricane	1	—	—	4	1	—	4	—	1	—	—	—	—	—	1	—	—	—	—	—	—
Spitfire	1	—	—	1	—	3	6	—	2	—	—	—	7	—	1	—	—	1	—	—	—
Battle	—	—	—	—	—	—	—	—	—	—	—	—	—	—	—	—	—	—	—	—	—
Blenheim B	—	—	—	—	—	—	—	—	—	2	—	—	—	—	—	—	—	—	—	—	—
Hampden	—	—	—	—	—	—	1	—	1	2	—	2	—	—	1	—	—	—	—	—	—
Wellington	—	—	—	—	—	—	—	—	—	2	—	—	—	—	—	1	—	1	—	—	—
Whitley	—	—	—	—	—	—	—	—	—	3	—	—	—	—	—	—	—	—	—	—	—
Coastal Cmd	—	—	—	—	—	—	1	—	—	2	—	—	1	—	—	1	—	—	—	—	—
TOTALS	2	—	—	5	1	3	12	—	5	11	—	2	8	—	3	2	—	2	—	—	—

	23 a	23 b	23 c	24 a	24 b	24 c	25 a	25 b	25 c	26 a	26 b	26 c	27 a	27 b	27 c	28 a	28 b	28 c	29 a	29 b	29 c	30 a	30 b	30 c
Blenheim	—	—	—	—	—	—	—	1	—	—	—	—	—	—	—	—	—	1	—	—	1	—	—	—
Beaufighter	—	—	—	—	—	—	—	—	—	—	—	—	—	—	—	—	—	—	—	—	—	—	—	—
Defiant	—	—	—	—	—	—	—	—	—	—	—	—	—	—	—	—	1	—	—	—	—	—	—	—
Hurricane	6	—	—	2	1	—	2	—	—	6	—	1	11	—	4	10	1	—	5	—	—	14	1	5
Spitfire	3	1	—	4	—	1	1	—	—	2	—	—	16	1	1	4	1	2	—	—	—	3	—	3
Battle	—	—	—	—	—	—	1	—	—	—	—	—	—	—	—	—	—	—	—	—	—	—	—	—
Blenheim B	—	—	—	1	—	1	2	—	—	1	—	—	—	—	—	—	—	—	—	—	—	—	—	—
Hampden	—	—	—	1	—	—	—	—	—	1	—	1	2	—	—	1	—	—	—	—	—	—	—	—
Wellington	—	—	1	3	—	3	—	—	—	—	—	—	—	—	1	2	—	—	3	—	1	—	—	—
Whitley	—	—	—	2	—	1	—	—	—	—	—	—	—	—	—	—	—	—	—	—	—	—	—	—
Coastal Cmd	—	—	—	—	—	—	3	—	—	1	—	—	1	—	—	2	—	—	2	—	—	10	—	—
TOTALS	9	1	1	13	1	6	9	1	—	11	—	2	30	1	6	19	3	3	10	—	2	27	1	8

TOTAL	a	b	c
Blenheim	0	1	3
Beaufighter	0	0	0
Defiant	0	1	0
Hurricane	65	4	12
Spitfire	48	3	12
Battle	1	0	0
Blenheim B	6	0	1
Hampden	8	0	5
Wellington	11	0	7
Whitley	5	0	1
Coastal Cmd	24	0	0
TOTALS	168	9	43

Day raids had not been abandoned, and on 1 October a Portsmouth assault needed intercepting. Next day when Bf 109s were plentiful over the south-east many flew high, only Spitfires being able to challenge them — if they could find them after wearisome battle climbs. Above 25,000 feet the two-stage supercharger in the Bf 109s' engine gave the German fighters a good advantage, while above 20,000 feet they could easily avoid accurate detection. Flying fast they took but 20 minutes to reach London, giving British fighters little time to react. Since it was impossible to distinguish the fighters from the fighter-bombers, the latter equipping or about to equip one gruppe of each Jagdeschwader, action was needed in nearly all cases.

Right *Intense night bombing of London resulted by October 1940 in many Londoners sleeping not just on the underground station platforms but, as here at Aldwych, on newspaper laid over the greasy tracks.* (IWM)

Below *The second Gruppe of Lehrgeschwader 2 specialized in shallow dive-bombing attacks. Its Bf 109s, marked with a black triangle (like 'H' here, of 4 Staffel), carried either four small bombs or one larger.* (Michael Payne)

To improve detection rates a special unit, No. 421 Flight, was formed, whose task was to operate high in an attempt to observe enemy activity. Single Spitfires were initially fielded, but after four were shot down pairs were substituted. In the tough, bright conditions of the combat zone pilots easily tired, giving credence to German belief that Fighter Command might become exhausted. October's weather prevented that possibility by producing many days when operations were impracticable except by single bombers selecting prime targets. Even so, 100 fighter

pilots were killed and 65 injured during the whole of October, in which time the Luftwaffe had aimed 7,160 tons of HE and dropped 4,735 canisters of incendiaries upon London.

Very effective raids relying upon cloud and rain cover were now increasingly practicable as the weather generally deteriorated. Some 50 raiders employing such tactics on 2 October crossed London's IAZ and not all escaped, including Do 17 U5+FA of KG 2 which was shot down near RAF Pulham. The Hurricanes of 17 Squadron involved were so short of fuel that two, (V7241 of Pilot Officer F. Fajtl and V7650 of Flying Officer H.P. Blatchford) had to force-land. Pilot Officer J.K. Ross, who delivered the coup de grace to the bomber, landed P3536 alongside his quarry for the satisfaction of seeing its crew taken prisoner, then headed for Debden, only to find his fuel state so low that he was lucky to reach Martlesham for refuelling. What that bomber's crew might have achieved was displayed at Banbury's gas works, but more importantly at Hatfield next day when a KG 77 Ju 88 crew, unable to find the Reading target below the 10/10 cloud at 500 feet, came by chance across de Havilland's Hatfield factory, where they slammed their bombs into the Technical School and assembly shop, where much of the work for early Mosquitoes was

promptly destroyed before the bomber was brought down by light AA fire.

At night on 3/4 October London was hit again, and the main hangar at General Aircraft's Feltham works, where Hurricanes were repaired, was damaged. A single raider started a fire at Hawker's Kingston factory on the 5th, and New Cross telephone exchange was also seriously damaged. During better weather that day Bf 109s and 110s operated high over Kent and the London area, then KG 77 mounted an afternoon raid on Southampton. Another day raid, this time by Ju 88s of II/KG 51 covered by Bf 110s of ZG 26, penetrated to Yeovil on the 7th despite the attention of British fighters, which shot down seven of ZG 26 and two Ju 88s before Bf 109s at the Dorset coast offered withdrawal support to their comrades. Four small day raids against London had resulted in fires in dockland and Rotherhithe. On the 9th it was Maidstone that particularly suffered, 87 buildings being damaged by fighter-bomber attack. Using cloud cover a single raider managed to damage English Electric's Stafford factory.

The use of Bf 109s as fighter bombers (Bf 109E-4 shown) radically changed the campaign. These high-fliers came in fast, bombed, and became excellent fighters. (Bundesarchiv)

By now it was clear that very large-scale, conventional, escorted bomber operations against Britain were all but over. Far, far more effective to employ high-speed fighter-bombers protected by fighters and all soon equally furious. Their bombing from great altitudes was inaccurate, but that had been equally true of many heavily escorted bombers. On 12 October — the date when Hitler abandoned a 1940 invasion of Britain — a 250-kg bomb dropped from a great height exploded in Piccadilly Circus killing five. Fighter Command would have to combat such activity. It would be costly, but it would

What might have changed the outcome of the entire campaign, even the war, would have been ample long-range drop tanks for Bf 109s as fitted to this Bf 109E-7. (Bundesarchiv)

never break the Command. Resolve to hold on would strengthen — and the demand to hit back. Two days later a strong night assault was mounted on industrial Coventry by Do 17s while, making maximum use of moonlight,

Had the Germans otherwise devoted the effort spent on the Bf 110 their success might have increased. This Bf 110 2N+ET was of I/ZG 26, Stavanger. (Michael Payne)

Cunliffe Owen's major repair works at Eastleigh, near Southampton, under attack on 13 October 1940. (Bundesarchiv)

some 200 Heinkels and Ju 88s rained enormous terror upon London, killing nigh on 600 and injuring nearly 2,500 people. Unbelievable, horrendous, isn't it? But the Battle of Britain was surely fast passing, and the Night Blitz was taking its place. Of one thing there was and remains no doubt: the victory was ours, but achieved at enormous cost, both national and deeply personal.

* * *

As the hours of darkness lengthened, the mists of autumn further shortened the daylight, the cost of victory was clearly evident. On the squadrons few from pre-war days had survived, and many of the youngest had perished within hours of joining the fight. There was time to contemplate — a love lost so soon, cruelly, suddenly. For many, all that was left were dreams, poignantly featured in one of the most haunting songs of the time:

'In the still of the night once again I hold you tight,
Though you're gone, your love lives on when moonlight beams.
And as long as my heart may beat,
Lover, we'll always meet here in my Deep Purple dreams.'

Such emotions laced for many the lonely hours. But one had to brace oneself for terrible storms ahead. Great effort had gone into ensuring that the harvest was safely stowed for a long, hard winter, and amid fears the Luftwaffe might determinedly incinerate the crops. Every apple was carefully stored, the fallen harvested too. Fast disappearing, the countryside verges changed into profitable strips, like every scrap of garden plot. Going the iron railings, along with aluminium objects, although their value for weapons was minimal. Everything that could be done to help win through was done in an ideal atmosphere of community co-operation. Going down, too, many merchant ships, resulting in rationing fluctuations. Yet nobody seemed to complain of hunger, and a leaner nation was probably a fitter nation. Long nights in the shelters and that intense cold at dawn as one emerged seemed acceptable —

provided the Luftwaffe had not produced real homelessness and not the 1980/90s version. Those were indeed memorably difficult times.

It is not surprising that for the 'over 60s' 'the war' remains a regular talking point, that the affluence of Britain as we enter the 1990s seems miraculous. Those who experienced the poverty of London's East End in the 1930s and '40s, in an area so brutally tortured by the Luftwaffe, and who can for example recall a Christmas when an ice-less cake was both total fare and present for a large family, can be forgiven for cynical attitudes towards current comfortable yet curiously unhappy life styles.

For all its pathos, terror, evil, that fighting summer was a tremendously exhilarating time which brought all so close; for bombs, unlike politicians, are not class-conscious. The possibility of instant annihilation or serious injury seemed not to cause much concern, took second place to the overriding determination never to surrender, to achieve victory. No missing work because the bus was late, buildings were burning, streets flooded. Mercifully, nothing like today's media instant expert was on hand analysing matters and advising without the necessary years of insight. There usually had to be a self-devised way round every problem. Self-sufficiency was essential and satisfying, while the actual fighting was left to wonderfully brave people being enveloped in so many fearful situations and whose courage you admired whether it be close by or miles above.

Does that perilous summer have any messages for the 1990s? Certainly it reminds us of how vital it is for warring nations to base their actions only upon accurate intelligence material — emphasized again during the Falklands conflict. How important it remains never to underestimate the foe. In an era when kind words, signatures on pieces of paper and troop movements cause euphoria and constitute a peaceful future, it does well to remember that such things were in evidence 50 years ago. History seems not to repeat itself, just produce new versions of old habits.

What has been so profoundly disturbing in the half century since the Battle is the readiness with which a one-time ally eagerly copied the equipment of another and, in a mere ten years after 1940, was threatening those whose governments had learnt nothing about keeping their powder dry — just in case. The challenge presented by the fighter-bombers in October 1940 was, by the mid-1950s, the grossly enlarged threat mounted by perhaps just three nuclear-armed Tupolev TU-4s lurking in a formation of 90 and all of which would need to have been smashed far from our shores just for some sort of life to survive. Ironic indeed that Duxford's 'Big Wing' idea of 1940 was resurrected in the 1950s there and then at other stations, that the wing would need to be away within a few minutes of 'scramble' and form up in time to be able to join other Sectors in order to ensure every incoming raider was disposed of. This a mere dozen years after the last fight for survival! By 1954 the threat was utterly grotesque — political ineptitude had produced a British fighter force whose best kill rate would have been only about 30 per cent. Against present multiple nuclear warheaded missiles defence is impossible. Only the certainty of mutual nuclear annihilation can keep us reasonably safe. Strange world, indeed.

Visiting places where once I stood to observe the 1940 battles, the firing, the invasion preparations, and recalling people I knew and loved so many summers past, I shall always find it difficult to believe that what happened did happen. Did Messerschmitts zoom, Heinkels throb, Spitfires whistle over Tower Bridge in their hundreds? Did a Dornier crash onto Victoria Station on the spot where still I often roam? Could a parachute mine dangle in Stepney near where the bus sometimes carries me home? Was Liverpool Street once wounded by the Luftwaffe in a manner reminiscent of its recent torture during redevelopment?

And what remains of those days that one can actually touch? Surprisingly little, apart from museum trophies, a Hurricane and the famous Spitfire P7350 which really did take part in the fight. Weary pillboxes can be found often brav-

ing onslaught by barbarians of the 1980s, incongruous slates remain on once-stricken roofs, some of which are supported by gaunt concrete-buttressed walls adjacent to no neighbour. At dear old Duxford, garden seats have replaced Spitfires and Hurricanes; and the shelter where I shook in my shoes when KG 2 tried to blow away Fowlmere has lately been bulldozed into oblivion.

And the people? Is the quite nice old chap gazing into the Rhine the one who tried to bomb you on that August night? Can the aged senior citizens among us really be those glamorous young men we so much admired and who won our freedom? Well, it is a long, long time ago, and hopefully a united Europe will ensure, if nothing else, that we shall live among Winnie's 'broad, sunlit uplands'. But, if you lived through that most memorable of all summers, you surely will ever remember it, and know for certain that This really was our Finest Hour.

Above left *What lasting image would any spectator of the fighting retain? For myself it has to be a sky covered by 'smoke trails' as folk called them, switching to 'vapour trails' when the first Flying Fortresses arrived in 1941.*

Left *What lasting sound would one recall? The frightening guns? The terrifying scream and crash of the bombs? No; for me it has to be the whistle of the Spitfires, the chatter of their guns, the exhilaration of seeing a real victory roll. When Battle of Britain veteran P7350 (which served with 266 Squadron from 6 September and 603 Squadron from 17 October 1940) still whistles by, I'm always grateful that I had a ringside seat to the greatest of all air battles and came through unscathed.*

Luftwaffe night attacks on London 7 September-31 October 1940

Raid commencing September	Aircraft claiming to attack London	HE used (tons)	Incendiary containers
7	247	335	440
8	171	207	327
9	195	232	289
10	148	176	318
11	180	217	148
12	43	54	61
13	105	123	200
14	38	55	43
15	181	224	279
16	170	189	318
17	268	334	391
18	300	350	628
19	255	310	533
20	109	154	79
21	113	164	329
22	123	130	476
23	261	300	611
24	223	256	384
25	219	260	441
26	180	218	224
27	163	167	437
28	249	325	303
29	246	294	136
30	218	287	104
TOTALS	4,405	5,361	7,499
October			
1	214	250	115
2	105	130	300
3	44	61	Nil
4	134	190	236
5	177	242	176
6	7	8	Nil
7	179	211	143
8	208	257	264
9	216	263	245
10	222	269	718
11	132	213	126
12	119	148	24
13	211	249	131
14	242	304	299
15	410	538	177
16	280	346	187
17	254	322	134
18	129	172	132
19	282	386	192

Raid commencing October	Aircraft claiming to attack London	HE used (tons)	Incendiary containers
20	298	356	192
21	100	115	52
22	82	98	40
23	64	65	Nil
24	64	75	Nil
25	159	193	193
26	203	253	176
27	114	127	40
28	146	176	111
29	186	236	109
30	125	178	92
31	67	48	83
TOTALS	5,173	6,479	3,208
GRAND TOTALS	9,578	11,840	10,707

Luftwaffe losses during offensive operations, and RAF losses during defensive operations 1-31 October 1940

By the end of September, and with the immediate prospect of invasion fast waning, Bomber Command had reverted to its strategic bombing campaign and Coastal Command too had largely switched to 'non-invasion' operations. A more direct comparison between British fighter and German attack losses becomes more feasible.

a indicates shot down b crashed and written off during/as a result of operational sortie
c seriously damaged

	1			2			3			4			5			6			7			8		
	a	b	c	a	b	c	a	b	c	a	b	c	a	b	c	a	b	c	a	b	c	a	b	c
Luftwaffe:																								
Do 17Z	—	—	—	1	1	—	1	1	—	1	—	1	—	—	—	2	—	—	—	—	—	1	—	—
He 111H	1	—	—	2	—	—	1	—	1	2	—	—	1	—	—	—	—	—	—	—	—	—	1	—
He 111P	—	—	—	—	—	—	—	—	—	—	—	—	—	—	—	1	—	—	—	—	—	—	1	—
Ju 88	—	—	—	1	—	—	3	—	—	2	2	—	2	—	—	2	—	—	2	—	—	2	—	1
Bf 109	2	—	—	4	—	—	—	—	—	—	—	—	6	1	—	—	—	—	8	4	—	—	—	—
Bf 110	1	—	—	—	—	—	—	—	—	—	—	—	2	—	—	—	—	—	7	—	1	—	—	—
TOTALS	4	—	—	8	1	—	5	1	1	5	2	1	11	1	—	5	—	—	17	4	1	3	2	1
RAF:																								
Blenheim	—	—	—	—	—	—	—	1	—	—	—	—	—	—	—	—	—	—	—	—	—	—	—	—
Hurricane	3	1	2	—	—	—	—	—	—	—	—	—	6	4	—	1	—	—	5	4	1	1	—	—
Spitfire	1	—	—	1	1	—	—	—	—	2	—	—	2	1	1	—	1	—	5	—	—	—	—	—
TOTALS	4	1	2	1	1	—	—	1	—	2	—	—	8	5	1	1	1	—	10	4	1	1	—	—

Days 9–16

	9a	9b	9c	10a	10b	10c	11a	11b	11c	12a	12b	12c	13a	13b	13c	14a	14b	14c	15a	15b	15c	16a	16b	16c
Luftwaffe:																								
Do 17Z	1	—	—	—	—	—	2	—	—	—	—	—	—	—	—	—	—	1	—	—	—	—	2	—
He 111H	—	1	—	—	—	—	—	—	—	—	—	1	—	1	—	—	—	—	—	—	—	1	—	1
He 111P	—	2	—	—	—	—	—	—	—	—	—	—	—	—	—	—	—	—	—	—	—	—	—	—
He 115	—	—	—	—	—	—	—	—	—	—	—	—	—	—	—	—	1	—	—	—	—	—	—	—
Ju 88	3	—	—	—	—	1	1	—	—	—	—	—	—	—	—	—	—	—	1	—	—	1	5	1
Bf 109	3	2	1	—	—	—	1	—	—	1	—	—	1	—	2	1	—	—	7	—	1	—	—	—
Bf 110	—	—	—	—	—	—	—	—	—	—	—	—	—	—	—	—	—	—	2	—	—	—	—	—
TOTALS	7	5	1	—	—	1	4	—	—	1	—	1	1	1	2	1	1	1	10	—	1	2	7	2
RAF:																								
Blenheim	—	—	—	—	—	—	—	—	—	—	—	—	1	—	—	—	—	—	—	—	—	—	—	—
Hurricane	1	—	—	2	—	—	2	—	—	7	—	—	—	1	—	—	1	—	12	—	—	1	1	—
Spitfire	—	2	1	1	2	—	4	3	—	1	1	2	—	1	1	—	1	—	4	—	1	—	—	—
TOTALS	1	2	1	3	2	—	6	3	—	8	1	2	1	2	1	—	2	—	16	—	1	1	1	—

Days 17–24

	17a	17b	17c	18a	18b	18c	19a	19b	19c	20a	20b	20c	21a	21b	21c	22a	22b	22c	23a	23b	23c	24a	24b	24c
Luftwaffe:																								
Do 17Z	—	1	—	—	—	—	—	—	—	1	—	—	1	—	—	—	—	—	1	—	—	—	—	3
Do 215	—	—	—	—	—	—	—	—	—	—	—	—	—	—	—	—	—	—	—	1	—	—	—	—
He 111H	1	2	1	—	—	—	—	—	—	—	1	—	—	—	—	—	—	—	—	—	—	—	—	—
He 111P	—	—	1	—	—	—	—	—	—	—	—	—	—	—	—	—	3	—	—	—	—	—	—	—
Ju 88	2	5	3	—	1	1	—	1	1	—	1	1	1	1	1	—	2	—	—	1	—	1	—	1
Bf 109	3	1	—	—	—	—	—	—	—	5	—	1	—	—	—	3	—	—	—	—	—	—	1	—
Bf 110	—	1	—	—	—	—	—	—	—	1	—	—	—	—	—	—	—	—	—	—	—	—	—	—
TOTALS	6	10	5	—	1	1	—	1	1	7	2	2	2	1	1	3	5	—	1	2	—	1	1	4
RAF:																								
Hurricane	2	—	—	—	—	—	—	—	—	—	—	3	—	—	—	2	—	—	—	—	—	—	—	—
Spitfire	2	—	—	—	—	—	—	—	—	2	—	—	—	—	—	2	—	—	—	—	—	—	—	—
TOTALS	4	—	—	—	—	—	—	—	—	2	—	3	—	—	—	4	—	—	—	—	—	—	—	—

Days 25–31 and GRAND TOTALS OCT.

	25a	25b	25c	26a	26b	26c	27a	27b	27c	28a	28b	28c	29a	29b	29c	30a	30b	30c	31a	31b	31c	GT a	GT b	GT c
Do 17P	—	1	—	—	—	—	—	—	—	—	—	—	—	—	—	—	—	—	—	—	—	0	1	0
Do 17Z	1	—	—	—	—	1	—	—	1	—	—	—	—	—	—	—	—	—	—	2	—	14	8	5
He 59	—	—	—	1	—	—	—	—	—	—	—	—	—	—	—	—	—	—	—	—	—	1	0	0
He 111H	—	2	—	2	—	—	1	—	2	2	—	—	1	—	—	—	—	—	—	—	—	14	10	6
He 111P	—	—	—	1	1	—	—	—	—	—	—	—	—	—	—	—	—	—	—	—	—	1	6	2
He 115	—	—	—	—	—	—	1	—	—	—	—	—	—	—	—	—	—	—	—	—	—	1	1	0
Ju 88	2	—	1	—	1	—	2	—	—	1	—	1	1	1	—	1	1	—	—	—	—	31	20	6
Bf 109	11	—	—	3	—	—	7	—	—	4	1	—	14	—	1	4	—	—	—	—	—	88	10	7
Bf 110	1	—	—	—	—	—	—	—	—	—	—	—	—	—	—	—	—	—	—	—	—	14	2	1
TOTALS	15	3	1	7	2	1	11	—	2	7	1	1	16	1	1	5	1	—	—	2	—	164	58	27
RAF:																								
Hurricane	4	4	—	4	—	—	3	—	—	—	—	—	3	1	2	1	—	1	—	—	—	57	15	17
Spitfire	2	—	—	1	—	1	6	—	—	—	—	—	1	—	—	6	—	1	—	—	—	43	12	9
Blenheim	—	—	—	—	—	—	—	—	—	—	—	—	—	—	—	—	—	—	—	—	—	0	2	0
TOTALS	6	4	—	5	—	1	9	—	—	—	—	—	4	1	2	7	—	2	—	—	—	100	29	26

Sorties flown by RAF Fighter Command
16 September-31 October 1940

Date	Day		Night	
September	Patrols	Sorties	Patrols	Sorties
16	78	428	?	?
17	121	544	44	45
18	200	1,210	63	65
19	108	237	12	16
20	124	540	40	46
21	118	563	43	46
22	65	158	46	50
23	116	710	70	70
24	126	880	46	50
25	137	668	37	39
26	120	417	34	34
27	138	939	27	27
28	110	770	53	65
29	121	451	25	25
30	168	1,173	48	50
October				
1	122	673	29	29
2	125	807	35	35
3	68	138	—	—
4	61	171	1	1
5	136	1,074	4	4
6	67	181	3	3
7	129	822	77	78
8	203	639	33	33
9	115	439	42	42
10	133	712	49	49
11	154	900	41	41
12	144	756	30	39
13	121	552	?	?
14	?	?	42	45
15	106	598	40	41
16	73	234	5	5
17	100	563	9	9
18	36	135	2	2
19	63	286	15	18
20	87	457	12	13
21	113	262	24	24
22	70	360	9	11
23	32	79	11	11
24	119	463	33	33
25	131	775	54	54
26	134	678	40	40
27	166	967	33	33
28	117	606	20	20
29	148	649	44	45
30	91	535	6	6
31	53	145		

Total numbers of aircraft available on fighter squadrons at 18:00 hrs on given dates

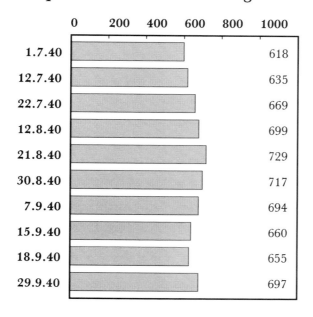

	0	200	400	600	800	1000
1.7.40				618		
12.7.40				635		
22.7.40				669		
12.8.40				699		
21.8.40				729		
30.8.40				717		
7.9.40				694		
15.9.40				660		
18.9.40				655		
29.9.40				697		

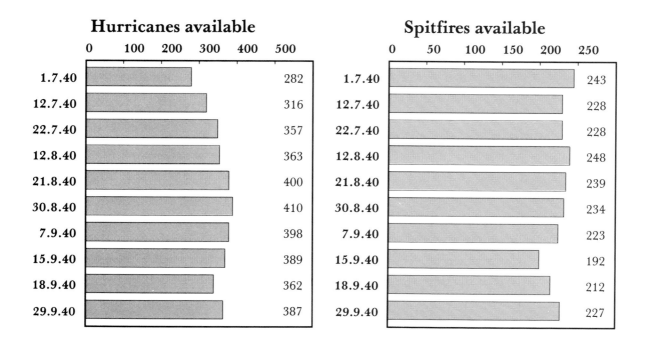

Hurricanes available

	0	100	200	300	400	500
1.7.40				282		
12.7.40				316		
22.7.40				357		
12.8.40				363		
21.8.40				400		
30.8.40				410		
7.9.40				398		
15.9.40				389		
18.9.40				362		
29.9.40				387		

Spitfires available

	0	50	100	150	200	250
1.7.40						243
12.7.40						228
22.7.40						228
12.8.40						248
21.8.40						239
30.8.40						234
7.9.40						223
15.9.40						192
18.9.40						212
29.9.40						227

1968: the film-maker's Battle of Britain

Left *Special Effects do their bit at North Weald to simulate the bombing of an aerodrome.*

Right *A damaged Heinkel passes low over invasion troops all dressed up and ready to go.*

Left *Thanks to their serving with the Spanish Air Force, Merlin-engined 'Me 109s' fly for the cameras off the White Cliffs.*

Left *Ex-Spanish Merlin-engined Heinkel 111s under attack by a smoking Spitfire.*

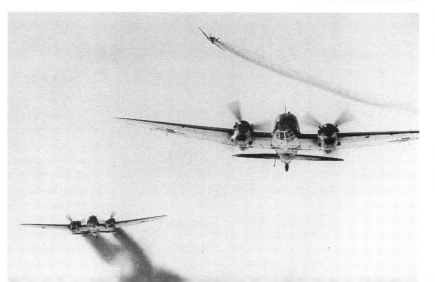

Right *Briefing for a bomber crew. There's another use for one of the Prop Department's 'Flak 88' ammo boxes!*

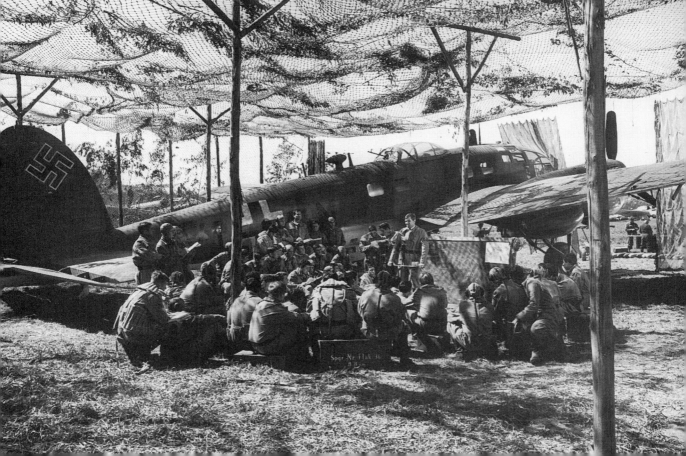

The Battle of Britain Museum, Hendon

Left *At Hendon may be visited the main Battle of Britain Museum. The Luftwaffe passed over Hendon aerodrome at 14:00 on 25 October 1940 securing this photograph of the present Museum site (centre). (Bundesarchiv)*

Below *Hendon's Museum holds a genuine Battle of Britain Hurricane, P2617, which after being used by 607 Squadron in France was Usworth-based with '607' from early June to September. It then flew from Tangmere, passing to 1 RCAF Squadron on 26 October, and later was used as a trainer by Nos. 8 and 9 Flying Training Schools. In August 1944 it was chosen for preservation.*

Right *The RAF Museum's Spitfire 1, SD:V K9942, was with 72 Squadron from 24 April 1939 to 7 June 1940 when it was involved in an accident. After lengthy repair it served with 57 OTU, 53 OTU, was briefly placed in naval hands and was chosen for preservation in April 1944.*

Below right *The Hendon Museum holds one of the few Bf 109Es left, although its pristine state makes it look almost unreal.*

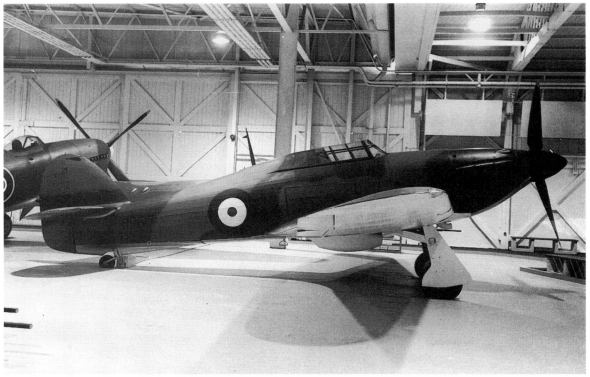

APPENDIX 1

Serial numbers of aircraft flown during operations. Listed here, and linked to index numbers in the text, are airframe serial numbers of aircraft used in many of the engagements — according to the relevant squadron Operations Record Books.

1. Hurricanes N2461, N2463, N2532, N2588, N2724, P3481, P3522, P3677, P3679
2. Hurricanes L1824, L1849, N2621, N2665?, P3484, P3788
3. Hurricanes P2955, P2957, P3400
4. Hurricanes P2920, P3393
5. Spitfires L1004-H, L1009-B, P9495-K, R6694-F, R6695-P, R6765-T
6. Spitfires K9905, K9909, K9915, L1094, N3101, N3128, P9436, R6618, R6619 and two more abortive
7. Spitfires N3173, P9387, P9549, R6707, R6708, R6709
8. Spitfires N3223, L1069, L1095, R6637, N3023, P9322
9. Spitfires P9503-D, R6629-E, R6630, R6694-F, K9931-R, N3284-J, P9545-Q, P6765-T, R6695-P
10. Hurricanes L2075, P2755, N2588, N2524, N2670, P3679
11. Spitfires P9393, P9399, P9398 Mungo Park's, P9379, K9951, L1089
12. Spitfires R6700, L1075, N3230?, K9991, N3293, K9795
13. Spitfires L1069 (Barren), L1095 (Mitchell), N3223, R6699, P9322
14. Hurricanes N2486 (Dixon), P2691, P3082

15. Hurricanes P3681, 2435, L1670, P3363, P3302, P2753
16. Hurricanes P3124, P3872?, P3617, P2948, P3599, P2978
17. Hurricanes P2753, P2690, P3302, P3363, L1670, P3681
18. Spitfire 1b R6625, R6770, R6688, N3234, K9944, R6882
19. Hurricanes P3152 (S/L Donaldson), P3316, P3312, L1750, P3320, L2005, P3275, P3304, P3301, P3307
20. Hurricanes N2402, P2970, P3479, P3473, P3356, P2985, P2922, P3587, P3612, P3354, P2970
21. Spitfires P9549, P9387, R6708, N3173, R6893
22. Spitfires P9450, L1035, L1073, N3230, P9507, P9447, R6694, N3293, K9991, P9369, R6975
23. Hurricanes included P3273, P3065, P3882
24. Hurricanes included P2966, P2963, P2768, P3109, P3160, L1584
25. Spitfires L1045-G (S/L A.T. Smith), R6976-A, P9503-D, R6694-F, N3284-J, P9495-K, P9540-M, R6806-N, R6695-P, P9545-Q, R6621-S, R6765-T
26. Hurricanes P3164 (S/L J.R. Peel), P2955, P2957, P3521, P2770, P3391
28. Defiants L6974, L6983, L6995, L6999, L7001, L7009, L7014, L7015, L7016
29. Hurricanes N2461, P3522, P2921, P3144, P3936, N2458, P3481, P3677, N2671, P3112, P3679
30. Hurricanes P3410, P3781, P3468, P3327,

P3351, P3964

31. Hurricanes P3122, P2921, N2524, P3679, N2461, N2458, P3481, N2670

32. Hurricanes N2337, P2963, P3380, P2768, P3160, P3487, P2801, P3162?, P3151, P3158, P2966, P3161

33. Spitfires R6621-S, L1044-H, R6986-A, R6595-O, P9495-K, P9496-L, R6806-M, R6695-P, P9330-V

34. Spitfires R6812, N3192, R6710, R6899, R6816, P9549, R6707, N3173, R6893

35. Spitfires R6799, R6620, R6712, N3164, P9516, R6617, N3101, K9915, R6777

36. Hurricanes N2458, P3146, P3481, N2596, P2921, P3112, P3936, N2671, P3677

37. Hurricanes P3109, P3487, P3158, P3111, P2801, N2587, P3160, P3380, P2768, N2337, N2328, P3109

38. Spitfires R6893, N3173, R6707, P9387, R6899, R6895, R6814, P9367, R6913, R6816, N3097

39. Spitfires L1055, P9421, R6865, N3293, L1073, L1039, P9447, N3231

40. Hurricanes P2980, P3047, P3170, P3172, P3395, P2686, P3396, P3684, P3296, P3678

41. Hurricanes P3618, P3819, P3702, P3219, P3617, P3823, P3462, P3402, P2827, P2947, P2983

42. Spitfires R6692, P9322, N3023, R6690, R6699

43. Spitfires N3091 (Malan), P9336, P9380, R6779, R6706, P9306, P9398, P9397, L1001, K9878, R6772 (Park), P9547

44. Spitfires P9428 (S/L Hood), P9429, N3038, N3163, N3132, N3234, P9430, N3126, N3264, N3112, K9890

45. Hurricanes P3704, P3776, P3709, P3705, P3706, P3775

46. Spitfires as item 44

47. Spitfires K9991, R6688, R6975, P9569, R6645, L1029, R6659, P9540

48. Hurricanes P3547, P3612, P3879, P3587, P3153, P3579, P2977, P3473

49. Hurricanes P3816, P3059, P3141, P3646, P3397, P3820, P3083, P3041, L1868, and -?-

50. Spitfires R6976-A, P9503-D, R6629-E, L1004-H, N3284-J, P9496-L, P9495-K, R6806-N, P9545-Q, R6765-T, R6963-W, R6630-X

51. Spitfires K9991, N3293, R6700, R6995, P9369, L1029

52. Hurricanes L1750, P3310, P2826, L2005, P3301, P3940, P3312, L1975, P3065, P3271 (W/C Beamish)

53. Hurricanes VY-Q (Allard), VY-W (Marshall), VY-M (Ellis)

54. Hurricanes P3164 (S/L Peel), P3896, P2955, P3391, V7294, P3163, P3221, P3736, -?-, P2951, P2918, P2696, P3381

55. Hurricanes P3971, V7221, P3386, P3216, P3267, P3460

56. Hurricanes P3164 (S/L Peel), P3163, P3896, P3521, P3391, P2957, P3221, P3736?, P2951, P2918, P2696, P3167

57. Hurricanes P3823, P3462, P3664, P2827, P2989, P3223, R4097, P3819, P2978, P3617, P3767, P3222

58. Hurricanes P3058, P3775, P3662, P3078, P2981, R4091?, P3620, P3642, P3623, R4088, and -?-

59. Spitfires P9322, R6699, R6977, R6986, R6979, N3024, R6691, R6769, L1082, K9841, R6986, R6690

60. Hurricanes P3164, P3896, P3163, P3521, N2496, P2957, P3221, P3736, -?-, P2951, P3545, P2918

61. Hurricanes P3202, P3781, P3786, P3468, P3527, P3214, P3971, V7221, P3386, P3216, P3267, P3466

62. Hurricanes N2921 (Brothers), P3679, 2755, P3956, 2524, P3147, P3146, N2458, N2596, V7223, P3522, P3481

63. Spitfires R6683, X4018, R6975, R6623, N3293, P9450, N3230, X4060, R6991

64. Spitfires R6840, R6839, P9306, R6773, R6757, R6772, K9871, P9951, R6759, R6962, P9492

65. Hurricanes P3598, V7233, P3593, P3387, V7231, P3404, P3389

66. Hurricanes P3164 (S/L Peel), P3391, V7294, P3521, 2495, P3896, R4177, P3221, P3736, P2951, P3167, R4176,

P2918

67. Hurricanes P3402, P3462, P3664, P2827, P2989, P3226, R4097, P3819, P2978, P3176, P3222, P3124

68. Hurricanes P3363, R4092, P3885, P3382, P2960, L1917, P8818, P3393, P3383, P3783, L2057

69. Spitfires P9322, N3223, N3024, N3113, L1082, R6769, L1096, K9841, R6915, R6977, R6896, K9997

70. Spitfires R6976-A, P9553-E, X4028-F, K9818-H, R6599-J, X4067-K, K9947-M, N3124-N, R6891-Q, K9975-S, K9970-V

71. Hurricanes P2587?, P2801, L1983, L1992, P3162, P3109, P2966, P3160, N2328, P2768, L2075, P2871

72. Spitfires K9997, N3223, N3113, L1008, L1096, R6915, K9841, R6699, R6692, R6977, N3024

73. Spitfires R7017, R7019, N3097, R6814, R6981, X4019, R6898, R6892, R7015, R6893, R6708

74. Spitfires R6975, X4067, R6623, R6683, R6605, L1038, P9447, N3230, R6990

75. Hurricanes R4109, P3786, P3527, R4102, P3202, R4107, P3971, P3386, V7221, P3972, V7206, L1739

76. Hurricanes N2602, P3886, L1917, P3363, 2690, P3382, P2920, P3358, P3884, P3383, L1990

77. Spitfires K9953, N3091, R6840, K9878, R6716, X4061

78. Hurricanes R4109, P3786, P3527, R4110, R4107, P3220, R4108

79. Hurricanes P3232, P3228, 2690, P3363, P3382, P3886, P3884, L1990, L1951, P3393, P3383, P3358

80. Spitfires R6975, X4067, R6623, R6683, R6605, L1038, P9447, N3230, R6990

81. Hurricanes P3402, P3462, P2983, P3177, P3223, R2681, P3176, P3219, P3804, R2680, L2089

82. Hurricanes P3232, P3228, P3363, L1670, N2602, L2102, P3358, P3393, L1951, P3230, L1990, P3263

83. Spitfires R6986, R6690, N3024, L1065, N3113, L1008, L1096, R6915, N3223,

R6977, R6699, L1082

84. Hurricanes P3479, N2429, P3587, N2440, P3384 and others

85. Spitfires R6803, R6610, R6884, K9915, N3101

86. Hurricanes 2459, 2458, P3481, P3171, V7223, P3146

87. Hurricanes P2587, L1983, P3161, P3162, P3158, L1992, P3380, L2075, P2871, P3109, P3160, N2328

88. Spitfires also scrambled were R6961, N3024, N3113, R6915, N3223, R6699, L1082, R6986, L1008

89. Spitfires X4201, N3108, N3123, N3126, N3162, N3266, P9428, P9430, R6603, R6605, R6756, R6885, R6611

90. Hurricanes P3580, P3650, L2012, P3832, L2018, P3583, N2557, P2717, P3308, P2994, L2122, P3827, L2014

91. Three Blenheims of 235 Squadron were about 150 miles out to sea heading for the Danish coast when they met about 40 He 111s. P/O Jackson-Smith and his gunner in T1803 shot down one. The others, L9404 (F/O Laughlin), T1804 (Sgt Hall), damaged another before the trio continued their sorties.

92. Blenheims 1F L1236, L8699, L1128, L1113, L1374, L1229, L1240, L8724, K7118, L1261, L8698, L6624

93. Hurricanes N2359, P3891, P2558, V7408, up 15:00; P3673, P3892, N2674 up 15:20

94. Hurricanes P3276, P2686, P3678

95. Hurricanes P3871 (W/C Beamish), P3490, V7411, P3065, V7410, L1975, P3309 included

96. Spitfires K9964, R6990, N3230, X4067, N3293, R6623, P9554, L1068, R6683, P9964

97. Hurricanes V7207, P3394, P3215, 2687, V7285

98. Spitfires N3242, R6985, N3277, P9466, R6988, R6896, P9363, N3239, N3279, P9320, R6967, N3191, P9494, X4016

99. Hurricanes R4109, P3527, P3786, P3202, P3220, R4107, P3971, P3386, V7221, V7206, P3466, V7366

100. Hurricanes L1951, P3263, P3358, P3884, L1990, P3393, P3232, P3228, P3363, V7253, P3836

101. Hurricanes P2910 (S/L J. Grandy), P2866, P3660, P3376, P3316, P3870, P3656, P3655, P3123, L1595, P3615, P3855, P3866

102. Spitfires R6708, R6709, R6893, R6898, R7021, R7017, P9389, P9367, L1042

103. Spitfires K9895, L1038, L1068, N3230, N3293, P9450, P9554, R6975

104. Spitfires R6987, X4059, R6712, R6618, R6620, (F/O 'Paddy' Finucane), R6982

105. Spitfires R6768, P9312, R6920, K9864, N3095, R6762, R6861, N3240, N3127, X4030

106. Hurricanes N2461, P3481, P3900, P3112, N2524, P3936, P3679, N2755, N2921, P3205

107. Hurricanes included R4193, P3029, V7222, N2482

108. Hurricanes P2548, P3170, P3169, P3042, P3653, P2751, P3396, P2686, P3276, P3173, P3784

109. Hurricanes L1742, N2621, P3202, P3216, P3220, P3386, P3466, P3971, R4109, V7221, V7366 and -?-

110. Hurricanes L1951, L1990, P3228, P3232, P3263, P3358, P3363, P3393, P3884, V7253, V7305

111. Spitfires K9839, K9881, K9969, L1002, L1005, L1019, L1040, N3227, P9381, P9463

112. Hurricanes reinforced by P3655, P2910, P2866, P3660, P3870, P3123, N2986, L1595, P3855, P3861

113. Hurricanes P3276, P3782, P3396, P3229, P2548, P2980

114. Spitfires K9895, L1068, N3293, P9540, P9554, R6700, R6975, X4067

115. Hurricanes L1992, L2075, P2587, N2768, N2871, N2963, P2966, P3111, P3158, P3161, R4192, R4194, R4221

116. Hurricanes 2921, P3112, 2461, V7363, 2524, P3679, P3481. V6535, R4106, P3147, P3900, V6536

117. Hurricanes P2760, N2617, P8816, P3803, N2329, L1865, P3059, P3208, R4105, P3815, L2038, V7234

118. Spitfires X4166-B, X4028-F, K9818-H, R6599-J, P9311-L, K9947-M, N3128-N, X4011-O, P9451-P, R6891-Q, X4064-T, R6802-Z

119. Hurricanes 'A', 'K', 'L', 'R', 'T', 'X'

120. Spitfires X4108, R6901, R6973, L1042, R7017, R6709, R6899, R7021, R6989, R6893, R6701, X4163

121. Hurricanes P2921, N2524, P3936, P3147, P3112, P3679, V7363, V6536, V6535, R4081, P3481, P3900

122. Hurricanes R4220, P2966, R4192, P2871, R4221, P3231, P2768, L1592, P3161, P3811, P3901, P3111

123. Spitfires R6623, R6975, X4067, N3293, R6990, P9450, P9596, P9557

124. Hurricanes R4109, P3786, P3627, P3202, R4107, P3466, P3386, P3179, P3903, V7366, V7208

125. Hurricanes P8818, P3263, P3393, P3230, L1990, P3228, P3886, V7303, N2602, V7253

126. Spitfires L1019, K9969, X4160, K9839, N3223, X4161, X4110, N3198, P9381, L1040, L1005, K9910, N3228, L1002

127. Spitfires P9466, R6957, X4036, N3283, X4035, X4023, N3280, X4035, X4023, N3280, P9494, X4009, N3279, N3239

128. Spitfires R6899, R7021, R6893, R6709, R6898, R6973, P9367, L1042, R6901, X4108

129. Hurricanes L2005, L1750, P3306, P3320, P3940, P3312, V7411, R4181, R4182, R4183, R4184

130. Hurricanes R4220, P2871, P3231, R4192, V7339, R4116, P3811, V7314, R4119, R4194, P3901, P3111

131. Spitfires K9909, R6775, (F/O J.K. Quill), N3101, N3163, R6683, R6803, R6982, X4059, R6712, R6818, R6714, N3164

132. Spitfires R6969, R7021, R6898, R6899, R6708, X4163

133. Hurricanes included VY-H, VY-E, VY-F, VY-KK, VY-G, VY-B

134. Defiants L7025, L6985, L7005, L7003,

N1536, L7024, L6967

135. Hurricanes V7380, P3309, P3739, P3119, 2826, V6537, R4185

136. Spitfires R6919, R6917, R6776, R6889, R6958, R6923, R6833, R6761, X4231, R6888, R6897, R6890, R6770, R6882

137. The three aircraft involved, of 235 Squadron, were T1804 shot down, L9261-P, and Z5736 which crash landed

138. Hurricanes P3194 (W/C Dewar), P3594, N2798 (F/L Gleed), V7225, P3993, P3755, P3118, V7307, P3404, P3174 (P/O Beamont), P3389, P3394, P3593

139. Spitfires R6986, X4165, R6631, N3223, R6915, P9661, L1082, R6769, X4104, R6691, L1008, K9997, X4107

140. Hurricanes P3788, P3878, P3536, P3168, P3894, P3027, P3168, P3033, V7416

141. Hurricanes N2755, N2920, V6547, N2433, P3936, V6546, P3679, V7425, V6547

142. Defiants L6985, L7028, L7005, L7026, L7024, L7025, N1536

143. Hurricanes R4089-R, P3889-S, P3156, P3142-M, P8809, R4087-X, P3887, P3143, P3157, R4184, P3159, P3960

144. Hurricanes V6549, V6542, P3466, -?-, P3386, V7308, V6548, V7303, V7306, P3903, P3179

145. Spitfires L1027, K9910, X4162, P9381, N3228, L1040, P9411, R6834, P9446, N3226, K9839, X4256

146. Spitfires X4009, P9494, N3279, X4182, X4183, R6959

147. Hurricanes P3102, P2760, L1578, P5194, R4223, V7234, P3397, V6545, R5193, R4105, L2038

148. Hurricanes V7314, P3162, R4194, V7239, R4119, R4220, P3231, P2871, R4116

149. Defiants L7021, L7028, N1576, N1574, N1672, N1569, N1673, N1556, L6957, L7026, L7018, L6963

150. Defiants N1672, N1576, N1556

151. Spitfires R6899, R6709, R6892, R6893, X4163, R6898, X4053, X4054, X4108, X4235, R6973, R6832, N3110

152. Hurricanes P2751, P3042, V7379, V7258, P2548, V7302, P3044, P3396, P3276, V7377, P3019

153. Hurricanes P3150, V7349, V7343, P3467, V7350 also VY-Q (S/L Townsend), VY-A, VY-G, VY-H, VY-K, VY-M

154. Hurricanes V7342, P3384, N2668, N2402, R2689, R4124, P5190, R4198, N2523, P3579

155. Spitfires R6899, R6898, X4053, R6892, X4163, R6973, R6974, P9367, N3110, X4054, X4235

156. Hurricanes P3150, N2645, V7343, V6581, L2071 also VY-A, VY-B, VY-D, VY-G, VY-K, VY-M, VY-Q (S/L Townsend)

157. Spitfires N3267-S, L1021-M (F/O R.H. Hillary), L1024-R, R6808-Z, P9459-N

158. Spitfires R6993-W, X4028-F, K9974-M, N3124, P9433-E, R6976-A, X4064-T, R6891-Q, K9818-H, X4011-O also DW-X and DW-Y

159. Hurricanes P3150, N2645, V7343, V6581, L2071 also VY-D, VY-G, VY-K, VY-L, VY-M, VY-Q (S/L Townsend)

160. Spitfires R6735-W, R6753-G, L1021-M, (Hillary, force-landed), L1040-R

161. Spitfires X4064-T, K9818-H, P9433-E, R6976, X4028-F, R6891-Q, P9311-L, X4239-R, X4966-B, N3124-N, DW-X, and DW-Y

162. Hurricanes L1750, P3301, R4184, R4182, V7369, P3813, P3119, V7384

163. Hurricanes P3150, V7343, N2645, V7349, L2071 also VY-D, VY-G, VY-H, VY-K, VY-M and VY-Q

164. Hurricanes P5179, P3213, P3537, V6640, P5188, P3551, P3032, P3115, P3717, P3804, P3921, P2883, L1965

165. Spitfires K9947, P9492, P9469, X4321, P9878, R6773, N3119, L1031, X4067, P9434

166. Hurricanes P3061, P2961, P2982, P3207, P3715, P2831, P3084, P3090, P3218, P3814, P2884, P2967, P3864, P3087

167. Hurricanes R4088, P3620, R4094, P3890, P3643, L1706, V7296, V7250, P3705, P3706, P3049, P3708, P3709, R4189, V7298

168. Hurricanes V7332, P2863, V7378, P3384, R4197
169. Hurricanes V7302, P3395, P2548, P3042, V7375, P2751, V7251, V7376, P3396
170. Spitfires R6888, R6912, R6890, R6882, X4231, R6924, R6958, R6809, R6923, R6833, R6917
171. Hurricanes V7343, N2645, V7349, L2071, V6581, P3150, also VY-G, VY-H, VY-K, VY-M, VY-P, VY-Q
172. Hurricanes P3032, P3115, P2883, P3804, V6640, P3537, P3551
173. Hurricanes P3312, V6537, V7384, P3739, P3813, V7630, R4184, R4185
174. Hurricanes R4089, P3156, P3142, P3889, P3888, P8810, R4084, P8811, P3159, R4085, V6621, P3268
175. Spitfires R6899, X4238, R6892, X4163, R6898, R6709
176. Spitfires N3056-B, R6752-E, R6754-F, L1020-L, X4264-M, X4273-K, X4271-N, X4274-P, X4264-R, N3267-S, X4250-X, R6626-Y, R6853-W
177. Spitfires K9940, K9935, K9938, P9338, X4013, P9460, X4241, P9958, X4105
178. Spitfire lbs R6888, R6924, X4159, X4059, R6776, R6917, R6923, R6833
179. Hurricanes V7408, V7416, P3673, P3539, P3033, R4122, P3027, P3892, P2741, P3878, P3536, P3023
180. Hurricanes P3756, P3114, N2599, V7201, P2965, P3066, P3063, P3062, P3053, P3094, P3064, P3024
181. Hurricanes P3049, V7298, P3704, P3705, P3708, P3735, L1703, P3645, V7254, L1706, P3578, R4088
182. Hurricanes P3143, V6556, R4085, P8811, V7436, P3056, P3142, V7304, P8809, P3148
183. Hurricanes P5179, V6637, P2588, P2686, P3032, P5181, P5172, P2865, P2883
184. Hurricanes V7360, V7202, P3756, P3066, V6531, P3201, P2599, P3053
185. Hurricanes R4175, R4179, V7243, V7284, V7290, V7289, P3974, V7242, P3700
186. Hurricanes R4229 (S/L Grandy), V6610, V7313, V6559, P3594, P2863, V6628, V6534, V6614, P5206, P3088, P3579

APPENDIX 2

High-scoring RAF fighter pilots 1 July-31 October 1940

The RAF generally avoids establishing small, élite groups within its ranks. Many interception successes during the Battle resulted from teamwork; some pilots were individually very successful in combat. *Certain* success nevertheless is often difficult to confirm. Where a victory was shared it is here shown as '1/2'. While few pilots used only one aircraft, quite a number flew the same machine many times. Likely scores, listed here, are based upon surviving combat reports, ORB listing and surviving relevant Luftwaffe and Fighter Command records. Likely scores of 5 or more 'kills' are listed.

Rank	Name	Sqn(s)	Score	Examples of aircraft flown	Remarks
Sgt	Allard, G	85	9, 2 x 1/2	N2477:VY-L	
P/O	Atkinson, H.D.	213	6	P3200, R4099	KIA 25.8.40
S/L	Badger J.V.C.	43	4, 2 x 1/2	P3971	
P/O	Barclay, R.G.A.	249	5	P3807	
Sgt	Beard, J.M.B.	249	5	P2866	
P/O	Beaumont, W.	152	5, 3x 1/2	R6829, R6831	
P/O	Bennions, G.H.	41	8	R6684, X4343	
P/O	Berry, R.	603	8, 3 x 1/2	P9459-N, R6626-Y	
F/O	Blair, K.H.	151	4, 1/2	P2826, P3309	
Sub Lt	Blake, A.G.	19	6, 1/2	P7423	KIA 29.10.40
Sgt	Boddington, M.C.B.	234	5, 1/2	N3057, P9494	
P/O	Bodie, C.A.W.	66	8, 2 x 1/2	P3029, X4321	
F/L	Boitel-Gill	152	8	K9954	
F/L	Boyd, A.D. McN.	145, 600	6, 3 x 1/2	P3381 (145 Sqn)	
F/L	Brothers, P.M.	32, 257	5, 1/2	N2921 (32 Sqn), V7254 (257 Sqn)	
F/O	Carbury, B.J.G.	603	15, 1/2	R6835, X4263	
P/O	Carpenter, J.M.V.	222	5	P9378	
F/O	Clyde, W.P.	87, 601	5, 1/2	P3389 (87 Sqn) P3230 (601 Sqn)	
F/L	Connors, S.D.P.	111	5	V7222	
Sub Lt(A)	Cork, R.J.	242	5	P2831, P3515	

Rank	Name	Sqn(s)	Score	Examples of aircraft flown	Remarks
F/L	Crossley, M.N.	32	9, 1/2	N2461, P3146	
P/O	Cunningham, W.	19	5, 2 x 1/2		
P/O	Curchin, J	609	7, 2 x 1/2	N3223, R6699	
P/O	Currant, C.F.	605	7, 3 x 1/2	P3580, V6783	
F/O	Count Czernin, M.B.	17	7, 5 x 1/2	V7408	
F/L	Dalton-Morgan, T.F.	43	7, 1/2	P3784	
P/O	David, W.D.	87, 152	6, 1/2	P3405 (87 Sqn)	
F/O	Davis, C.R.	601	11, 1/2	P3363, P3382	KIA 6.9.40
F/O	Davis, C.T.	238	5, 2 x 1/2	P3462	
F/L	Deere, A.C.	54	4	N3183, R6895	
P/O	Doe, R.F.T.	234, 238	15	V6814 and V6801 (238 Sqn), X4036 (234 Sqn)	
F/O	Dundas, J.C.	609	7	R6769, N3113	
F/L	Dutton, R.G.	145	7, 3 x 1/2	P3521	
F/L	Ellis, J.	610	6	R6806-N, R6993-W	
F/O	Eyre, A.	615	5, 2 x 1/2	P3151, R4194	
Sgt	Farnes, P.C.P.	501	6	P2760	
Sgt	Feary, A.N.	609	5	R6691, X4234	
P/O	Feric, M. (Pol)	303	7	V6681	
F/L	Forbes, A.S.	303, 66	7	R4217 (303 Sqn), X4324 (66 Sqn)	
Sgt	Frantisek, J. (Pol)	303	17	R4175, P3975	KIA 8.10.40
P/O	Freeborn, J.C.	74	6	K9863, R6706	
F/L	Gibson, J.A.A.	501	8	P3102	
F/L	Gillam, D.E.	616, 312,	7, 1/2	X4181 (616 Sqn)	
Sgt	Glowacki, A.	501	8	P3815, P3820	
P/O	Goodman, G.E.	1	5, 1/2	P2686, P3678	
F/L	Gracie, E.J.	56	5	P3554, P3570	
P/O	Gray, C.F.	54	14, 2 x 1/2	R6893	
P/O	Gribble, G.D.	54	5, 2 x 1/2	P9387, R6899	
P/O	Grier, T.	601	9, 5 x 1/2	P5208, P3393	
F/O	Haines, L.A.	19	5, 2 x 1/2	X4352	
Sgt	Hallowes, H.J.L.	43	9, 1/2	P3386	
Sgt	Hamlyn, R.F.	610	8	X4028-F, R6891-Q	
Sgt	Harker, A.S.	234	5	R6957	
F/O	Henneberg, Z.	303	8	V6684	
P/O	Hillary, R.H.	603	4	L1021-M	
S/L	Hogan, H.A.V.	501	5, 3 x 1/2	R4228, V7433	
F/L	Howell, F.J.	609	5, 1/2	R6769, X4104	
Sgt	Howes, H.N.	85, 605	6	P3107 and P3965 (605 Sqn)	
F/L	Hughes, P.C.	234	14, 3 X 1/2	X4009	KIA 7.9.40
Sgt	Karubin, S.	303	5	P3901	
Sgt	Kilner, J.R.	65	5, 1/2	P9516, R6713	
F/L	Kingcombe, C.B.F.	92	6, 2 x 1/2	R6622, X4051	
Sgt	Lacey, J.H.	501	15, 1/2	P8816	

Rank	Name	Sqn(s)	Score	Examples of aircraft flown	Remarks
F/O	Laricheliere, J.E.P.	213	6	-?-	
P/O	Lewis, A.G.	85, 249	9	V6617 (249 Sqn)	
Sgt	Llewellyn, R.T.	213	11	P3113	
P/O	Lock, E.S.	41	16, 1/2	N3152, X4409, R6610	
F/O	Lovell, A.D.J.	41	5	N3266, P9429, X4021	
S/L	MacDonald, A.R.D.	64	5, 1/2	R6995, L1055	
P/O	MacKenzie, K.W.	501	5, 1/2	V6799, V6806	
F/L	Malan, A.G.	74	6	R6773, K9953	
P/O	Mayers, H.C.	601	7	L1917, P2620, R4218	
F/L	McArthur, J.H.G.	238, 609	6	R6915 and X4165 (609 Sqn)	
Sgt	McDowall, A.	602	11	K9910, L1040, N3228	
F/L	McKellkar, A.A.	605	14, 1/2	P3308, V6878, V6789	
F/O	McMullen, D.A.P.	54, 222	10, 3 x 1/2	P9389 (54 Sqn) X4341 (222 Sqn)	
P/O	Meaker, J.R.B.	249	5, 2 x 1/2	P3123, P3834	KIA 27.9.40
P/O	Millington, W.H.	72, 249	9, 2 x 1/2	V6614	KIA 30.10.40
F/O	Mungo-Park, J.C.	74	6	K9878, R6772	
P/O	Neil, T.F.	249	7, 2 x 1/2	P3316	
P/O	Oxspring, R.W.	66	5, 2 x 1/2	R6800, X4052, X4421	
F/O	Paszkiewicz, L.W. (Pol)	303	6	V7235	KIA 27.9.40
F/L	Rabagliati, A.C.	46	6	P3597, V6544	
Sgt	Rolls, W.T.E.	72	7	K9841	
F/L	Sing, J.E.J.	213	6, 1/2	P3780	
P/O	Stapleton, B.G.	603	5, 2 x 1/2	L1040-R	
P/O	Stephen, H.M.	74	8, 2 x 1/2	P9492, P7361	
F/O	Strickland, J.M.	213	5, 1/2	P3979, V6544	
Sgt	Szaposznikow, E.	303	8	P3120, V7244	
S/L	Townsend. P.W.	85	6	P2716:VY-F, P3166:VY-Y	
F/L	Tuck, R.R.S.	92, 257	10, 1/2	N3268 (92 Sqn), V6555 (257 Sqn)	
F/Sgt	Unwin, G.C.	19	10	X4425, P9546	
P/O	Upton, H.C.	43, 607	10, 1/2	V7206 (43 Sqn)	
F/O	Urbanowicz, W. (Pol)	145, 303, 601	14	R4177 (145 Sqn), V7290 and R2685 (303 Sqn)	
P/O	Urwin-Mann, J.R.	238	8	P3226	
P/O	Vigors, T.A.	222	5	X4341, K9947	
F/O	Villa, J.W.	72, 92	10, 4 x 1/2	X4252 (72 Sqn), X4419 (72 Sqn)	
F/O	Weaver, P.S.	56	7, 1/2	P3554	KIA 31.8.40
F/O	Webb, P.C.	602	6	L1019, R6834	

Rank	Name	Sqn(s)	Score	Examples of aircraft flown	Remarks
F/L	Webster, J.T.	41	8	R6635, R6661	KIA 5.9.40
Sgt	Whall, B.E.P	602	6	K9969, R6601	KIA 7.10.40
P/O	Wlasnowalski, B.	32, 607, 213	5	V7223 and P3679 (32 Sqn)	
P/O	Woods-Scawen, C.A.	43	7	P3964	KIA 2.9.40
P/O	Zumbach, J. (Pol)	303	8	P3700, V7242	

APPENDIX 3

Pilots and aircrew of Fighter Command killed in action during the Battle of Britain

RAF	Pilots	Other Aircrew
British	370	32
Belgian	5	—
Czechoslovakian	7	—
French	—	—
Polish	29	—
RCAF	3	—
RNZAF	—	3
TOTALS	414	35

APPENDIX 4

RAF personnel casualties 1 July-31 October 1940

	Killed	Wounded	Missing in action	PoW
Fighter Command				
To 1.7.40	51 (42)	42 (36)	180 (151)	28 (26)
	120 (95)	31 (24)	3 (2)	
1.8.40	81 (67)	63 (57)	224 (182)	34 (31)
	141 (111)	39 (31)	6 (2)	
1.9.40	136 (114)	139 (129)	329 (269)	43 (38)
	157 (123)	46 (35)	8 (2)	
1.10.40	238 (204)	230 (223)	377? (315)	47 (42)
	171 (135)	50 (38)	10 (4)	
31.10.40	317 (278)	266 (256)	365 (305)	54 (47)
	207 (159)	55 (41)	14 (9)	
Bomber Command				
To 1.7.40	233 (91)	68 (24)	656 (237)	139 (52)
	233 (101)	49 (22)	10 (2)	
1.8.40	331 (129)	84 (31)	747 (27)	219 (78)
	260 (110)	65 (27)	15 (3)	1 pilot interned
1.9.40	497 (189)	98 (39)	723 (270)	325 (120)
	332 (144)	73 (28)	35 (8)	2 pilots interned
1.10.40	539 (205)	108 (42)	878 (331)	407 (145)
	393 (169)	83 (32)	43 (10)	3 interned
31.10.40	616 (230)	134 (52)	945 (363)	438 (157)
	447 (197)	98 (37)	39 (9)	1 interned
Coastal Command				
To 1.8.40	132 (55)	31 (10)	213 (93)	6 (4)
	44 (25)	23 (12)	16 (9)	
1.9.40	166 (68)	37 (12)	216 (93)	25 (12)
	80 (44)	27 (14)	16 (9)	
1.10.40	180 (75)	39 (14)	250 (107)	36 (16)
	82 (45)	33 (15)	21 (11)	
31.10.40	199 (82)	45 (16)	315 (133)	41 (18)
	87 (46)	38 (17)	20 (12)	

Grand total of personnel losses to noon 31.10.40:

1,688 (667)	936 (387)	2,303 (940)	683 (270)
1,194 (664)	329 (171)	103 (42)	31 (8) interned

Bracketed figures = pilots. All totals to noon on date listed.

Second line entries relate to casualties resulting from flying accidents.

Source: Returns to Air Ministry War Room July-October 1940.

Adjustments to the figures were to be repeatedly made, over a long period. No final summary along the lines of this seems to have been prepared.

APPENDIX 5

The heaviest raids — civilian areas (excluding London area) 1 August–31 October 1940.

Loads delivered as recorded by the Ministry of Home Security and involving 40 or more high explosive bombs (about 70 per cent 50-kg, remainder mainly 250-kg). Listed monthly, in order of number dropped.

August

24	Ramsgate 500 (45), mainly in sea, a jettison load clearly over-estimated, and ibs; also 60 HE and 6 ob around Broadstairs	
24	Bridge Blean RD, Kent 400 (29), 4 ob	
16	Sevenoaks 229 (30)	
2	Bridge Blean RD 200 (4), ibs	
15	Reigate 158 (14)	
26/27	Birmingham CB 152 (22), ibs	
15	Malling RD, Kent 150 (96), 1 ob	
12	Folkstone 150 (1), ibs	
16	Northfleet 104 (2)	
24	Portsmouth 100	
25/26	Birmingham CB 96 (16), 1 ob, ibs	
15	Swale RD, Kent 98 (8)	
16	Strood RD, Kent 84 (2)	
28	Rochford RD 78 (24)	
18	Swale RD 75 (2)	
15	Chatham 72 (6)	
15	Sunderland 71 (1)	
18	Strood RD 69	
15/16	Birmingham CB 64 (1), ibs	
16	Malling RD 63 (3)	
13	Ventnor 60 (18)	
12	Portsmouth 21 (36), 3 ob	
16	Custon RD 53	
25/26	Rugby RD 56	

11/12	Bristol 50	
14/15	Bristol 50	
29/30	Liverpool 49 (8), 1 ob, ibs	
16	Gosport 48 (5)	
23/24	Birmingham 48, 250+ ibs	
13/14	Birmingham CB 47	
31/1.9	Bradford 41 (8), 10 ob	
31/1.9	Strood RD (45)	
31	Birkenhead 35 (8), 1 ob	
12	Gosport 40 (1)	
20	Shardlow RD 38 (2), ibs	

September

25	Bristol 300	
8	Dover and Deal RD 159 (24), 1 ob, ibs	
1/2	Bristol 125, 1 ob, ibs	
1/2	Swansea 84 (22)	
15	Tonbridge RD 77 (30), ibs	
15	Dover and Deal RD 77 (17), ibs	
4/5	Liverpool 76 (3), 2 ob, ibs	
4	Chatham 75 (6)	
15	Portland 70 (10), 4 ob, ibs	
4	Rochester 55 (6)	
3/4	Liverpool 45 (4), 3 ob, ibs	
4/5	Strood RD 43 (2), 2 PM, ibs	
17	Thurrock 44 (1), 1 ob, ibs	
7	Dover and Deal 36 (5), ibs	
16	Dover and Deal RD 31 (10)	
4/5	Bristol 40, 5 ob, 1,000+ ibs	
3/4	Bristol 36 (4)	
29	Bagshot RD 39 (1)	

October

26/27	Birmingham 108 (5), 2 ob, ibs	
21/22	Coventry* 100 (35), ibs	
12/13	Coventry 98 (1), 1 ob, ibs	
14/15	Coventry 94 (40), 2 ob, ibs	
19/20	Coventry 94 (34), ibs	

25/26 Birmingham 78 (3), 1 ob
15/16 Birmingham 73 (9), 3 ob, ibs
19   Battle RD, Kent 61 (5)
8   Eastleigh 20 (27)
29/30 Birmingham 39 (3), 1 ob

Raids during the entire period involving 30 to 39
HEs = total 17
20 to 29 HEs = 45

* By way of comparison, in the well-known heavy
Coventry raid of 14/15 November 1940 the dropped
loads were assessed officially as: 50 PMs, 1,120 HEs
and 280 UX and unknown incendiary load. German listing shows 503 tonnes of HE and 31.716
tonnes of incendiaries. London's heaviest raid during the Blitz period came on 16/17 April 1941
according to the Germans — total 890 tonnes of HE
and 151.20 tonnes of incendiaries. The heaviest fire
raid came not as generally supposed on 29/30
December 1940 (22.248 tonnes of incendiaries) but
on 8/9 December 1940 (114.768 tonnes of fire
bombs).

Notes: ibs = incendiaries (number never easy to
assess)
e.g. 33 (45) = 33 HE (45 more unexploded or
delayed action, HE)
RD = Rural district; unless thus stated, incident
occurred in given town/city
ob = oil bomb (petroleum based liquid in 50-kg
HE bomb case)

APPENDIX 6

Tonnage of bombs dropped on the United Kingdom

| | British Assessment | | German Listing | | |
	Tonnes	Percentage of German figures	HE tonnes	Incendiary tonnes	Total
August	6,770	257.7	2,462	165.456	2,627.456
September	9,975	111.4	8,528	429.336	8,957.336
October	6,910	74.5	9,027	252.432	9,297.432

British over assessment was due to the belief that many bombs fell at sea. The 'Ramsgate incident' highlights that. There was also great difficulty in locating unexploded bombs, particularly in rural areas, where some unquestionably remain.

London's heaviest raids — British Assessment
15/16 October 1940 — 1,186 HE bombs, the most up to 31 October
20/21 October 1940 — 691 HE bombs, the second heaviest raid
16/17 October 1940 — 535 HE bombs — one 1,800-kg bomb reported

APPENDIX 7

Estimate of the number of bombs dropped — British figures

1940	HE	oil	parachute mines*
June (night)	1,388	14	9
July	1,921	162	19
August	5,103	318	45 (9)
September	18,327	688	122
October	476 x 50-kg bombs 280 x 250-kg + 17,550 unclassified HE	1,253	113 = 5,845 MT

*Prior to 17 September when the dropping inland of parachute mines began on a major scale these weapons were almost all sea mines dropped in error on coastal regions.

ABBREVIATIONS

Bf   109, 110 — generally accepted as the correct designation of the wartime Messerschmitt 109 and 110

CE   Channel convoy eastward bound

CH radar   Chain Home radar station

CW   Channel convoy westward bound

Establishment   Number of aircraft/personnel, etc., approved as total unit/ squadron strength but not necessarily held

FN   East coast convoy sailing north to Forth

FS   East coast sailing south from Forth

FTR   Failed to return from operational sortie

GP   General purpose HE bomb — SAP/AP bombs were for hardened targets

grt   Gross Registered Tonnage

HE   High explosive bomb

He   Heinkel (111)

JG   Jagdeschwader (i.e. Luftwaffe fighter group)

KG   Kampfgeschwader (i.e. Luftwaffe bomber group, consisting of three or four Gruppen subdivided usually into three-Staffel and denoted by Roman numerals, i.e. I, II, III, with a Stab or HQ Flight.

KIA   Killed in action

PM   Parachute mine

UX   Unexploded bomb

SELECT INDEX